G000150332

Life, Sex and Death

A distinguished and revered elder of the British Psycho-Analytical Society, William Gillespie is one of the few British psychoanalysts who began analytic training in Vienna in the early 1930s. Later he became well known for his pioneering work in England on the study of sexual perversion, and for his views on female sexuality, on regression in old people facing death, and on instinct theory. Characteristically prepared to support unpopular views if the evidence warrants it, he courageously described his experiences of extrasensory elements in dream interpretation in spite of his fears that his unconventionality might damage his psychoanalytic reputation.

William Gillespie is celebrated not only for his scientific contributions but also for his administrative skill, integrity and tact in managing the International Psychoanalytical Association and the British Psycho-Analytical Society, where he was trusted and respected by both Melanie Klein and Anna Freud.

In a biographical introduction the editor, Michael Sinason, looks back on the productive ninety years of Gillespie's life, writing movingly of his early life in China and Scotland and showing his development as a psychoanalytic thinker, organiser, administrator, husband and father. In addition, Charles Socarides discusses the innovations introduced by each of the papers in the collection and shows how Gillespie's ideas influenced his own contributions and affected the field as a whole.

Dr Michael D.A. Sinason trained in psychiatry at the Maudsley Hospital. His main clinical work has been the psychoanalytic approach to psychotic illness and he became a full member of the British Psycho-Analytical Society in 1993.

Dr Charles W. Socarides is in private psychoanalytic practice in New York. He has written extensively in the area of sexual deviations and is the author of several books, including *Homosexuality* and *The Preoedipal Origin and Psychoanalytic Therapy of Sexual Perversions*.

THE NEW LIBRARY OF PSYCHOANALYSIS

The New Library of Psychoanalysis was launched in 1987 in association with the Institute of Psycho-Analysis, London. Its purpose is to facilitate a greater and more widespread appreciation of what psychoanalysis is really about and to provide a forum for increasing mutual understanding between psychoanalysts and those working in other disciplines such as history, linguistics, literature, medicine, philosophy, psychology and the social sciences. It is intended that the titles selected for publication in the series should deepen and develop psychoanalytic thinking and technique, contribute to psychoanalysis from outside, or contribute to other disciplines from a psychoanalytical perspective.

The Institute, together with the British Psycho-Analytical Society, runs a low-fee psychoanalytic clinic, organises lectures and scientific events concerned with psychoanalysis, publishes the *International Journal of Psycho-Analysis* (which now incorporates the *International Review of Psycho-Analysis*), and runs the only training course in the UK in psychoanalysis leading to membership of the International Psychoanalytic Association – the body which preserves internationally agreed standards of training, or professional entry, and of professional ethics and practice for psychoanalysis as initiated and developed by Sigmund Freud. Distinguished members of the Institute have included Michael Balint, Wilfred Bion, Ronald Fairbairn, Anna Freud, Ernest Jones, Melanie Klein, John Rickman and Donald Winnicott.

Volumes 1–11 in the series have been prepared under the general editorship of David Tuckett, with Ronald Britton and Eglé Laufer as associate editors. Subsequent volumes are under the general editorship of Elizabeth Bott Spillus, with, from Volume 17, Donald Campbell, Michael Parsons, Rosine Jozef Perelberg and David Taylor as associate editors.

ALSO IN THIS SERIES

Dr William H. Gillespie in the garden of his London home in 1988.

NEW LIBRARY OF PSYCHOANALYSIS
23

General editor: Elizabeth Bott Spillius

Life, Sex and Death

SELECTED WRITINGS OF WILLIAM H. GILLESPIE

Edited and introduced by Michael D.A. Sinason

With an overview by Charles W. Socarides

London and New York

First published 1995
by Routledge
11 New Fetter Lane, London EC4P 4EE

Simultaneously published in the USA and Canada
by Routledge
29 West 35th Street, New York, NY 10001

© 1995 Selection and editorial matter, Michael Sinason; chapter 2, Charles W. Socarides; other articles, the copyright holders.

Typeset in Bembo by LaserScript, Mitcham, Surrey
Printed and bound in Great Britain by
Biddles Ltd, Guildford and King's Lynn

All rights reserved. No part of this book may be reprinted or
reproduced or utilised in any form or by any electronic,
mechanical, or other means, now known or hereafter
invented, including photocopying and recording, or in any
information storage and retrieval system, without permission in
writing from the publishers.

British Library Cataloguing in Publication Data
A catalogue record for this book is available from the British Library

Library of Congress Cataloguing in Publication Data
A catalogue record for this book has been requested

ISBN 0–415–12804–8 (hbk)
ISBN 0–415–12805–6 (pbk)

Contents

Part Three: Other writings and references

Acknowledgements

Ideas about the format of this collection were debated for some time before a decision was made and I am indebted to Clifford Yorke and Elizabeth Bott Spillius for their part in the moulding process. Elizabeth has sustained the project throughout with her expert advice. Charles Socarides responded enthusiastically to the idea of contributing a chapter tracing the effects of William Gillespie's papers in the field of sexual perversions and this added momentum towards completion. Jill Duncan, Librarian of the British Psycho-Analytical Society, and her assistant Paula Lavis have helped in the preparation of the manuscript and in updating and completing the references. I am grateful to Pearl King for historical information and to Edwina Welham for help in choosing the photographs. William's daughter Veronica Ions has assisted in checking the accuracy of the biographical information and in seeking out family photographs. Most of all I would like to thank William Gillespie for the opportunity to get to know him through the shared task of editing this collection of his papers and for his patience and forbearance when there were unavoidable delays. Sadie Gillespie was a constant source of encouragement and her supreme effort during August 1994 enabled William to recover from a near-fatal fall and thus see the book completed.

I would also like to thank the following for their kind permission to reproduce copyright material: the Archives of the British Psycho-Analytical Society; the *International Journal of Psycho-Analysis* for Chapters 3, 4, 5, 7, 9, 10 and 12; Random House, New York for 'The Structure and Aetiology of Sexual Perversion', first published in S. Lorand and M. Balint (eds) *Psychodynamics in Therapy*; Oxford University Press, London for 'Psychoanalytic Theory of Sexual Deviation with Special Reference to Fetishism', first published in I. Rosen (ed.) *The Pathology and Treatment of Sexual Deviations*; International University Press, New York for 'Extrasensory Elements in Dream Interpretation', first published in G. Devereux (ed.) *Psychoanalysis and the Occult*; and the *British Journal of Medical Psychology* for Chapter 13.

PART ONE

Introduction to the papers

1

Biographical introduction

DR MICHAEL SINASON

I first met William Gillespie as the fleetingly glimpsed husband of my training analyst Sadie Gillespie. A few more impressions were gathered from exchanges on the telephone when I had to leave a message. William was courteous and precise in his tone and manner but also engagingly blunt and direct in sorting out any ambiguities in my messages. He seemed an able 'minder' for his wife in the event that this should be needed in the course of the analysis. These impressions did not alter when, some years after the end of my training analysis, I came to know Sadie and William socially, but I was also then able to enjoy William's wry sense of humour and sharp character assessments. I had also, of course, heard during my training about William's years as President of the British Society and President of the International Psychoanalytical Association. William, however, rarely referred to the famous analysts or the political events as I expected. I eventually discovered that this was based on a deep dislike and distrust of grandiosity or pomposity that meant that he was averse even to acknowledging his achievements let alone to trumpeting them. Sometimes Sadie or colleagues would complain to William about his modesty, but he would then impishly enjoy quoting Churchill's memorable but cruel characterisation of Clement Attlee as 'a modest little man with much to be modest about'.

When the plans for this book began to take shape I made a strong bid to include with the papers two chapters which would redress the balance and allow William's contributions to British and international psychoanalysis to be voiced. In this chapter I provide a biographical outline so that the reader can map his outstanding clinical and organisational achievements on to the nine decades of his personal life. In the next chapter, Charles Socarides reviews William's contributions to the psychoanalytic literature and identifies the influence his papers have had on the understanding of sexuality, the perversions and the destructive instincts and on the direction of subsequent

3

work in these fields. Most of the facts about William's life that follow were provided for me by William from autobiographical notes he made about ten years ago, from other material in the British Society Archives and from conversations I had with William. I am also indebted to Sadie Gillespie, Pearl King, Jill Duncan and Elizabeth Spillius for their assistance with information for this chapter and for their contribution to other aspects of the preparation of the book. William's daughter Veronica helped to find early family photographs to supplement those in Sadie and William's own collection and those in the archives of the British Psycho-Analytical Society.

Despite the Scottish origins of the Gillespie family name, William's grandfather was a bank manager in the Northern Irish town of Newry, County Down. In the Protestant community there were many religious divisions and in 1858 he left the Church of Ireland to join the Irish Presbyterian Church, which he actively served, eventually becoming, in 1930, at the age of 91, a presbyter, the term for an elder in the governing body. He lived to see William's son in 1934 but died the following year.

William remembers his grandfather as an imposing Victorian with a fine beard and the delectable habit of distributing gold half-sovereigns on his birthdays. He sent all but one of his seven children to university to study medicine, theology or both. Two of the three children who became doctors worked as medical missionaries and two were members of the clergy, so the majority were professionally concerned with religion. The education of these children was a formidable financial undertaking. It was, however, funded in a manner more expected of the impecunious. Each child sent to university had to reimburse him later on so that the next in line could be financed. Although this strategy was accepted as part of the practice, in large families, of shifting some responsibilities of parenting to older siblings, such shifts leave the older children with a dislocated but lingering experience of deprivation, and William's father did not escape this.

William's father was born in 1867. He took an arts degree in Dublin and followed this up with theological training at Galway University. He was fluent in Greek and Hebrew. After his ordination he spent most of his life as a clerical missionary in China. William's mother was also born in County Down but his parents did not know of each other's existence until they met in Manchuria! She had gone to work as a 'Zenana' missionary, working, that is, for the Women's Association for Foreign Missions. She too had started as a member of the Church of Ireland but transferred her allegiance to the Irish Presbyterian Church. Her father had been a petty officer in the Royal Navy and then went into the Coastguard Service stationed on the island of Arran, where she developed a love for Scotland that affected her decision later to live there. William's mother was the eldest in her sibship and her two younger sisters also worked as Zenana missionaries in Manchuria. His mother lived to nearly 90 years and both

4

these aunts lived far into their 90s. William's mother relished the family connection with the Duke of Hamilton and told William how she remembered her father receiving letters from the Duke addressed to 'My dear Cousin'. His mother's maiden name was Isabella Burgoyne Grills. One of the Burgoynes was the general in the American War of Independence who was defeated at Saratoga. His mother illustrated that the ancestry of the Burgoynes dated back to the fourteenth century by quoting a doggerel:

I, John of Gaunt
Do give and do grant
To Johnny Burgoyne and all of his loin
Sutton and Potten until the world's rotten.

There are two tiny villages called Sutton and Potten only a mile or so apart in Bedfordshire, near Biggleswade, which appear to be the places designated by John of Gaunt.

William's father arrived in China in 1893 and married two years later. Their first child, Annie, was born in 1896, followed by two girls in rapid succession, Harriet and Ethel, the latter being born in July 1899. Soon after this, in the summer of 1900, there occurred the Boxer uprising. Though it is regarded in the West as a simple expression of anti-foreignism, its roots lay in the inability of Confucian orthodoxy to provide for the needs of the common man. In Shantung, where economic conditions were poor, young men banded together studying the ancient arts of self-defence – 'Chinese boxing' – so that they could protect the poor from exploitation. Later, they became increasingly hostile to officials and foreigners. The movement caused great disruption and hardship and some loss of life to the missionaries in China, not least in Manchuria.

During the last years of the nineteenth century foreign missionaries in large numbers went deep into Shantung villages, where they converted people, tore down traditional temples, and built churches. The Boxers were initially much more hostile to the Chinese Christians and those Chinese officials, who aided the foreigners. However, the Empress Dowager tried to deflect the movement's growing violence away from the dynasty and towards the foreigners and their reformist officials, who were seen as trying to subvert Manchu rule. In the early months of 1900 the Boxers swept across the countryside of north China, burning and looting missionary settlements and slaughtering thousands of Chinese Christians. Boxer ranks were swelled with mobs of destitute vagrants who had been driven off their land by famine, flood and drought. In their desperation they found the Boxer sorcery, mysticism and promise of supernatural powers (which would make them immune to bullets) most seductive.

On 13 July 1900, the Boxers stormed into Peking and laid siege to the

William's father (centre) and fellow missionaries with their congregation.

eleven foreign legations, while the Chinese government ignored the foreigners' desperate pleas for protection. Finally, in mid–August, allied troops broke through from Tientsin to relieve the haggard, frightened prisoners of the besieged legations, and Boxer resistance quickly disintegrated, leaving the troops of the international force to take revenge on the Chinese by looting and raping. However, fortunately, the Gillespie family had gone on holiday leave in February of that year, so they were not personally involved, although their house, where the three girls had been born, was destroyed.

   In December 1904, when his mother was 40 years old, William was conceived. He was born on 6th August 1905 and was given the same forenames, William Hewitt, as his father. William was born in Pei-Tai-Ho, which is not in Manchuria but in China proper. The family were spending the summer there because it was an attractive seaside resort much patronised by the missionaries for holidays. It is situated just south of the Great Wall, about 160 miles directly east of Peking, approximately on the 40th parallel. The first three years of William's life were spent in China, although the experiences inevitably disappeared into the mists of infantile amnesia. However, he visited Pei-Tai-Ho again later and remembers the beautiful sand, the heat and the rock pools.

6

William (in pram) and his sisters in China, 1906.

Westerners who went to China in the nineteenth century branded the Chinese an inferior race and reviled them as heathens whose souls had to be transformed before they could become fully human. Every revolt against oppressive rule was bloodily put down, with the effect of creating ever more revolutionaries. City and village drifted apart in early twentieth-century China. The cities became Westernised and a part of the world market system which foreign imperialism had created. Shanghai, for example, became more a European than a Chinese city. The villages, although affected by the new cities, retained much of their traditional heritage. William remembers meals being served by the 'boy' – actually a mature man – whom he came to like but could not communicate with well owing to his parents' policy that the children were on no account to learn Chinese lest they be led astray by their heathen ways. Every European family had three servants, which was *de rigueur*, for no Chinese would have accepted employment without this minimal establishment. There was the cook, who also did the shopping, the 'boy' – a sort of butler – and the lowest rung was occupied by the coolie, who did all the dirty jobs.

The strains of this social structure broke out one night when William's father was away 'itinerating'. The cook crept up to his sister Ethel's room and said that he was cold and wanted to get into her bed to get warm. Ethel, innocent though she was, knew enough not to allow this and went through to her mother's bedroom. His mother immediately woke William, took both the children into her room and armed herself with a hammer. She then shouted to the cook that if he tried to come in she would kill him. William and his sister can still remember her Chinese words. The cook thereupon fled the house. He was subsequently arrested and William's father later had to question Ethel to prepare himself to give evidence, asking her 'You wouldn't have allowed him to get into your bed, would you?', to which she replied 'Of course not – a Chinese!' The official family explanation was that the cook had gone mad.

In the summer of 1908, the whole family returned to England, since his father's furlough was then due. They travelled by train on the Trans-Siberian Railway through Russia and Germany to a destination in Sevenoaks, 23 miles south-east of London. This choice was governed by the presence there of Walthamstow Hall, a school for the daughters of missionaries, where William's three sisters were enrolled. The older two spent most of their schooldays there as boarders whereas Ethel came with her father, mother and William when they returned to China four years later. William's father spent most of the intervening time travelling in Ireland, as was the custom of missionaries on furlough, propagandising the work of the mission, encouraging others to join it and raising funds for its work.

The family moved to Ireland for some of this time, staying in the seaside town of Warrenpoint some six miles from his grandparents in Newry. This period made a great impression on William and established his unequivocal identification of himself as Irish. During this stay he was taken by his father to Belfast to see the famous *Titanic* which was near to completion and therefore to her disastrous sinking on 15 April 1912, her maiden voyage.

Family portrait. Teddy bear given to William by his father for his sixth birthday, 1911. Left to right: Harriet, Anne, Father, William, Mother and Ethel.

By the summer of 1912 William had returned to China with his mother and sister Ethel to meet up with his father, who had returned earlier. He was now 7 years old and much more able to appreciate the nature of the journey they were undertaking. He remembers it as the most exciting experience of his childhood. This time they travelled with the cheaper Norddeutscher Lloyd shipping line rather than P&O as most British did, to cut costs for the mission. Many of the passengers were German and William remembers a young man of 18 who was bound for Penang to avoid compulsory service in the German Army. The ship sailed round the Bay of Biscay to Genoa and Naples and through the Suez Canal to the Red Sea. He remembers the searchlights in the Suez Canal and the over-whelming heat in the Red Sea, with only slow electric fans to stir the hot air limply. From Penang they sailed to Shanghai, after which they trans-ferred to a smaller Japanese ship that took them to Dairen, a port in southern Manchuria, where his father was on the quay to meet them.

The reunited family travelled by rail to Kwan-Chung-Tzu, the town where William's sisters had been born and in which his father worked for most of his life and later died. Its name was later altered to Chang-Chun and then again to Hsin-King. However, this was not the end of their journey since Kwan was not his home at this time and he was living in Kirin, some sixty miles to the east. Kirin is on the great river Sungari but it was not on a railway, so the last part of the journey was by Chinese cart, the traditional method of travel and one habitually used by his father and the other missionaries when 'itinerating'. A Chinese cart is a miniature covered wagon, with solid wheels and no springs, pulled slowly by a mule. Since the road led through the mountains William has vivid memories of the landscape as he approached his father's house in Kirin.

The house itself was memorable because, unusually in China, it had two storeys, and also because its amateur architect was another missionary who had forgotten to provide for an internal staircase. One had to be added as an afterthought, which made it a perennial joke. There was access to the roof from the upper floor and William learned from his father to recognise the stellar constellations and the resplendent Venus and Jupiter.

After about a year, the family returned to their house in Kwan-Chung-Tzu, since William's father had finished his assignment to Kirin. Kwan was divided into Chinese, Japanese and Russian parts and William's house was a conventional one-storey house with a big garden, in the Chinese sector. In the summer William and Ethel and the other missionary children would play cricket, rounders and French cricket. In winter, everything was covered in six feet or more of snow and they constructed dugouts in it. This may have been inspired by the Great War because in August 1914 the children were told a war was starting, although it was very unclear who was going to fight whom. In the summer of 1915 William returned to England with his mother and sister. His father accompanied them to Harbin where they picked up the Trans-Siberian Railway. It was, of course, impossible to travel through Germany in 1915. At the frontier they transferred into a Swedish train. The contrast with the dirty Russian train was dramatic. All was clean and comfortable and the food delicious, whereas they had been obtaining food until then on the platforms of the stations from the peasants who brought it there. They travelled through Sweden and Norway to Bergen and then embarked on a ship for Newcastle. There was a very real danger of torpedoes and mines and William remembers a diplomat in their party whose bag was weighted so that it would sink irrecoverably if they were hit. The family then travelled to Chester to stay for a short time with his uncle and aunt, and there they were reunited with William's two older sisters.

The plan was for the family to make a new home in Edinburgh, and this was where William spent the next fifteen years of his life. Edinburgh was chosen partly because of Isabella's attachment to Scotland, acquired when she spent part of her adolescence in Arran, but the more compelling reason concerned the medical training of his eldest sister Annie. This was not for the outstanding reputation of the Edinburgh medical school but was based on the fact that in 1915 women medical students were completely segregated from the men in Edinburgh, whereas in Belfast they studied together. Fortunately for Annie, this policy was altered soon after she began her training. William was enrolled at George Watson's Boys' College, a very well-known Edinburgh school, and his two other sisters in George Watson's Ladies' College. A flat had been secured for them at 37 Warrender Park Road, part of a typical Edinburgh stone-built terrace of houses. Their flat was on the top, fourth, floor. The flat was quite big and provided separate rooms for him, his mother and three sisters. Lighting was by gas, first gas jets then gas mantles. There was no electricity. Heating was by open coal fires and one or two gas fires.

As William's Chinese clothes were distinctly peculiar he had been taken to a tailor in Chester to be fitted out. One of the items bought on the recommendation of the tailor was a bowler hat. When he wore it in Edinburgh (at the age of 10) it brought him as much ridicule as his Chinese clothes would have and it was regularly knocked off his head. School did not begin immediately on the family's arrival and they had time to get to know two families from Ulster with a clerical background. Both had flats, one above the other, in the immediate neighbourhood. These families were drawn together by being Irish in a Scottish world, and they helped each other deal with the social stresses. One of the children was beginning at Watson's, like William, having previously been at school in Belfast. He was labelled 'White Paddy' because he had fair hair while William was named 'Black Paddy' since he had dark brown hair.

William's formal education, as well as Ethel's, had until then been undertaken by his mother. It was good, although not orthodox, so that when he was tested at Watson's it was discovered that he knew how to read and write English well but had no formal knowledge of grammar whatsoever. William remembers a spelling test in which they each had to correct their neighbour's paper. One of the words was music and when he got his paper back this word was marked wrong, for it read 'musics'. He justly accused his neighbour of having added the redundant 's'. His teacher declared that this was a very serious accusation, to which he replied that it was nevertheless true and pointed out that the 's' was obviously written with a different pencil from the 'music'. This is an early pro-forma of the blend of courage, bluntness and perspicacity built into William's character that has shown itself in his handling of adversity in the subsequent eight decades. The settings and the people have changed much but this characteristic has won William many of his admirers as well as, of course, some adversaries.

Before leaving China, William had no basis on which to assess his own abilities and no motive for doing so, but at Watson's he soon found himself at or near the top of the class, and became quite determined to stay there when he discovered that it was possible to win scholarships, which saved his parents from paying school fees. Later, in higher forms, there were bursaries to be won, which carried a few pounds as well as free education. From then on his parents did not have to pay school fees, and he bought his mother a clock with his first bursary money.

Churchgoing went without saying, generally twice every Sunday, besides Sunday school. St George's United Free Church was reckoned to be the nearest approximation to the Irish Presbyterian Church, which did not exist in Edinburgh. For a time William considered his father's career as a missionary to be the only truly worthy one, although his father did explain to him that this was not the only way to lead a good life and serve God.

The reality of the Great War was brought home by Zeppelin raids, several of which had Edinburgh as their target. When an air raid occurred at night the family had to go down to the flat at the bottom of the house. On one occasion a bomb went right through the house where both families of their Irish friends lived, although it did not explode, and another bomb damaged his school. It was just after William entered senior school at the age of 13 that the Armistice occurred, 11 November 1918. This allowed William's father to be reunited with his family. A Chinese labour force had been organised to help clear up the dreadful mess in France and Belgium left behind by the war and his father volunteered to go with them, mainly as an interpreter, though officially as an army padre in khaki. They spent the summer holiday together in Ireland and his parents celebrated their silver wedding. William's conflicts regarding his recurrent separations from his father are revealed in an exchange he had at this time. He asked his father what was the meaning of his invariable grace before meals: 'For these fees thy gifts O Lord make us truly thankful.' This apparently innocent question was not well received, since his father could not see how he could fail to know that what he really said was: 'For the use of these thy gifts.' This unconscious hostility to his father's employment as a missionary, which so often caused the family to have to live apart, was clearly shared by his sisters, since they admitted afterwards that they had been equally puzzled but had never dared to enquire what he meant. It was at this same period that his father explained to William that he was not under any moral obligation to follow in his footsteps as a missionary. Soon after, his father left the family again for China in a transport full of returning Chinese. The plan was that his mother would follow in a year or two, by which time his youngest sister Ethel would be 21, the eldest Annie would be a qualified doctor and William was to stay in one of the boarding houses that were attached to Watson's.

These plans were not to be fulfilled, however, because fate dealt the family a cruel blow that radically changed their lives. One day when

William returned home from school Annie took him aside and told him that their father had been killed as a result of a murderous attack by intruders at their home in China. For a long time he kept having dreams that his father had returned, that it was all a mistake. Letters took a long time to come from China and the general feeling of the unreality of the disaster was reinforced by their receiving several letters written by him before the attack.

The full story eventually reached them. There had been a number of earlier occasions when the house had been broken into during the night and his father had chased the intruders successfully in his pyjamas. He had a low estimate of Chinese courage and thought that they would always flee if chased by a 'foreign devil' like himself. This time, however, he appears to have cornered them in the kitchen. One of them took up a kitchen cleaver and hit him over the head with it and then they made their escape. The severe wound was not immediately fatal. A surgeon was called in from Mukden and it was decided that one eye must be removed. This was successfully done and his father was reported, characteristically, to have joked about his state as a one-eyed missionary. However, infection set in and he must have developed a panophthalmia, from which he died a few days after the attack.

The death of William's father changed all of their lives profoundly. Suddenly, at the age of 15, William was the only male member of the family. Annie was just then taking her final medical examinations, and because of her need to become a breadwinner straight away she by-passed the usual unpaid house-jobs in medicine and surgery and went instead to work in the County Asylum in Chester where her Uncle Galbraith was the medical superintendent. Annie remained working there for many years, ultimately as deputy medical superintendent. Harriet started taking jobs as governess in wealthy families and Ethel was finishing university and training as a teacher. William became closer to his mother, feeling under an obligation to look after and protect her even though she was only 55. The violent death also changed William's outlook on religion since his faith in God the Father Almighty was fundamentally shattered by God's failure to preserve this good and faithful servant. William's first change was to shift from wanting to be a missionary, to the idea of being a medical missionary, but the depth of his disappointment was shown by his evasion of 'first communion' despite taking instruction that was supposed to lead to his confirmation. He never thereafter took part in a communion service.

There is also an indication that there was a significant change in William's character at this time. He found himself using his flair for solving mathematical problems to gain popularity with his fellow prefects by giving them the answers they wanted. One day a close friend, whom he somewhat idealised, reprimanded him for this showing off in a way that left

William feeling completely crushed. William dates his tendency to hide his light under a bushel from that event, which therefore probably took on enormous unconscious significance, perhaps as an accusation from his dead father for his oedipal victory.

William's actual achievements were, however, not muted in any way. He stayed on for a seventh year to prepare for the Open Bursary competition of the University of Edinburgh. He took exams in English, mathematics, science and Greek and emerged top scholar of the school, winning by 9 points out of 400 over any of his rivals. Whilst at university studying medicine he won a further scholarship and a prize that helped to pay his way. In his second year of medical school there was the general strike of 1926 and many students answered the call for volunteers to run essential services. William was allocated the job of tram conductor. On one occasion a group of strikers invaded the upper deck and one of them attacked him, giving him a bloody nose for which he received double pay for the day's work. William was not sure of the justice of being a strike breaker and refused to continue, but remembers that other students were enrolled as special constables and armed with truncheons.

William saw himself as a budding physician, with a leaning towards psychiatry because his uncle and sister were both working in the asylum in Chester. During his last year he competed for a clinical essay prize offered by the British Medical Association. His sister Anne had a number of patients in Chester suffering from the after-effects of encephalitis lethargica; she let him examine them and write them up and he won the prize. He took his finals in the summer of 1929 and qualified with honours. He asked his clinical chief Edwin Mathew if he would accept him as his house physician. Mathew agreed but the post was already promised, so that there would be a wait of six months. William therefore decided to find a job that would fulfil the obligation to conduct 'special study or research', which had been a condition attached to the Vans Dunlop scholarship he had won. He was accepted by George Robertson, the Professor of Psychiatry, to act as houseman in the Jordanburn Nerve Hospital, which was just then opening as an annexe to the Royal Edinburgh Hospital, more familiarly known as Morningside Asylum. It was also decided that he would during this period undertake the three-month intensive course for the Diploma in Psychiatry. After this he went on immediately to the Royal Infirmary to spend six months as house physician to Edwin Mathew. During this time, whilst William was president of the doctors' mess, they were visited by the Prince of Wales. William therefore had the chance to meet the future King Edward VIII, whom he invited to sign his name on the mess table alongside those of all the residents.

By this time William had done a good deal of reading of both Freud and Jung in translation. An opportunity arose for a travelling scholarship for a year, worth £400, and with a condition that one had to know the appropriate foreign language. William had decided that 'depth psychology', as psychoanalysis was called, was the worthwhile approach to psychiatry, and he was personally convinced that Freud was right about the importance of sexuality in the unconscious motivational structures of the mind. In addition he judged that Vienna, as the city of music, would have considerable appeal. Accordingly he applied to study psychiatry and neurology for a year in Vienna, prudently concealing his underlying interest in psychoanalysis. He knew no German whatever, but he bought Linguaphone records and, on the basis of having studied the first six of these and his private determination to acquire it, boldly claimed a knowledge of German. His expertise was not, fortunately, put to the test and he was awarded the scholarship.

The train journey to Vienna was a long one but William remembers the thrill of pulling into the station and seeing its German spelling: WIEN. He had booked a room in a hotel on the Ringstrasse where he stayed for a few days while looking around. He had learned of the American Medical Association of Vienna and found its headquarters in the Café Edison. The Association organised lectures and demonstrations given in English by leading members of the Viennese medical faculty and he enrolled for several of these, for example on endocrinology and pathology. William made contact at the Café Edison with a number of American post–graduate students, some of whom were interested in psychoanalysis. One of these was named Sippy, the son of the inventor of a famous diet for peptic ulcers. He, it turned out, was having an analysis with Paul Federn, one of the most senior of Freud's followers, and Sippy gave William an introduction to Federn. The interview was conducted in a darkened room and William remembers him as a rabbinical figure with full beard and full red lips. He was friendly and helpful and understood that William wanted to gain experience of psychoanalysis and that this entailed first a personal analysis. He asked William if he had any problems in himself that he wanted analytic treatment for, to which he received an emphatic 'no'. Nowadays such an answer would be itself evidence of such problems, since 'normality' is regarded in psychoanalysis as the most stubborn of defences, but it did not deter Federn, who said he would try to find someone for him. He soon put him in touch with Eduard Hitschmann, another of Freud's oldest adherents, then aged 60, as he told William.

It will be appreciated that psychoanalytic technique as practised in Vienna in 1931, certainly by the old school and with candidates for training, was not quite what it is today. Hitschmann was prepared to take William on for one hour a day, six days a week, at a fee of 20 schillings (equivalent to about 12 English shillings), mainly, William thinks, because he wanted to improve his English. When Hitschmann realised William's

William in Vienna, 1931.

lack of actual sexual experience he thought this should be remedied without delay and suggested he should find some dissatisfied 'bourgeois' wife and be initiated by her. The bourgeois wife idea did not appeal to William, who wanted someone of his age, then 25, or younger.

It was Hitschmann who helped William to fulfil the obligations of his scholarship by introducing him to Heinz Hartmann, who was in charge of one of the sections of the University Psychiatric and Neurological Clinic. He met Hartmann in his ward, found him full of charm and welcome, was officially enrolled as a post-graduate student under Professor Pötzl and attended Hartmann's ward rounds daily, gradually learning German as he went along. William attended a practical course on hypnotism given by Hartmann, which proved to be the most interesting and useful of those available. In the clinic he met Erwin Stengel and the daughter of Alfred Adler. He was also present at a large medical meeting addressed by the famous Eugen Bleuler from Zürich. Wagner-Jauregg's comment on it was that it was '*halb Selbstverständlichkeiten, halb Unverständlichkeiten*' – literally, half self-evident facts, half incomprehensible ones!

Hitschmann told William that he should continue his analysis during his summer vacation by spending his vacation in the same resort, namely Velden am Wörthersee in Carinthia, which he duly arranged. William was allowed to go to an occasional minor psychoanalytic meeting or lecture, but as the end of his year approached it became necessary to plan the next step, which involved finding some means of living whilst continuing his analytic training in London. He applied to the London County Council for a post as junior assistant medical officer at one of their mental hospitals, which carried a living-in salary of £600 a year. In December 1931 he presented himself for selection and was appointed to Claybury Hospital, which is situated in Essex, far to the east of London. There was another vacant post, at Tooting Bec Hospital, which is much nearer the centre and so better suited to his main purpose, which was to continue with his psychoanalytic training. William approached the man who had been given the job to see if he would agree to an exchange, but it turned out that he too preferred Tooting Bec because of his intense interest in music and his wish to attend concerts in London. However, by great good luck Edward Mapother was present; he knew William's fellow applicant and told him not to be a fool, for Claybury was a real mental hospital, whereas Tooting Bec was a specialised hospital for senile patients, and this was sufficient to change his mind.

Having secured his desired hospital post it remained for William to see if he would be accepted for training at the British Psycho-Analytical Society. He first met Ernest Jones, to whom he had been recommended by the Vienna Society. He remembers seeing Jones, in his beautiful Regency house in Regents Park, a little man sitting at an enormous desk piled up with papers. He asked William searchingly why he had started his training in Vienna instead of London. Jones regarded the London training as greatly superior and William was careful to say that it was necessitated by the requirements of the travelling scholarship. Jones tried out William's German, which was pretty fluent by then. He added that his French was poor but that he did not think this mattered since the French psychoanalytic literature was not of much importance. This did not go down too well with Jones, who had studied the French psychiatric literature in some depth. Following this interview he was sent to Wimpole Street to see Edward

Glover, who was much more urbane and very Scottish, and he was officially enrolled as a student of the British Psycho-Analytical Society.

William's duties at Tooting Bec were often medical rather than psychiatric, since all the patients were of advanced age and deaths were frequent from bronchopneumonia. However, William found that many of these patients were very ready to talk and what they said was of great interest from the point of view of psychopathology. Some showed the typical picture of senile or arterio-sclerotic dementia, but not all, and both the demented group and the others frequently had psychotic features, mainly depressive, paranoid and hypochondriacal and often a mixture of these. It occurred to him that a study could be made of these patients which could provide the material for the thesis that he had to write for his MD, the examination part of which he had passed in Edinburgh before leaving for Vienna. Since his daily duties were light he had plenty of time to sit down and listen to the patients and to record what they said. An underlying theme gradually emerged. Much of the psychopathology could be understood as defensive manoeuvres aimed at denying death as a fact of life, for example fear of persecutors threatening the patient's life from without.

This early exposure to the consequences of both biological and functional psychotic deterioration allowed him to appreciate fully Freud's reason for conceiving of a biological basis for the two fundamental and opposed drives, *Liebenstrieb* and *Todestrieb*, translated by Strachey as life and death instincts. Much later this experience contributed to his ability to appreciate fully the significance of Melanie Klein's writings about the strong aggressive and destructive fantasies in infants and young children. William did not publish material from this thesis until 1963, when he included it in a paper in the *British Journal of Medical Psychology* entitled 'Some Regressive Phenomena in Old Age'. He says in this paper 'Natural death comes from something inside, whether it be disease or "death-instinct"; but the typical senile psychotic patient is apparently oblivious of this real internal peril, and is convinced that he is going to be murdered by some outside agent.' This corresponds closely to Melanie Klein's description of the structure of the 'paranoid–schizoid' position in which hate and hostility is projected outwards and experienced as being directed at the self from outside.

It is likely that this early opportunity to see the effects of both biology and psychological processes on the genesis of psychosis enabled William to be appreciative of both the contributions of the Viennese and the followers of Klein. Certainly, he was later to be seen as a friend by both Anna Freud and Melanie Klein. I have included this paper and a talk published in the *Bulletin of the British Psycho-Analytical Society* in 1973, entitled 'The End of Life', as the last two papers in this collection. Despite the fact that the clinical material for both these writings was drawn from the beginning of

William's psychoanalytic life, these experiences had impressed on him from the outset the power and importance of the forces ending life, and these ideas have shaped his approach to all the clinical phenomena to which his attention was turned throughout his subsequent career.

After a couple of years at Tooting Bec William was offered the opportunity of a three-month secondment to the Maudsley Hospital, which was also run by the London County Council. Since this was the Mecca of psychiatry in England he eagerly accepted. His contact with Aubrey Lewis and the other staff confirmed him in the desire to move there permanently, which he eventually achieved in 1935. Sir Aubrey Lewis was Professor and Chairman of the Department of Psychiatry of the Institute of Psychiatry from 1945 to 1966. Lewis consistently argued that 'fields within which psychiatric research is carried on are so wide that there is scope for many kinds of interest and ability'. This capacity of Lewis to create a climate in which to draw to the Maudsley individuals who would become pioneers in their own fields meant that it retained its appeal as a suitable hospital base for William's work until his retirement in 1970 at the age of 65.

On the basis of the year of personal analysis with Hitschmann in Vienna William was allowed to take on a patient under supervision as soon as he became a registered student of the British Society. This first training patient was supervised by Sylvia Payne. The female patient firmly believed she was being poisoned by her mother, but she had been diagnosed at the London Clinic of Psychoanalysis by Edward Glover as a case of anxiety hysteria. After six months, during the first summer break, she had a severe breakdown, was seen at the Maudsley Hospital, was diagnosed as paranoid schizophrenic and was admitted to a mental hospital, where she remained. His replacement patient remained in treatment and William was eventually allowed to take on a second, male, patient, this time under the supervision of James Strachey. Strachey was the first non-medical psychoanalyst that William had met and he found his literary and musical background very appealing. Probably on the basis of Strachey's report, the Training Committee decided that William would need to have further personal analysis before he could qualify. He was allotted to John Rickman but William objected to such a unilateral decision, even though they were customary at the time. William requested to go to Ella Sharpe, who was conducting the training analysis of other students whom he knew and who thought very highly of her. His request was granted and Miss Sharpe agreed to take him on. He found this analysis more painful but also more rewarding than the first and it lasted much longer. As a former teacher of English she was able to address the finer nuances of language in a way that was impossible with Hitschmann.

William remembers his attempts during the analysis to understand the 'hunger pains' which had been troubling him since he began his medical training. Whilst he was at Tooting Bec he had asked the radiologist to X-ray his stomach since he suspected a peptic ulcer. As nothing had shown up, he was inclined to view this a psychosomatic symptom. When, much later, Ella Sharpe heard that a duodenal ulcer was eventually discovered and treated successfully by a partial gastrectomy, she was quite distressed, since any missed organic pathology was a sore point for a non-medical analyst. William was eventually passed for qualification and became elected an associate member of the British Psycho-Analytical Society in 1937.

By 1937 William had also taken the examination for membership of the Royal College of Physicians, a requirement for Maudsley posts then, and was working part-time in the out-patient department with Aubrey Lewis. All new patients were seen by either Aubrey Lewis or William and this meant seeing at least six patients in a half-day for assessment, but often more. On one occasion he saw thirteen, which did no good at all to his duodenal ulcer! There was a strong bias in the British Psycho-Analytical Society at this time, according to which only analysts who had also trained in the psychoanalysis of children were regarded as first-class citizens. This was one of the consequences of Melanie Klein's powerful influence, which was strongly supported by Ernest Jones. William did not want to undertake this time-consuming and expensive further training, so he compromised and applied for a Commonwealth Fund Fellowship to train for a year in child guidance under William Moodie. After completing this, he was offered a part-time job in the children's department at the Maudsley instead of his previous collaboration with Aubrey Lewis. He also took on other part-time jobs including a couple of years' doing diagnostic work at the Institute for the Scientific Treatment of Delinquency.

The headquarters of the British Psycho-Analytical Society at that time was in Gloucester Place, and he attended a course of lectures on psychosis by John Rickman which was open to other interested professionals besides the psychoanalytic students. One of these was Dr Helen Turover, to whom he was immediately attracted. Helen had two analyses but was distinctly ambivalent about both her analysts and she never attempted to train as an analyst. She moved in bohemian artistic circles that were new and exciting to William. These included 'bottle parties' she took him to in the Soho studio flat of one of her painter friends. He remembers that he liked the fact that she was small, since he was himself only 5 feet 7 inches tall. However, she was seven years older than he was and for a while this conflicted with his strong previous stipulation that his girlfriends had to be younger than himself, even if only by a month. Nevertheless they liked exploring art, music and sculpture together and enjoyed the freedoms and common ground that came from both being in analysis at the same time. They soon became very close.

Helen was from a Polish Jewish family. Her father was an orthodox rabbi in a small town near Warsaw, and a Zionist. After his rejection by his Hassidic community the large family moved to Warsaw and became extremely poor and undernourished, so that Helen had developed some degree of rickets. She blamed her father for their deprivation but admired her mother for the way she worked to make ends meet. At the time of Helen's birth Poland was part of Russia and she started life bi-lingual. When she was in her teens the family moved to Antwerp, where Helen learned both French and Flemish. A fifth language was added when World War I turned the family into 'Belgian refugees' in London. Her capacity for mastering languages was exceptional and she did well at school and became a medical student at Charing Cross Hospital.

By the end of 1932 William and Helen had decided to marry, which they did just before Christmas, honeymooning in Menton in a hotel recommended by a sister of Helen's who lived in Paris. This was the only one of her siblings in Europe, the others having gone to America. The couple moved from Helen's Bloomsbury flat to lease a small terraced house in Primrose Hill, deliberately chosen to be near Regents Park and the zoo, because they wanted to have children straight away since Helen was then 34.

Their first child, Andrew, was born on 28 August 1933, slightly premature but none the less robust. In the summer, just before Andrew's first birthday, they went on holiday in County Down, staying in Warrenpoint where William's grandfather and Aunt Ethel had moved from Newry. At this time William's grandfather was 94 and still physically quite well, although he was beginning to have memory difficulties and he died a year later. William and Helen's second child, Veronica, was born on 17 November 1936 and was their last, because the pregnancy had exacerbated heart and kidney damage produced by Helen's childhood scarlet fever.

The failure of Neville Chamberlain's 'appeasement' of Hitler and the take-over by Germany of Czechoslovakia and Austria led to dramatic changes in the affairs of the British Psycho-Analytical Society. Ernest Jones made strenuous efforts to get the necessary documents to evacuate Sigmund Freud, his daughter Anna and other Jewish members of the Vienna Society to England, because he saw that their lives were at risk. These refugees included Hitschmann with his wife and daughter, but they later proceeded to the United States, as did the majority of the Viennese analysts. Among those who remained were Willy Hoffer and his wife Hedwig, who was also an analyst.

By the time Freud came to London he was 82 and suffering the last stages of cancer of the jaw. He lived for only little over a year, dying just after the outbreak of World War II. William did not attempt to see him, in view of his condition, and so did not ever actually meet him. When William was in analysis with Hitschmann in Vienna he was told that Freud would not see him owing to his sensitivity about his mouth condition and the dreadful prosthesis he had to wear, by which he felt plagued.

The large influx of Viennese analysts led to a difficult state of affairs in the British Psycho-Analytical Society because they were nearly all strongly opposed to the innovations introduced by Melanie Klein. Klein had come to London from Berlin in 1926 on the encouragement of Ernest Jones, who believed that her work in the analysis of children was very important and valuable. Indeed, one of his motives seems to have been to have her analyse his own children. By the time William moved to London in 1932 her influence was very great and was strongly supported by her own psychoanalyst daughter, Melitta Schmideberg. When William started to go to Scientific Meetings of the Society he found that the emphasis was entirely different from that of Vienna because of the influence of Melanie Klein. He describes the situation as 'Sex was out and aggression was in, genital was out and pre-genital was in'!

Opposition to Klein's views had begun to be expressed by about 1935, an opposition led by Edward Glover and later joined by Melitta. Glover bitterly resented the assumption promoted by the Kleinians that only those trained in the analysis of children as well as those concerned with the analysis of psychosis should be regarded as first-class analysts. What is more important, he feared that Klein and her followers were steadily taking over the training in the Society and would thus ensure the dominance of their views. William remembers the phalanx of women analysts, Susan Isaacs, Paula Heiman and Joan Riviere, who were Melanie Klein's main supporters, all wearing black, and taking up the same position in the meeting room each time. This phalanx was both defensive and offensive and in these heated discussions they carried the heavier guns. This did not mean that they were in the right but they were the most lucid and powerful exponents.

Glover's opposition to Klein was powerfully reinforced by the Viennese, many of whom tended to regard Klein as no better than a deviationist whose work and views merited unqualified denunciation. The Society therefore became acrimoniously divided and it was Glover's failure to get Klein and her adherents expelled that led to his resignation from the Society in 1944. In the same year Jones officially retired as president, a position he had held for thirty-one years, ever since he founded the Society in 1913.

The onset of war in 1939 brought William's psychoanalytic practice to an abrupt end. He had been an associate member for the two years required in order to be considered for full membership, and the final requirement was to read a clinical paper to the society and for this to be approved. One of his patients had been a young man with a fetishistic perversion and he decided to write a paper on this work for the membership presentation.

The reading of a 'membership paper' was universally regarded as a severe ordeal, especially as Jones was always in the chair and opened the discussion, sometimes with great acerbity. However, Jones appeared to like the paper and so William became a full member in 1940. The paper became his first psychoanalytic work to be published, appearing in the same year in the *International Journal of Psycho-Analysis*.

In the summer of 1939 with the prospect of war looming it was expected that there would be massive air raids on London, with widespread psychiatric casualties in its surviving population. Since the Maudsley is in central London, a few miles south of the Thames, it was to be closed and the doctors and nurses divided into two groups, one to be stationed in a hospital in Sutton and the other at Mill Hill, occupying the houses and grounds of the public school there. William arranged to go to Mill Hill, where the clinical staff were headed by Aubrey Lewis, and it was there that he heard the fateful announcement on the radio by Neville Chamberlain that Britain was at war with Germany. Initially they worked preparing the school, now a hospital, for the attentions of the *Luftwaffe*, putting up blackout curtains and pasting strips of brown paper on to the windows to minimise the effects of blast. The expectation of immediate bombing of London turned out to be mistaken but there was still strict enforcement of the blackout measures. William nevertheless thought it prudent to establish his family somewhere much safer and they bought a house in Cranleigh, Surrey, not far south of Guildford, where Helen went to live with the two children. It was relatively easy for William to visit at this time because petrol rationing had not yet been imposed.

Although William's psychoanalytic practice had to be abandoned when he was mobilised, there was no difficulty in attending meetings of the Psycho-Analytical Society in Gloucester Place. The active membership was considerably depleted by the war service of the men and the evacuation to the country of many of the women members, including Melanie Klein. Jones too retired to his country house in Sussex in 1940. Nevertheless, there were plenty of members left of every shade of opinion, and controversy continued to rage. It was with the aim of bringing the controversy back to a scientific level that the so-called 'Controversial Discussions' were organised, and the discussions, minutes, resolutions and relevant personal correspondence have now been edited by Pearl King and Riccardo Steiner and published as No. 11 in the New Library, *The Freud–Klein Controversies 1941–45*.

Jones's official retirement allowed the members to change the constitution to limit the tenure of its important officers. This was, however, only achieved with considerable difficulty. William teamed up with John Bowlby and older analysts like Adrian Stephen and Rickman to ensure that the new president could only be in post for three years. This contributed to Glover's resignation, because he had hoped to take over the mantle left by Jones. With the new constitution in force Sylvia Payne was elected President, John Bowlby became Training Secretary and William became Director of the Clinic. Adrian Stephen was the son of Sir Leslie Stephen, who had edited the *Dictionary of National Biography*, and he, along with his two sisters, Virginia Woolf and Vanessa Bell, were part of the 'Bloomsbury Set'.

Hitler's pact with Stalin and the division of Poland between them resulted in the full strength of the German war machine being deployed in the West. France, Belgium, Holland, Denmark and Norway were occupied and the British had to rescue their army from the beaches of Dunkirk. At Mill Hill, William started to see the effects of this blow to morale as they began to receive from the armed services the psychiatric casualties that the civilian population had failed to produce. Thereafter Mill Hill became a military hospital taking psychiatric casualties from all the armed forces. William's ward began to specialise in hysteria since there were many cases of conversion symptoms and hysterical amnesia from the trauma of war. In the wartime setting, psychoanalytic treatment was out of the question, since rapid results were demanded. William obtained spectacular results with hypnotic suggestion sometimes reinforced by the use of intravenous barbiturates. One case of astasia–abasia who was unable to walk or stand was walking round the grounds with him 48 hours after admission. However, it soon became apparent that these marvellous 'cures' were spurious since they nearly always relapsed when the question arose of sending the man back to his unit. All that could be accomplished was to abolish the symptoms and then give the man his 'ticket' – that is, to recommend discharge from the armed forces at a military medical board. When the 'ticket' was achieved the therapeutic result held.

Following Dunkirk, bombing began in earnest in London and its environs. A bomb fell quite close to William's house in Cranleigh and he became increasingly concerned for the safety of his family. In the case of invasion he knew well what would be the fate of his Jewish wife and half-Jewish children. Many London children had been evacuated to parts of the country more remote than Cranleigh. The risk of bombing was perhaps tolerable but the prospect of invasion was quite another matter. Some children began to be evacuated to America. Helen had two brothers in Washington and she and William began to be urged by them to send their children. Andrew was not quite seven, Veronica three and a half. William and Helen had the heart-rending dilemma of trying to decide whether to put first their children's physical survival or their emotional wellbeing.

They went to the United States Embassy to investigate their situation. There was no problem about the children, who were British by birth, but

Helen, despite being British first by naturalisation and secondly by marriage, was, for the Americans, on their Polish quota and could not go with them. William was excluded by being mobilised and on essential war work, but out of curiosity he made the enquiry and discovered that he would be on the Chinese quota, which was even more impossible than the Polish. William jokes that this is the only time he was seriously regarded as Chinese! In the end they decided that the children would go to stay with Helen's younger brother Raphael, who was an engineer and doing well as a patent lawyer. He too had been educated in London for a time, they knew each other well and Helen was fond of him. His wife Denise was very active in the Jewish Hadassah organisation and was a very efficient organiser, but it was uncertain how she would be as a substitute mother. The arrangements for evacuation were very secret because of the danger to shipping from submarines. Helen went with the children to Glasgow where they embarked with other children who were being escorted to America. It was to be five years before they were reunited. In between, their only contact was by letter and photographs.

After about a year William was able to find medical work for Helen in Mill Hill, first in a special research unit and then on the psychiatric wards. They were therefore very fortunate in being able to continue their married life together and had a reasonably pleasant war apart from the unhappiness about their separation from their children. During this time William had his partial gastrectomy, an operation which then carried a 10 per cent mortality risk, but after the operation he was told that his ulcer had been on the point of rupturing into the pancreas. When he came out of hospital he was skeletal, but he made a good recovery and it enabled him to be free of the hunger pains that had plagued him for twenty years. After this he and Helen took charge of a new children's department located in a house in the grounds of the Mill Hill School (actually it had been the school tuck shop). This venture was made difficult by the arrival of a new menace, namely the V-1 'buzz bombs', which meant the evacuation of the children into trenches that had been dug in the grounds. William and Helen also ran an out-patient department at the Maudsley itself once the RAF achieved air superiority.

The war in the west dragged on longer than expected after the Normandy invasion because the Germans put up a stubborn resistance despite being attacked on two fronts. Eventually, when victory came, William was able to arrange for his children to come home. He went with Helen to Southampton to meet the *Aquitania* and saw Andrew at the railings. William remembers having to search for Veronica, who was hiding, and finally finding a little blonde girl sitting on the vast staircase, nursing a doll. She agreed she was Veronica but he was not surprised that she was totally unable to recognise him. There followed some difficult years of adjustment and the family learned the hard way of the profound effects that result from a five-year separation for young children.

The Mill Hill and Sutton hospitals were disbanded and William returned to an intact Maudsley, which had a new children's department, including a so far unused in-patient unit that had been planned and built just before the war under the auspices of Mildred Creak. William wanted a half-time appointment so that he could rebuild his psychoanalytic practice and he obtained this, although Aubrey Lewis tried to persuade him to work there full time. In 1944 William had succeeded Glover as Director of the London Clinic of Psycho-Analysis and he worked with Sylvia Payne and John Bowlby to devise a new training scheme. This was designed to enable the warring factions in the Society to work alongside each other, for the main conflicts centred on the control of training. The solution did not enforce a unity of training but instead created two parallel streams. These were to some extent independent but both were under the control of the Training Committee, which itself, under a 'gentlemen's agreement', was to contain representatives of all three parties: the followers of Anna Freud, those of Melanie Klein and a third uncommitted group known then as the Middle Group. This unaligned group had an important mediating function for quite some years, and key figures such as the president and the training secretary were deliberately drawn from its members.

When William had resumed his private practice in 1945 he found that his colleagues referred him a number of patients with sexual deviations, since they remembered his 1940 paper on fetishism. Papers reporting on this work appeared in the *International Journal* in 1952 and 1956, and he also wrote a chapter on this subject for a book edited by Sandor Lorand and Michael Balint. In 1963 he was asked to contribute a paper to a symposium on homosexuality at the International Congress, which was published in the *International Journal* in 1964. In the same year he wrote a chapter for a book edited by Ismond Rosen, *The Pathology and Treatment of Sexual Deviation*, which became, in this country, the definitive source book for clinicians working in the field of sexual perversion.

These six publications are included in this collection because of their originality, and the historical review paper, in Chapter 2, by Charles Socarides brings out the full extent to which these papers were innovative, going beyond Freud, and were also landmarks for future navigators in the field. Included together with these papers are two written by William on the subject of female sexuality. This topic had become increasingly controversial in feminist circles in the 1960s, where Freud's views were often strongly opposed. There had also been an open controversy on the subject between Freud and Ernest Jones. Another significant influence was the publication in 1966 of the research by Masters and Johnson and the subsequent discussion of it by American psychoanalysts. William argued that Freud's authoritative pronouncements on the clitoral versus vaginal orgasm had been proved wrong by this 'sexual laboratory' research. William's paper, 'Concepts of Vaginal Orgasm' (1969), was written for the fiftieth anniversary of the date of the foundation by Ernest Jones of the *International Journal of Psycho-Analysis*.

Under the new constitution, which limited tenure of office to three years, Bowlby ceased to be Training Secretary in 1947 and William was appointed his successor. He had been made a training analyst shortly before this and had been allotted his first student. After the war the number of students greatly increased and the accommodation at Gloucester Place became increasingly inadequate. William had moved his consulting room a number of times in the Harley Street, and Wimpole Street area and one day noticed a sign on a house facing the north end of Mansfield Street advertising a long lease for sale. This was Mansfield House, 63 New Cavendish Street, which has been the home of British psychoanalysis ever since. William mentioned it to Rickman, who became very enthusiastic. The house, empty for some time, had formerly been occupied by the Swedish Legation. It was grand and imposing, with beautiful painted ceilings, and cost £25,000 for a 999-year lease from the Howard de Walden Estate. Although his presidency ended in 1950, Rickman took the most active part in finding the money and making the move, which occurred in 1951.

William was liked by Anna Freud, perhaps initially because of his early training in Vienna and later because of their collaborative work in the International Psychoanalytical Association. He also got on well with Melanie Klein, and in fact after the war he and Helen had bought a house in Carlton Hill, the street next to the one where Mrs Klein lived, in Clifton Hill. William often drove her home after meetings and remembers discussing with her the difficulty of finding a successor to Rickman as president. In the event William was nominated and duly elected in the summer of 1950, becoming, at the age of 45, the youngest president the society was ever to have. At the time William became president the duties were extremely heavy. He presided at every fortnightly Scientific Meeting of the Society, he was Chairman of the Board of the Institute, and in addition he was ex-officio on the Training Committee and interviewed all the new applicants for training. He was very uncertain about his ability to do the job, but in fact his reputation as a fair and independent thinker was already well established by then, and he contributed significantly to stability in the affairs of the Society because he was trusted by both the warring factions.

Apart from his age, William has said that there was another reason that he was unsure of his acceptability as president. This was because of a 'short communication' he had made to the Society in 1948 on the subject of extrasensory factors in dream interpretation. The prevailing psychoanalytic approach to matters of the extrasensory such as thought transfer or telepathy was one of profound scepticism. William's paper was based on a number of striking experiences he had with several patients in the preceding two years. To his surprise it was very well received. Thirteen people participated in the discussion and it emerged that a number of them took such experiences for granted, although this was never debated publicly in scientific meetings. Despite the genuine scientific curiosity that emerged on that occasion William feared that his reputation could be marred by allusions to and associations with the supernatural and the occult.

Similar fears clearly had prevented any other analyst from presenting such occurrences up to that point, and, as far as I know, ever since. In 1990, when I was Honorary Secretary of the Scientific Committee, the possibility of a presentation of some new ideas on the subject came up and I tried to facilitate this, but eventually the fear of tarnished reputations led the analyst to withdraw the paper. This illustrates the courage William had in presenting the work, and the paper is remembered by many people in the Society to this day for this, as well as for its clinical interest. While preparing this collection I was asked by several people to include the paper, because for them it represents William's genuine independence of mind and scientific integrity, and this was also the reaction of the Society when he presented it.

I have included the paper amongst William's later writings on the life and death instincts because of the links he makes in this paper with schizophrenic symptoms such as 'thought insertion' and 'ideas of influence'. Working analytically with schizophrenics can be severely disorienting because of the disconcerting breaks in the usual boundaries of self and other. William explores the possibility that the uncanny ability of the paranoid patient to understand the unconscious hostile motives of another person is based on the patient's experience of becoming aware of the other person's thought processes.

A few years after he had given the paper, the dissemination of information in psychoanalytic circles led to an approach by an American analyst, George Devereux, who was planning a book on psychoanalytic contributions to the problem of extrasensory perception. He persuaded William to allow his paper to be included, since the book also contained five papers by Freud in which the matter was mentioned. William eventually agreed since the book was due to be published only in America, so that the clinical illustrations he was giving would be unlikely to be seen by his patients. However, despite the hope that the book would emphasise the scientific content and interest of the papers it was eventually published with the unfortunate title *Psychoanalysis and the Occult* which maximally stirred up the non-scientific allusions!

International Psychoanalytical Congress, London 1953. Front row: Maxwell Gitelson, Princess Marie Bonaparte, William Gillespie (Chairman), Anna Freud, Jeanne Lampl-de-Groot. Second row: Ernest Jones.

The International Psychoanalytical Association had been founded in 1910 and Freud had designated Carl Jung to be its first president, to be succeeded after World War I by Karl Abraham and then Ernest Jones. In 1953 the biennial congress of the International Psychoanalytical Association was held in London, at Bedford College. Hartmann was President of the Association and William was still President of the British Society, the hosts of the Congress. At this Congress it was proposed that William be nominated for the office of Vice President of the International, and he was elected. Four years later at the Paris Congress he was elected President of the International and invited, along with a limited selection of guests, to a dinner in the palace of Princess Marie Bonaparte at St Cloud. There was a white-gloved footman for every two guests, and gold cutlery. The princess showed William and Helen photographs of 'Lily-Bet' (later to be Queen Elizabeth II) in her childhood and of Philip, who had spent some of his boyhood with the princess.

Straight after his election, William was lobbied by a group of eminent French analysts, including Lacan and Lagache, who had resigned from the Paris Society and thus automatically from the International Association. They had been refused readmission after their case had been examined by a special committee. William had met Jacques Lacan years before in London when he delivered his paper on the mirror stage of development.

International Psychoanalytical Congress, Paris 1957. Row facing, from right:
Rudolph Loewenstein, Kathleen Jones, William Gillespie (President of IPA),
Princess Marie Bonaparte, Ernest Jones.

He had a number of private meetings with Lacan after that to hear his
version of what had happened in Paris. William appointed a Special
Committee to examine the Paris problem and wanted to secure endorsement of their careful and thoroughly documented report by the Central
Executive Committee at the 1961 Congress in Edinburgh. There was
bitter and determined opposition to the readmission to the International of
any of the analysts who had resigned. At an anxious counting of heads in
the small hours the opposition finally conceded defeat and so, after a
probationary period, the new Association Psychanalytique de France was
born. This was a notable achievement of William's presidency, but in
addition, with the assistance of Pearl King, whom he had appointed as
Secretary of the International, he initiated a revision of the International's
statutes. One of the changes introduced was the creation of a new category
called a Regional Association, which was designed to deal with the
anomalous position of the American Association, previously accorded an
autonomy in training matters unlike that of any other of the Component

Societies. A measure of the success of William's skills in problem solving and diplomacy can be gained from the fact that when he stepped down from the presidency he was elected as vice president again and continued to be re-elected to this office for a further twelve years, until, at the Paris Congress of 1973, he refused to stand again for office.

During the ten years between 1963 and 1973 William wrote the last three papers included in this collection, venturing into the controversial area of Freud's 'death instinct' theory and its adoption and clinical application by Melanie Klein and her adherents. The 1971 paper, 'Aggression and Instinct Theory', was contributed to a symposium, and 'The End of Life' was a public lecture that appeared in the *Bulletin of the British Psycho-Analytical Society* in 1973. William argues that Freud was right to identify the existence of biological and psychological representatives of an instinct of destruction as well as one of construction, but thinks that Freud was mistaken in regarding it as a universal urge to return to the inorganic state. On the contrary, William's view is that the capacity for destructiveness is often mobilised when the individual feels that there is a threat to life, and that it is aimed at preservation of life, although its effects can sometimes bring about the reverse. He has pointed out that Freud's fundamental drives, Eros and Thanatos, have representatives in the genetic structure of the fertilised ovum. Some genetic 'instructions' dictate growth, development and differentiation but there are evidently other instructions that call a halt to growth. Without adequate 'life force', in William's view, the infant will die; without appropriate 'death instinct' growth will be uncontrolled, as in cancer. For the species, uncontrolled growth would be its death, and limitation of procreation is essential for survival. For these reasons William sees the death instinct as separated from the life instinct, as Freud described it, but also as intrinsic to healthy life rather than something evil that we should strive to control or eliminate.

The next Congress was held in London at the end of July 1975. The Christmas before this Helen felt unwell and began to lose weight, and she was admitted for an exploratory operation to the Middlesex Hospital. William was phoned at home by the surgeon to be told that she had cancer of the pancreas with secondaries already in the liver. This cancer is rapidly fatal and she died before the summer Congress.

Although William did not expect, at the age of 70, to marry again, he found to his surprise that he did. A practising analyst, Sadie Mervis, had come to him some four years before for a refresher analysis. This analysis was coming towards its termination when Helen became ill. In the following months it became plain that William and Sadie shared an attachment that went beyond transference feelings, and they were later married. The unorthodox ending of the analysis was not acceptable to either the analyst William or the analyst Sadie. In any event Sadie felt that

31

she needed further analysis. She went to Dr Hanna Segal for a five-sessions-per-week analysis for ten years. This analysis often strained the marriage, but it has become stronger and deeper and more enriched ever since.

Sadie had trained originally as a speech therapist, following a degree taken at Witwatersrand University in Johannesburg, South Africa. She had gone for psychoanalytic training to Wolf Sachs, who was conducting a one-man training scheme in South Africa with the blessing of Ernest Jones. Sachs unfortunately died in 1949 and after the Zurich Congress of that year Sadie applied for training in London. After completing the training she was soon recognised to be a very good analyst, and after completing the newly introduced membership course, which was an alternative route to full membership, she was soon appointed as a training analyst.

Their marriage stimulated Sadie to a more active and public professional life while William was planning retirement from his. At the age of 65 his Maudsley appointment had automatically been terminated, but he had continued his psychoanalytic practice combined with some teaching. In 1974 a new chair was set up at University College, London, endowed by Mr David Astor. The post was a yearly appointment under the designation 'Freud Memorial Professor of Psychoanalysis'. William was asked to serve on the committee that would establish the appointment. This was not easy since the person had to be a practising psychoanalyst who could give up the major part of his practice for one year, as the post was nominally full time. The first holder was Roy Schafer for the year 1975–76, and the following year William realised he was being considered, and so resigned from the committee. The post appealed to him as a stepping stone towards retirement from psychoanalytic practice. He was appointed and gave a series of public lectures focusing on various aspects of Freud's work and its relationship to other disciplines. He also held a number of college seminars and lectures and greatly enjoyed the links he made with college academics who were not psychoanalysts.

William has been honoured in many other ways in recent years. On 9 July 1975 the British Psycho-Analytical Society elected him an 'Honorary Member of the Society' in grateful acknowledgement of 'the outstanding contributions which he had made to the science, practice and development of psychoanalysis both within the United Kingdom and internationally'. Anna Freud invited him to give the first of a series of annual lectures at the Hampstead Clinic to commemorate the anniversary of Freud's birthday. He entitled it 'Fifty Years with Freud' and talked of his own experience of psychoanalysis over half a century. This talk was published in the *Bulletin of the Hampstead Clinic* in 1983. William has also had a splendid sculpture made of his head and shoulders by Eileen Klein, the wife of Sydney Klein. The Institute has purchased a cast made in bronze and this was unveiled and presented to the British Psycho-Analytical Society on 16 July 1986. It has now been placed on the elegant first turn of the staircase in Mansfield House. The latest recognition that William received was at the Plenary Session of the 37th IPA Congress, held in Buenos Aires on 2 August 1991, when he was made an 'Honorary Vice-President' of the International Psychoanalytical Association for his outstanding work.

William Gillespie has made an astonishing contribution to the scientific, cultural and administrative life of the British Psycho-Analytical Society and the International Psychoanalytical Association. In addition to being President of the International Psychoanalytical Association he has twice been the President of the British Psycho-Analytical Society. He has held high office in one or other or both organisations continuously since 1944, when he was Director of the London Clinic of Psychoanalysis. Now, fifty years later, his input as 'Honorary Vice President' is still sought despite the vagaries of his physical health. William had an almost fatal fall at the beginning of the Gillespies' 1994 August holiday. The hospital was in an unfamiliar town and most friends were on vacation. Sadie was by his bedside daily from dawn to midnight keeping him in touch with his condition in order to mobilise his temporarily traumatised drive to live. She knew that if he did not recover his mental capacities he would not wish to live, but they fought for life together and he has made a remarkable recovery, later much facilitated by the good wishes and attention of friends and family.

The paper at the end of this collection, entitled 'The End of Life', is an affirmation of William's unique ability to deal with death as a necessary accompaniment of life and neither to seek it, nor to seek to avoid it. His analytic experience leads him to regard human destructiveness as arising from perceived threats to the life of the individual rather than a wish to be rid of some innate, 'bad' death instinct, which he likened to the concept of 'original sin'. William's lust for life combined with his willingness to face death is encapsulated in two lines of a poem he likes by Walter Savage Landor, entitled 'Finis':

I warm'd both hands before the fire of life;
It sinks, and I am ready to depart.

2

William H. Gillespie's psychoanalysis of sexual perversions: an appreciation and integration

DR CHARLES W. SOCARIDES

Some personal remarks

It came as a pleasant surprise to be invited by Dr Sinason to write a historical review of Dr Gillespie's contributions on sexual perversion, describing the development of his concepts as well as commenting on their heuristic importance to the psychoanalytic research and therapy of these ineluctable conditions. As a beneficiary of Dr Gillespie's scientific observations over the years, and having incorporated many of his psychoanalytic discoveries into my own theories, I found it a welcome opportunity to express my indebtedness.

The task of reviewing Dr Gillespie's notable achievements was both challenge and fulfilment, as well as a considerable labour. I found myself in need of a 'token' to enchant and animate the intellectual work which lay before me, as well as a personal mandate from him for my review, as we had never met. I made my acceptance contingent on one proviso: namely, that I be provided with a picture of Dr Gillespie himself. The photograph duly arrived and lived up to my expectations: a man with the unequivocal appearance of earnestness and judgement, passion and patience, as well as liveliness of demeanour – qualities so evident in all his writings.

These personal needs met, I began to place Gillespie's papers in their historical context. It was soon apparent that it was impossible to write of Gillespie's contributions in isolation; for his discoveries and observations, always defined with surgical sharpness and precision, span over fifty-five years of work, and constitute an essential part of a tapestry woven by over a dozen of our most gifted psychoanalysts. Since his work played a key role in the evolution and advance of my own ideas, I decided to review his major accomplishments from the point of view of my own personal scientific experience. I shall now examine some of his major contributions, making a critical evaluation of their meaning and content, as well as

35

describing how they compare and integrate with the work of other investigators.

Gillespie is an anatomist of the psyche, if you will, who by careful observation has made a detailed examination of structure, separating the parts of an earlier, disorganised body of information in order to discover the position, structure and economy of each part as well as its relationship to the whole. As a medically trained psychoanalyst, his interest has been to look, again and again, at familiar phenomena and report on their macroscopic and microscopic form and structure. In so doing he has explained functional impairment in terms of 'what kind of difficulties stand in the way of normal sexual development' (Gillespie, 1940, p. 403). While he has rarely written of his actual therapeutic techniques, therapy is implied by his psychopathological diagnoses.

Like many of us of this period, Gillespie began his psychoanalytic career at one of the psychiatric hospitals devoted to the care of elderly/chronic patients with psychiatric problems. The study of such patients often appeared unrewarding to most physicians at the time, but Gillespie discovered 'fascinating pathological findings in such patients' and reported on them first in a MD thesis, then much later in a paper on regression, delivered at a symposium on regression in 1963 (Gillespie, 1963). In this connection I am reminded that Charcot, too, had, according to Freud, a great number of 'chronic nervous patients at his disposal', which enabled him to make use of his 'own special gifts'. Charcot, according to Freud,

> used to look again and again at the things he did not understand, to deepen his impression of them day by day, till suddenly an understanding of them dawned on him. In his mind's eye, the apparent chaos presented by the continual repetition of the same symptoms then gave way to order: the new nosological pictures emerged, characterised by constant combination of certain groups of symptoms. . . . He might be heard to say that the greatest satisfaction a man could have was to see something new – that is, to recognise it as new; and he remarked again and again on the difficulty and value of this kind of 'seeing'.
>
> (Freud, 1893, p. 12)

Gillespie's earliest seminal discoveries, going beyond Freud, supplied psychoanalysis with seeds which, once planted, have led to considerable progress in understanding: (1) the role of castration anxiety in producing perversion; (2) the significance of oedipal versus pre-oedipal factors; (3) the role of aggression in perversion; (4) the part played by splitting mechanisms as well as projection, and introjection; (5) superego functioning in perversion; (6) early concepts of classification of perversions.

It becomes clear that Gillespie has been not only an innovator and a discoverer, but a pioneer investigator whose work encompasses the entire history of accomplishments of psychoanalytic thought on perversions.

'A Contribution to the Study of Fetishism' (1940)

Strongly influenced by Sylvia Payne's 'Some Observations on the Ego Development of the Fetishist' (1939), Gillespie, as a young psychoanalytic practitioner, decided to publish his first psychoanalytic paper on the subject of sexual perversion. He believed that there was some urgency for presenting his clinical material, as World War II was upon us and most of us would be unlikely to have a large number of fetishists to report upon for some time, and that the best way of approaching the problem was to 'pool' our own experiences, even though they might be limited to a single case for the moment. This correct assumption was voiced by Greenacre, even as late as 1968. She noticed a difficulty facing every investigator in the area of perversion, namely, that there is a 'multiplicity of forms and varying intensities of the perversions, from the slightly deviant to the extreme or even bizarre [which] confuse us in our understanding of its essential character'.

It remains still a matter of psychoanalytic history that few psychoanalysts have the opportunity to treat or report on very many perverse patients during their psychoanalytic careers. Gillespie remarked that Payne did not think of fetishism as a perversion, but as something which 'saves the individual from a perverse form of sexuality' (Gillespie, 1940, p. 401). 'The component impulse which has prevailed,' she stated, 'if not placed under special control, is a sadistic impulse' (Payne, 1939, p. 169). The aim was to 'kill the love object'. What Gillespie offered at this time was the analysis of one of his own cases which confirmed Payne's earlier conclusion but added much more, for this initial paper was a cornucopia of multiple clinical observations which have withstood the test of time and have been frequently referred to in subsequent publications, by both Gillespie and others. Departing from classical theory, he challenged established psychoanalytic findings about the role of oedipal conflict and castration anxiety as exclusive agents in the production of a sexual perversion. He not only confirmed Payne's earlier findings that fetishism is a product of castration anxiety to be related almost exclusively to the phallic phase, but also suggested that 'the main dynamic force really [comes] from more primitive levels, which undeniably contribute to give its ultimate form to the fetish' (p. 402). In agreement with Freud's earlier comment (1919) that for the time being, 'we must be content to explain what occurs rather than what does not occur' (p. 402), he frankly admitted that we lacked specificity as to the aetiology of these problems; but he asserted 'the time seems to have

arrived when we must attempt to answer these more searching questions'
(p. 402). Influenced by Melanie Klein's discoveries of the introjection-
projection phases of early development, he began to speculate as to the
origins of these perversions in the earliest periods of life.

This early paper set the course for Gillespie's psychoanalytic journey
into perversion. He concluded as follows:

1 There was a strong indication that the mental mechanisms and psychic
   laws for the production of fetishism lay in the pre-oedipal phase of
   development, although the presence of oedipal pathology made this
   conclusion somewhat uncertain at this time.
2 The fetish serves to protect the love object from the dangers inherent
   in the fetishist's sadistic love with its annihilating tendencies.
3 The male fetishist has a profound unconscious identification with the
   female – an observation which was to be fully documented in later
   studies of perversion.
4 The fetish itself represents both the penis and a protection against the
   child's fear of penetration by the father's penis into the male body of
   the fetishist.
5 There is an overproduction of frustration and rage in fetishistic patients
   and, as a consequence, a close relationship may exist between
   masochism and sadism.
6 Most fetishists have an unconscious homosexual fantasy – a dread of
   the father taking an active role in their anal penetration. The unconscious fantasy is that of the patient delivering a 'dirty' (faecal) baby.
7 The fetishist is in the grip of a fantasy: the penis is a source of food, or
   of nutrition; this can be expressed in terms of the equation: 'penis =
   breast = baby'.
8 The fetish symbolised the female phallus, an observation already made
   by Freud (1905, 1927).
9 Sadism plays an important role in fetishism.
10 Introjection-projection mechanisms are prominent in such patients.
11 While the fetish may come into being as a result of castration anxiety,
    equally important as a determinant are the oral-aggressive impulses
    directed towards the father's penis, incorporated in the mother.

With typical modesty, Gillespie made a stunning assertion of far-reaching
consequences in emphasising the crucial importance of the possible pre-
oedipal origin of sexual perversion in general:

  Finally, reverting to the problem of phallic versus pregenital, I should
  like to make the following suggestion with regard to the aetiology of
  fetishism. May it not be that what we have actually to deal with is
  neither the one thing nor the other, but a combination of the two? I

do not simply mean that I want to have it both ways – what I am suggesting is a specific constellation, to use Dr. Glover's conception. I do feel that there are points about this case which give strong support to this view: in particular, the extraordinary compound (for it is much more than a mere mixture) of phallic, oral and anal aggressive and erotic phantasies.

To put it in another way, I would suggest that fetishism is the result of castration anxiety, but of a specific form of castration anxiety, a form produced by a strong admixture of certain oral and anal trends.

(Gillespie, 1940, pp. 414–15)

To appreciate properly the significance of this scientific leap, it should be noted that at this point in psychoanalytic theory, one invariably explained perverse psychopathology from a libidinal frame of reference, that is, in terms of oral, anal or phallic fixation. Furthermore, an increasing integration in psychoanalytic theory and practice in the field of perversion had yet to take place. For example, in a panel report (Arlow, 1954) entitled 'Perversions: Theoretical and Therapeutic Aspects', Arlow reported:

The aggressive drive, the significance of which, in comparison to the libido, was appreciated only within recent years in analysis, was in the forefront of the reformulations in the theories of perversions. . . . The importance of identification of narcissistic object-choices as defences against destructive wishes directed toward the object appeared in almost every contribution [in the 1954 panel report]. . . . The deleterious effects of distorted object relations which damage the developing superego through the corrupting influence of seduction, suggestion, and permissiveness show how considerations of problems of ego psychology were honoured . . . progressive advances in this field of psychoanalysis . . . have lagged behind the more dramatic successes affected in the area of neurosis.

(Arlow, p. 345)

Gillespie's speculations, therefore, well antedated newer concepts of ego psychology, object relations theory, the role of aggression, newer concepts of narcissism. Infant observational studies were only beginning.

More recently I have suggested, in an attempt at classification of perversions (Socarides, 1979, 1988, 1990), that the *forms of fetishism* consist of a wide range of conditions: from those which derive from very archaic primitive levels to those which are a product of more highly differentiated ones. Each individual case is hierarchically layered with dynamic mechanisms stemming from multiple points of fixation and regression (Socarides, 1960, 1988). Today we may conclude that a clinical picture of fetishism itself does not necessarily describe the *origin* of the particular mechanism responsible for it. When we study fetishism today, psychoanalytically, it is incumbent upon us to study the developmental stages through which the individual has passed, his level of fixation, the status of his object relations, and his ego functions, as well as the degree of separation–individuation (Mahler, 1965, 1967, 1968, *et al.* 1975) which has been achieved during the first three years of life.

Thus, a multiplicity of forms and varying intensities of the fetishistic perversions, from the slightly deviant to the extreme or even bizarre forms which have long confused us in understanding its essential character, can now be systematically examined and investigated, and treatment prescribed.

'The General Theory of Sexual Perversion' (1956)

This paper, first presented at the International Psychoanalytical Congress in Geneva (1955), boldly presented the status of our theories and understanding of sexual perversions as of thirty-nine years ago. I recall that Gillespie's unequivocal assertions provided much insight and encouragement to my own neophyte psychoanalytic studies in the area of the study of sexual perversion. My own work would have been impossible without the clarifying contributions made by Gillespie, and others at that time, including those of Sandor Lorand, Gustav Bychowski, Robert Bak, Masud Khan, Edward Glover, Otto Fenichel, Anna Freud and Phyllis Greenacre.

Grounded simply in what Otto Fenichel cited in his important work, *The Psychoanalytic Theory of Neurosis* (1945), I found myself irresistibly drawn to the work of Gillespie. For this paper was remarkably comprehensive, taking into account infantile sexuality and affirming that the problem of sexual perversion lies in the defence against oedipal difficulties. It underscored the concept that in sexual perversion there is a regression of libido and aggression to pre-oedipal levels rather than a primary fixation at these levels. It stressed the importance of ego behaviour and ego–defence manoeuvres as well as the Sachs mechanism (1923). Gillespie delineated the characteristics of the ego which make it possible for it to adopt a certain aspect of infantile sexuality, thereby enabling it to ward off the rest. The superego had a special relationship to the ego which made the latter tolerant of this particular form of sexuality. 'A split in the ego often coexists with a split in the sexual object', he noted, so that the object becomes idealised and, therefore, 'relatively anxiety-free, and relatively guilt-free in part' (Gillespie, 1956a: 402).

I found that I could apply the seven principal points in Gillespie's general theory to my treatment of perverse patients, especially to the numerous homosexuals whom I treated in psychoanalysis. For example: (1)

he believed that the raw materials of perversion are drawn from the constituent elements of infantile sexuality. (2) 'A clinical perversion, however, is generally specialised in an elaborate way, leaving only one or two routes open for achieving sexual excitement, discharging sexual tension, and establishing a sexual object relationship' (Gillespie, 1956a, p. 402). (3) A perversion represents a defence against the Oedipus complex and castration anxiety. (4) Defensive systems induce: (a) a regression of libido and aggression to pregenital levels with a resulting increase in sadism and its associated anxiety, and (b) guilt feelings and defences against sadism and anxiety 'designed to protect both the self and the object' (p. 402). (5) A special characteristic of perversion is the libidinisation of anxiety, guilt and pain as a method of defence. (6) No less important than the vicissitudes of instinct are the ego's behaviour and defensive manoeuvres. (7) In perversion the ego has adopted a certain piece of infantile sexuality and is enabled in this way to ward off the rest.

Gillespie believed that the ego is able to do this, first, because the superego is especially tolerant of this form of sexuality and (even more important) second, 'because of a split in the ego and in the object . . . an idealised object and a relatively anxiety-free and guilt-free part-ego are available for the purposes of a sexual relationship, which takes place, so to say, in an area where the writ of reality-testing does not run' (Gillespie, 1956a, p. 402).

In his 'General Theory', Gillespie was the first to call attention to a relatively unknown paper, that of Hanns Sachs, written in German in 1923, which, by virtue of Gillespie's knowledge of German, provided him and psychoanalysis with the first valid explanation of the *mechanism* of sexual perversion. Upon reading Gillespie's paper, I determined to have the Sachs paper translated into English, and have since made it widely available to psychoanalytic students for their perusal and application to clinical material (translation by Hella Freud Bernays, 1964).

Gillespie had the insight to perceive, from the writings of Hanns Sachs, that a perversion preserves a particular, suitable portion of infantile experience or fantasy in the conscious mind, through the vicissitudes of childhood and puberty. The rest of the representatives of the instinctual drives have succumbed to repression instigated by their all-too-strong need for gratification or stimulation. The pleasurable sensations of infantile sexuality in general are now displaced on to the conscious, 'suitable portion of infantile experience' (Sachs, 1923). This conscious, suitable portion, Gillespie noted, is now supported and endowed with a high-pleasure reward – so high, indeed, that it competes successfully with the primacy of the genitals. Certain conditions appear to make this fragment particularly suitable. The pregenital stage of development upon which the pervert is strongly fixated must be included in it. The extremely powerful partial

41

drive must find its particular form of gratification in it. This particular fragment must have some special relationship to the ego, which allows it to escape repression. One must keep in mind that in the ego, unconscious elements are present, e.g., guilt and resistance. Instinctual drives are in a continual struggle throughout the developmental stages of life. The complete subjugation of drive which gives pleasure to the ego is not possible. We have to resign ourselves to a compromise, allowing the pleasure to remain in a partial complex, to be taken up into the ego and to be sanctioned, while the remaining components are detached but repressed more easily. This separation or split, 'in which the one piece [of infantile sexuality] enters into the service of repression and thus carries over into the ego the pleasure of a pre-oedipal stage of development while the rest falls victim to repression, appears to be the mechanism of perversion' (Sachs, 1923).

The most difficult work of repression is almost always to effect a detachment from the infantile object–choice, the Oedipus complex, and castration fear. Thus, the partial drive does not continue directly into a perversion (homosexuality or other perversion) but must pass through the permutations of the oedipal conflict. This alternation of the original drive eventually wipes out traces of the Oedipus complex, eliminating both the important individuals involved and even one's own self-involvement. The product becomes the perverse fantasy which enters consciousness and yields pleasure. It follows that fantasies which lie outside the circle of infantile sexual gratification present themselves as a 'way out'. For instance, male homosexuals cannot deal with their extremely strong fixation on the mother. They fixate instead on their own sex, as a result of narcissism, and in a retreat from later castration anxiety. This fixation is incorporated into the ego and is acceptable to it. In essence, the ego has taken over a portion of what would otherwise be repressed. Nevertheless, the repressed portion may still remain strong enough to threaten a breakthrough and the homosexual or pervert may, at any time, develop neurotic symptoms.

Gillespie's interpretation of Sachs's meaning was invaluable to me, and I applied this information to the problem of homosexuality in the following way: homosexuality is a living relic of the past, testifying to the fact that there was once a conflict involved in an especially strongly developed component instinct in which complete victory was impossible for the ego and repression was only partially successful. The ego had to be content with a compromise of repressing the greater part of the infantile libidinal strivings (primary identification with the mother), intense un-neutralised aggression toward her, dread of separation, and fear of fusion at the expense of sanctioning and taking into itself the smaller part. For example, it became clear to me that the wish to penetrate the mother's body (which I found in the dreams and fantasies of homosexual patients) or the wish to suck, incorporate and injure the mother's breast underwent repression. In these instances, a piece of the infantile libidinal strivings has entered the service of repression through displacement and substitution. I could now assert that instead of the mother's body being penetrated, sucked, injured or incorporated, it is the male partner's body which undergoes this fate; instead of the mother's breast, it is the penis with which the patient interacts. Homosexuality, in effect, became the choice of the lesser evil.

I observed that two defence mechanisms, identification and substitution, played a crucial role, especially in my homosexual patients. The homosexual makes an identification with the masculinity of his partner in the sexual act (A. Freud, 1951, 1954). In order to defend himself against the positive Oedipus complex – that is, his love for his mother, hatred for his father, and punitive aggressive drives toward the body of the mother – the homosexual substitutes the partner's body and penis for the mother's breast. Homosexuals, it could be seen, desperately need and seek a sexual contact whenever they feel weakened, frightened, depleted, guilty, ashamed, or in any way helpless or powerless. In my patients' words, they want their 'shot' of masculinity. They then feel miraculously well and strengthened, thereby avoiding any tendency to disintegrative phenomena or separation anxiety. It also enhances their self-representation. They simultaneously feel reintegrated upon achieving orgasm with a male partner. Their pain, fear and weakness disappear for the moment, and they may feel well and whole again. The male partners whom they pursue appear to be representatives of their own self in relation to an active phallic mother.

There are two parts to this concept. The first is an identification with a partner of the same sex. In this way homosexuals achieve masculinity through identification with the partner's penis (A. Freud, 1954; Socarides, 1978, 1988). The man chosen as a partner represents one's forfeited masculinity (and self-representation) regained. The second is a substitution of the penis of the male partner for the mother's breast, an observation already made by other investigators. In every homosexual encounter, it could now be seen, there was a hidden continuation of the close tie to the mother through the breast = penis equation. The reassuring presence of the penis in place of the breast allows the homosexual to feel that he is maintaining the tie with the mother but at a safe distance from her. Furthermore, he divests himself of oedipal guilt by demonstrating to her that he could not have possible interests in other females; he is interested only in men. In addition, he is protecting the mother against the onslaught of other men's penises, allowing penetration into himself instead.

Interpretations along this line make a homosexual patient aware of his unconscious motivations and lead him to realise, in later phases of treatment, that he is engaged in an act of major self-deception, having been

43

victimised into sexual activity with individuals of the same sex by certain intricate, unconscious, psychic transformations. He has not given up his maleness at all; he urgently and desperately wants to be a man, but is able to do this only by identifying with the masculinity, penis, and body of his partner in the sexual act. Homosexuality, it could be seen, served to protect the personality against regression. If homosexual enactments did not take place, the patient would experience separation anxiety and regress to earlier points of fixation: in the severest of instances, such regressions constitute a threat of loss of ego-boundaries, and a fear of impending dissolution of the self. Overt homosexual acts are crucial for the survival of the ego when it is faced with the catastrophic situation of imminent merging with the mother and the pull toward the earliest phases of development.

Gillespie was one of the first to emphasise clearly: (1) the underlying unconscious anxiety of the perverse patient, ordinarily hidden from conscious awareness by the neutralising effect of perverse performances, and (2) the absolute necessity for this anxiety to be explored within the motivational context of its occurrence. He noted a dramatic appearance of severe anxiety, tension, depression and other symptomatology upon a patient's interruption of perverse practices. Gillespie had earlier underscored this central feature of perverse symptoms, namely that they represent a compromise formation against deeper anxieties, anxieties which heretofore had only been briefly alluded to, and their content never clearly defined. Anxiety, an outcome of interruption of activities, was only then beginning to be seen consistently in the course of treating patients in depth, and this anxiety had a definite content. While this anxiety was usually attributed to castration fears of the oedipal phase and a secondary regression to earlier points of fixation, it ultimately, in my opinion, could only be explained by a combination of both oedipal-phase conflict and an even more important pre-oedipal conflict, that is, anxiety and guilt in association with separation from the object (Socarides, 1988).

'The Structure and Aetiology of Sexual Perversion' (1956)

In this paper, published in the same year as his 'General Theory', Gillespie took increasing note of the importance of aggression to perversion formation. This contribution was published simultaneously with Robert Bak's (1956) far-reaching conclusions as to the role of aggression in perversion, published during the same year and in the same volume, one of whose editors was the leading theoretician in America in the area of perversions, Sandor Lorand.

Gillespie asserted that frustration, aggression and sadism were central to

44

any understanding of perversion formation. He and Bak were in agreement that the psychoanalytic understanding of perversion in mid-century had, unfortunately, rested almost entirely on the dominance of pregenitality in sexual functioning and on the traumata of the phallic phase, with only a gradually emerging interest in the traumatic influences of the prephallic era. These concepts had been largely investigated in connection with the role of the development of the libido and its vicissitudes; it was now time for a change. The concept of fixation and its relationship to libidinal development in the production of aggression secondary to frustration had been noted by Gillespie in his 1940 paper.

Bak, from his wide clinical experience, began an integration of aggression into sexual pathology as an 'equal partner' of libido. He suggested, expanding on Gillespie's idea, that we can assume in perversions an 'increased quantity of aggression, either constitutionally . . . or as a consequence of those very early environmental stresses that sometimes increase the impetus of the aggressive drives' (Bak, 1956, p. 232).

Both Bak and Gillespie clearly understood what was later to be documented by infant observational studies, namely that these reactions will depend upon a 'temporal factor', that is, the stage of structural development and the rate of establishing object relations. The earliest period of life, the pre-oedipal phase of development, and the stages of object relations of that period are of particular importance, suggesting that the group of perversions that are the 'most ego-syntonic', and, for the most part, escape our investigation, are those in which there are highly developed object relations and which originate from or near the Oedipus Constellation.

Operating from a Mahlerian theoretical frame of reference, I asserted that well-structured perversions are fixated in the rapprochement phase of the separation–individuation process, and therefore are definitely pre-oedipal in origin and are not a product of oedipal conflict. Traumatic overstimulation, occurring even in the undifferentiated phase of development, affects both libidinal and aggressive drives in their early nascent state simultaneously, with resultant tendencies to the development of various forms of perversion.

Bak's comments on aggression and perversion proved extremely valuable:

1 Overstimulation of undifferentiated libido and aggression is a determinant for heightened sadistic disposition with its character of 'unusual inner pressure and drivenness for gratification' (Bak, 1956, p. 233).
2 'Large quantities of excitation' during the early phases of ego development tend to lead to 'uncontrolled libidinal and aggressive discharge without interference from the ego' (Bak, p. 233).
3 Such discharges are important since the defences at this stage of

development are 'autoplastic, and largely based on a magic omnipotence which consists of denial of the outside world' (Bak, p. 233). This 'denial of the outside world' appeared to be equivalent to Gillespie's earlier statement that these activities occur 'where the writ of reality-testing has not run' (1956a, p. 402).

Bak's contribution was more clinical than Gillespie's. He described the function of aggression in various perversions. With regard to exhibitionists, he confirmed that the first task of the exhibitionist was to assure himself against castration. The acting out of his aggression and the exhibitionistic act itself served as a means to deny deeper, passive, feminine identification. The male exhibitionist identified with the female child, and expressed awe and ambivalence towards the paternal phallus. Given the greater degree of 'ego-syntonicity' of aggression in men (Bak, 1956), the passive feminine self was then externalised onto the object. The fetishist, on the other hand, used the fetish and revered it as a means of denying and protecting himself against destructive wishes directed against the object, especially the breast. The transvestite defended himself against the loss of the object by taking on its external appearance and, in so doing, denied castration and destruction. In homosexuality there was: (1) a shift from aggressive rivalry to love, making the object of aggression into the object of sexual desire; (2) 'intense attachment to the mother [which] leads to identification with her but contains an intermediate phase of aggression motivated by this attachment' (Bak, 1956, p. 238); (3) destructive impulses against the mother which were resolved, and at the same time, in the resolution, paved the way to a libidinisation of aggression against the rival. The homosexual thus succeeded in defending himself against retaliation from both sexes.

Both Bak and Gillespie made giant steps forward in this poorly understood area of pathology of perversions. These advances spurred me on to suggest a unitary theory of sexual perversions, first proposed in 1969 and published in 1979 and 1988.

Where my own theories tended to differ was around the aetiological significance of castration anxiety and oedipal fears versus those of pre-oedipality. The emphasis on castration anxiety by both Gillespie and Bak seemed to me to be a secondary overlay in the true, well-structured perversions. For all obligatory perversions, I continued to feel, were a pre-oedipal disorder characterised by an object-relations conflict, rather than a structural one involving the castration anxiety of the oedipal phase with regression to earlier, pre-oedipal positions of fixation.

When too much aggression is stimulated, Bak noted, it may lead to an 'overflowing' between self and object as the ego is in a process of development. This may well lead to a continuation of a feminine identification (already suggested by Gillespie in his first paper) and a predominance of the introjective-projective mechanism often cited by Gillespie. The type of perversion produced under such conditions, Bak asserted, was closely allied to schizophrenia, a special area of Bak's clinical interest. However, Bak concluded, 'Perversions in schizophrenics seem to represent different forms of defenses against the un-neutralised aggression threatening the object' (Bak, 1956, p. 235). In both Gillespie's and Bak's contributions, aggression was clearly established as equal to libido in the causation of perversions, with special emphasis placed on castration anxiety and the Oedipus complex. Common to all perversion is a dramatised denial of castration, a denial augmented by a projection of heightened aggression, and marked by a disturbance in sexual identification established as a defence against destruction of the object, as first suggested by Gillespie (1940).

Guilt over destructive aggression is handled by denial and by splitting of the ego and a 'denial of reality' in these patients. This had already been mentioned by Gillespie in his paper entitled 'Notes on the Analysis of Sexual Perversions' (1952). But how do perverts become masochists and sadists? Gillespie's answer was that the splitting mechanism determined the ego's handling of such aggression. These individuals (sadists), he stated, regard their perversion as perfectly harmless (negation), and insist that most people 'just do not have "the right idea" about it' (Gillespie, 1952, p. 399). They state that for themselves they abhor real cruelty and enjoy themselves only if their partners are enjoying their consensual role. The real object, according to Gillespie, is the 'instrument of whipping' (p. 399); the patient's attitude to whips is very similar to that of a fetishist to his fetish. All in all, the guilt in perversion is not guilty oedipal activity but is guilt neutralised through the mechanism described by Sachs.

'The Psychoanalytic Theory of Sexual Deviation with Special Reference to Fetishism' (1964)

Gillespie's (1964b) contribution to Ismond Rosen's textbook, *The Pathology and Treatment of Sexual Deviation*, repeated many of his earlier assertions but went on to define essential differences between neurosis and perversion, among other important contributions. He reiterated that while we may say that in a neurosis, a repressed fantasy breaks through into conscious expression only in the form of symptoms unwelcome to the ego, and is typically accompanied by neurotic suffering, in a perversion the fantasy remains conscious, being welcomed by the ego and pleasurable. The difference seemed to him to be one of 'ego attitude', positive or negative emotional signs, rather than one of content. This comparison always seemed to be insufficient for a total explanation of why the personality of the pervert accepts its perversion. Why is it that the ego of one individual is especially tolerant and has a welcoming attitude towards elements of primitive sexuality, while in others it is necessary to deal with them so sternly, either by the formation of neurotic symptoms or by the certain transformations of adolescence?

Was it simply due to Sachs's mechanism with its capacity for substitution displacement, changing into its opposites, etc.? Or was it, as I increasingly believed, due to the fact that when individuals react with anxiety to perverse fantasies instead of with pleasure, we are dealing with a different phenomenon? That is, we are not dealing with a perversion at all, but with the consequences of a structural conflict with regression to deeper oral and anal phases, and the threat of fusion with the maternal object. In contrast, in true perversions we are dealing with early developmental arrest, whether partial or complete, which is the bedrock of their development. The solution of this problem, which leads either to homosexual desire or to homosexual dread, remains for future clinical researchers. It lies in the answer to the essential question of how the ego can totally accept a true perversion. The questions posed by such an enquiry are formidable and the answers would do much to clarify our understanding of the 'choice' of perversion. What is the particular relationship between the ego and this particular piece of childhood sexuality that makes it acceptable? How has the ego managed to make a compromise? And what is the attitude of the superego, if indeed a superego as we conceive of it exists by the age of 3 or 4?

Perhaps the answer can best be understood if we refer to the superego as a *pregenital archaic superego* formation, as suggested by Sandler (1960). Gillespie offered the following explanation: perversion may represent the sexual attitudes of the parents of perverts and a faulty superego may have developed on the basis of a parental model. This had already been suggested by Johnson and Szurek (1952), Kolb and Johnson (1955), as well as Sperling (1956). In such instances, perverse and pregenital activities are treated with relative leniency, or even encouraged; through the unconscious perverse needs of the parents, an unconscious corruption of the superego is effected. Therefore, a particular piece of infantile sexuality, Gillespie felt, is acceptable to the ego because of the ego's judgement of what will please or at least pass relatively unchallenged by parental figures, eventually internalised by superego formation (Gillespie, 1964b, p. 133). He noted that the attempt to please the superego is especially prominent in those perversions with masochistic content.

In this paper, Gillespie emphasised Glover's (1933) suggestion that perversions may form a developmental series reflecting stages in the overcoming of anxiety concerning the individual's own body or external objects. They represent attempts at defence by means of excessive libidinisation against anxieties connected with introjection and projection. These

primitive mechanisms, Gillespie suggested, are related to psychotic formations and, following the lead of Glover (1933), he noted that certain
perversions have to be regarded as the negative not so much of neuroses
but of *psychoses* as they help patch over flaws in the development of reality
sense.

The question of whether perversions are a defence against neurotic
development or, indeed, of psychosis remained a pressing one in my own
mind. There was evidence for both, and in an attempt to clarify the issue,
I proposed a classification (Socarides, 1978, 1988, 1990). In so doing, I
utilised much of what Gillespie had previously asserted about whether a
perversion was oedipal or pre-oedipal in origin. I was, furthermore,
stimulated in this undertaking by Greenacre's (1968) notable paper entitled
'Perversions: General Considerations Regarding their Genetic and
Dynamic Background.' She stated:

> Recent studies of early ego development would indicate that [the]
> fundamental disturbance is . . . that the defectively developed ego
> uses the pressure of the maturing libidinal phases for its own purposes
> in characteristic ways because of the extreme and persistent
> narcissistic need . . . Probably in most perversions, there is a pro-
> longation of the introjective-projective stage in which there is an
> incomplete separation of the 'I' from the 'other' and an oscillation
> between the two. This is associated with a more than usually strong
> capacity for primary identification.
>
> (Greenacre, 1968, p. 302)

Three contributions, therefore, aimed at describing the origins of sexual
perversions and set the stage for attempting a comprehensive psychoanalytic classification of perversion: the first by Gillespie (1956a), the
second by Greenacre (1968), and the third by my writings in 1978 in
which I proposed a classification of sexual perversions.

To elaborate: Gillespie relied heavily on infantile sexuality and affirmed
that the problem of perversion lies in the defences against oedipal difficulties.
He underscored the concept that in perversion there is a regression of the
libido and aggression to pre-oedipal levels, rather than a primary fixation at
those levels. This theory, to recapitulate, provided an all-important insight
into ego-defences, the Sachs mechanism, the role of the superego in
perversion formation, splitting processes, and, now, the relation of perversion to psychosis.

My classification (1978–88), published in my book *The Pre-Oedipal
Origin and Psychoanalytic Theory of Sexual Perversions* (1988), utilised much
of what Gillespie had previously asserted, Glover's comments about the
relationship of perversion to psychosis, as well as Greenacre's formulations
(1968). By 1978, I had begun to utilise the theoretical frame of reference

proposed by Margaret Mahler and her associates in describing separation–individuation phases of childhood to explain my clinical findings.

The work of Mahler (1967, 1968) and her associates (Mahler *et al.*, 1975), among others, delineating symbiotic and separation–individuation phases of human development, when applied to clinical data already gathered through the psychoanalysis of adult perverts, helped to explain that the fixation of the pervert lay, in all probability, in the various phases of the separation–individuation process, producing a disturbance in self-identity as well as in gender identity; a persistence of a primary feminine identification with the mother; separation anxiety, fears of engulfment (restoring the mother–child unity); and disturbance in object relations and associated ego functions. By combining both clinical data and theoretical explanation, I conceived of a classification which I believed would answer many of the questions posed by some of my colleagues.

I proposed that there were three major forms of perversion. My classification was based on the following items: (1) the conscious and/or unconscious motivation, (2) the developmental stage from which the patient's nuclear conflict arose, and (3) the degree of pathology of internalised object relations in perverse patients. In effect, in my opinion, I had made inroads into Gillespie's vexing question as to whether the aetiology was pre-oedipal or oedipal; it was both if not more. I decided, on the basis of these three factors, to divide perversion into three major forms: (1) two types of pre-oedipal perversion, (2) oedipal perversion, and (3) schizoperversion (the coexistence of perversion and schizophrenia).

In the milder pre-oedipal type (pre-oedipal type I), the surface clinical picture was of oedipal conflicts and castration anxiety, which obscured the deeper and more important pre-oedipal ones, and regression did not involve severe impairment in object relations and other ego functions.

In the more severe pre-oedipal type (pre-oedipal type II), a pre-oedipal fixation was of prime importance, constantly dominating the psychic life of the individual in his search for an appropriate, gender-defined self-identity and a cohesive self. Oedipal conflict and castration fear might defend against deeper fears, and pre-oedipal fantasies might defend against the emergence of oedipal material. For a complete description of these different forms of perversion, I refer the reader to my book *The Pre-Oedipal Origin and Psychoanalytic Theory of Sexual Perversions* (1988) and to 'The Homosexualities: A Psychoanalytic Classification' (1990).

Refinements in my understanding of the forms of perversion led me to conclude that the true perversion is always a pre-oedipal disorder and does not arise from oedipal conflict with a regression to earlier phases. Crucial to the formation of perversion was the initial disturbance in gender-defined self-identity, a product of the inability to traverse successfully the separation–individuation phases of human life. Oedipal perversion could be seen as a different form of perversion, which I termed *perverse behaviour*, which could be treated similarly to the way in which the neuroses are treated. The latter occurs as secondary to a temporary regression and, in my opinion, does not represent a developmental arrest, whether partial or complete, but a regression to a point of infantile fixation.

Female sexuality and other contributions

Only twice did Gillespie move from his study of the male and his sexual difficulties to that of the female. In 1969, his paper on 'Concepts of Vaginal Orgasm' was representative of his constant awareness of developments in the field of sexuality in general and his willingness to accept new and substantial evidence for modification of psychoanalytic theory. He frankly affirmed that the findings of vaginal orgasm represented by Masters and Johnson in their experimental studies were certainly something to which psychoanalysts themselves should give thoughtful appraisal. He insisted that there must be a revision of the traditional psychoanalytic theory of vaginal orgasm, and that this must be made in accordance with the anatomical and physiological findings of these investigators. There can be no doubt that orgasm involves anatomical structures around the vagina, including vaginal barrel stimulation, *and* clitoral stimulation. How is such clitoral stimulation achieved in deep penetration? It is via a ligamentous connection between the labia and the clitoral hood which, through physical stimulation, allows for increasing sexual arousal. Ligamentous stimulation on the clitoris then spreads, of course, into the vagina, with rising excitement due to venous engorgement of both the muscular and vascular structures of the female, thereby leading to orgasm.

In 'Woman and her Discontents: A Reassessment of Freud's Views on Female Sexuality' (1975), he writes that Freud's inability to discover a female analogue to seminal-vesicle stimulation was a stumbling block to our theories. However, it is now known that not only the seminal vesicles are stimulated but that there is, of course, hormonal stimulation to the cerebral cortex, which, in the last analysis, is responsible for sexual arousal. Certainly, psychological factors intrude and disturb any and all neuro-muscular and vascular responses to stimulation.

In his paper entitled 'Contribution to Symposium on Homosexuality' (1964a), Gillespie reviewed some of our knowledge and theories relating to homosexuality and asked whether or not they could be accommodated to a general theory of perversions. He concluded that some of the manifest-ations of homosexuality may be properly classified with the perversions, while others may not. Perhaps the confusion, he noted, lay in some of Freud's original ideas of bisexuality, which, in my opinion and his, have now been discarded by many, if not most, psychoanalytic clinicians versed in the treatment of perversions. No one is born, in my opinion, with a constitutional desire for sexual relations with the same *or* the opposite sex; both are learned behaviour. Gillespie concludes that although there are 'no differences in principle between homosexuality and other perversions', there are certain specific features of homosexuality, such as its socially cohesive quality when aim-inhibited, which lead to social consequences not found in other perversions. As regards bisexuality, he refutes all the arguments for it.

He commented that we should separate homosexuals into those in whom there is a regression from oedipal levels, and, secondly, those whose homosexuality originates in pre-oedipal identifications. The first type is similar to the normal male 'bisexuality' in that there are mainly overt male homosexuals whose homosexuality can be considered as a part of oedipal bisexuality. 'The other type are predominantly overt homosexuals, and their heterosexual activity can be regarded as pseudo-heterosexuality arising from superego and ego ideal demands in a pre-oedipally determined homosexual' (Gillespie, 1964a, pp. 206–7). He concludes that the psychosexual development in such cases (the pre-oedipal) is basically that of a perverse overt homosexual. He recognises correctly that in some homosexuals their behaviour is 'natural to the individual because of a pre-oedipal fixation' (p. 207). He again asks the important question: 'Is homosexuality necessarily the outcome of an attempt to deal with the Oedipus complex, exploiting a particular piece of infantile sexuality for this purpose; or can it be better understood as a direct outcome of the pre-oedipal mother–child relationship?' (p. 207). He concludes that the best-established analytic findings confirm that in the homosexuality of both sexes, the mother relationship is a vitally important issue, and on this issue, I am in complete agreement with him.

Gillespie is secure in his position of regarding homosexuality as a perversion, and he is uncomfortable with the genetic studies which propose the 'normality' of homosexuality. He says we should beware of accepting uncritically the proposition that homosexuality is simply a perversion like any other, and that it is unwise to argue that 'homosexuality occupies a special place because it is based on universal constitutional bisexuality' (p. 208). Powerful psychoanalytic arguments are now appearing in the literature which emphasise the essential importance of pre-oedipal fantasies rather than an oedipal castration threat; in particular, fantasies involving oral fixations relating to the mother and her breast.

Lastly, I wish to comment only briefly on his paper entitled 'Aggression and Instinct Theory' (1971), and his observations on ageing and death. I am thoroughly in agreement with Gillespie in his view that 'the explanatory uses [Klein] makes of the death instinct theory inevitably gives the impression that ultimately it is this inherent "bad" element in the infant that gives rise to trouble, rather than, for example, any failure in mothering' (p. 157). I agree that Klein's view of the death instinct and its clinical application as an explanatory concept does indeed constitute a serious stumbling block, as he says, although its concepts of 'good and bad objects', splitting, and paranoid and depressive positions have important implications for all clinical work including perversions, and I, personally, have found them useful in interpreting some of the deepest pre-oedipal conflicts. While sexual masochism, in the context of orgastic pleasure and sexual arousal, leads us to considerations of death and pleasure-coated self-damage, I believe it does not convince one to postulate an 'instinct of self destruction'.

During a lengthy psychoanalytic experience, my concentration on Eros rather than Thanatos has deterred me from careful examination of the various manifestations of an instinct for self-destruction, although I have been tempted to delve into the theoretical issue. On the whole, death, in my opinion, does not come by a special operation of instinct but from a failure of adaptation. More careful enquiry may lead me to a different conclusion. I shall escape confrontation with this most formidable subject by taking refuge in a statement of an earlier mentor, Sandor Rado:

In environments that do not tax their adaptive powers, primitive organisms can be kept alive indefinitely. The germ cells of the extant metazoa have been alive for about one billion years. Freud's interpretation of life as a titanic struggle between the two forces, Eros and the death instinct, perpetuates ancient mythology. It depicts, once again, the eternal war between Vishnu, the preserver, and Shiva, the destroyer of the Hindu Trimurti; between the Persian Ormazd, the Lord of Light, and Ahriman, the Lord of Darkness; between God and Satan, the personified forces of love and hate, attraction and repulsion, etc. This perennial strife of the gods is continually fed by perennial human passion, or as Freud himself put it, by the Id. The battle of Eros and Death, as unfolded by Freud, is a moving spectacle, filled with suspense, agony and hope. The scientific investigator quietly reduces this Olympian drama to the observation that pleasure is the source of fulfillment of life, and death is its problem.

(Rado, 1956, p. 203)

Papers

A: The psychoanalytic theory of sexual development and sexual deviation

3

A contribution to the study of fetishism[1]

The clinical material upon which this paper is based is derived from an analysis which was interrupted by the war. I had hoped to have collected more material and reached more definite conclusions, but there is nothing to be gained now by postponement. In view of the paucity of cases recorded in the analytical literature, publication of my incomplete findings seems justified.

It is not my intention to deal with the literature of fetishism. It is not very extensive on the analytical side; and on the non-analytical side, although extensive, it is not very illuminating. Freud has expressed his fundamental contributions to the subject with great lucidity, and there is no doubt to my mind that they provide us with the most important line of approach. But I feel sure that he did not mean to suggest that the last word had been said on the matter. Further additions of great value have in fact been made, notably by Sylvia Payne. I should like to thank her both for the help she gave me in the early stages of the analysis and for her very stimulating recent paper on the subject.[2]

It will be remembered that Dr Payne laid special emphasis on the pregenital components determining fetishism, and on the importance of introjection-projection mechanisms. She said: 'In my opinion the fetish saves the individual from a perverse form of sexuality. The component impulse which would prevail if not placed under special control is the sadistic impulse' (p. 169). The aim, she said, is to kill the love object. Ample confirmation of these views is to be found in the analysis of my own case.

This brings me to what I conceive to be the crux of the problem of fetishism at the present time, and I want to present it in as lucid a manner as possible, at the risk of appearing elementary and obvious. The problem may be stated thus: is fetishism primarily a product of castration anxiety, to be related almost exclusively to the phallic phase, and concerned to maintain the existence of a female penis; or does the main dynamic force really come from more primitive levels, which undeniably contribute to give its ultimate form to the fetish?

Although Freud was the first to draw attention to the scopophilic and coprophilic components in fetishism, he made it quite clear that he regarded it primarily as a method of dealing with castration anxiety and preserving a belief in the phallic mother. At the same time, he says, it saves the patient from the necessity of becoming homosexual, by endowing the woman with the character that makes her tolerable as a sexual object. He admitted that he was unable to say why the castration fear resulting from the sight of the female genital causes some to become homosexual, others fetishists, while the great majority overcome the experience. For the present, he says, we must be content to explain what occurs rather than what does not occur. But this lack of specificity in our aetiology is one of the problems of which we are becoming more and more conscious, and the time seems to have arrived when we must attempt to answer these more searching questions.

According to Freud's conception, then, the castration complex is the alpha and omega of fetishism. I think it would be fair to say that Sylvia Payne's paper, while by no means neglecting the importance of castration anxiety, tended to emphasise the mental mechanisms and psychic layers which the work of Melanie Klein and her followers has brought so much into the foreground of our discussions in recent years.

The fact that my own observations are based on one case only tends to invalidate any generalisations one might be tempted to make; for clearly it is difficult to be sure which facts are typical of fetishism and which are peculiar to the particular patient, and perhaps have little relation to fetishism as such. But as any one worker is unlikely to have the opportunity of analysing a large number of fetishists, it would seem that the only way we can tackle the problem is by a pooling of our experiences, and the tentative conclusions derived from the study of one case may therefore be of some value. Even though I am thus limited to one case, it will not be possible for me to give anything like a complete case history. The analysis was a fairly lengthy one, covering a period of nearly three years, and the material produced was at all times profuse; often indeed embarrassingly so.

I propose, therefore, after giving a brief general sketch of the case for purposes of orientation, to concentrate on one particular facet, corresponding approximately to one phase of the analysis. This facet is one which, so far as I know, has not hitherto received much attention from analysts. I refer to the patient's struggles and difficulties in endeavouring to achieve a full genital potent relationship with a heterosexual love object. That is to say, I propose to examine the problem from the other end, as it were: instead of discussing what makes the patient a fetishist, to consider what kind of difficulties stand in the way of his normal sexual development. It is clear that these difficulties will throw a great deal of light on the factors responsible for fetishism.

The patient, whom I shall call A., when he came to me near the end of 1936, was a young man on the eve of his twenty-first birthday. He had already had a period of some eighteen months analysis with Dr Eder, towards whom he had developed a very emotional superficially positive transference. The analysis had been undertaken at his parents' request on account of his masturbatory activities, which were of a fetishistic nature. It had been abruptly cut short by Dr Eder's death in the spring of 1936. This event had at the time only a superficial effect; but by the time he came to me some eight months later, a severe reaction taking the form of a hypochondriacal depression had developed, and it was on account of this condition that he was referred to me.

When A., the third and last child, was born in 1916, his father was serving in the war. Hence A. saw little of him until the age of 3, and this fact played no small role in his psychological development. His parents were again separated when he was 12; this time it was his mother who went away for a period of about a year to join his older brother in Canada. Such a separation of the parents seems to be a not uncommon finding in fetishism, though I must confess that I am not clear what is its exact aetiological role, if any. Younger than the brother, but several years older than A., there was a sister.

A. was fed exclusively on the bottle, a fact with which he was fond of reproaching his mother. According to his account, hers is much the more dominant personality of the two parents. She is a very dynamic woman, much interested in intellectual matters, and for this A. greatly admired her, though analysis revealed underneath this admiration a deep reproach for her lack of a more flesh and blood relationship with him – a relationship which would have been realised had she given him the breast. At the same time, she was vivid and active, virile and virulent, as he expressed it. The father, on the other hand, according to A.'s account, was much more passive and placid. In this way it was possible for A. to become very confused as to the differences between the sexes. Typically, the thing was worked out on the mental rather than the bodily plane. This tendency to intellectualisation is a very characteristic feature in my patient. On the one hand it depends on an identification with the mother and a taking over of her attitude; but much more important from the dynamic point of view, I think, is its value as a defence mechanism against bodily anxieties. In fact, I came to realise that his intellectualisation plays a role similar to his fetishism in combating castration and related anxieties. Intellect is something which a woman can have equally with a man; so that if one concentrates on intellect one can deny the fateful anatomical difference. Similarly, by taking activity as the criterion of maleness, he could demonstrate to his own satisfaction that the female was more male than the male. Besides castration anxiety, however, another very important motive unconsciously underlying the production of this theory was the need to convince himself that the mother was strong enough to be safe against the danger of his own (and also his father's) sadistic attacks, so that she could survive them and still be there at the end of it all. Here again there is a very close connection with the fetish; if anything was established with certainty about this it was that the fetish serves to protect the loved object from the dangers inherent in the fetishist's sadistic love with its annihilating tendency.

I cannot enter into a detailed life history of this patient, but I must say a word about the development of his fetishism. Apart altogether from re-constructions, it seems first to have become recognisable in the form of a fascinated interest in schoolboys wearing O.T.C. (Officers Training Corps) uniforms, at the age of 10 or 11. This interest was felt to be an unhallowed and forbidden one, ostensibly on account of his mother's strongly pacifist views; and indeed he had the same feeling at a much earlier age about playing with toy soldiers, an activity which was not forbidden but one nevertheless of which he felt his mother disapproved. A very interesting light was thrown on this when he had a dream about a house with a dark attic, like a lavatory, in which he and his brother found boxes containing amber stones, and later, rifles. They feared an attack by a little miniature man, who was a murderer. There were many other details and associations to this dream, but the point for my present purpose is that after I had interpreted 'attic' as 'attack' A. recalled that at the age of 8 he remembered seeing an old uniform of his father's in an attic, and his mother saying: 'Take that horrid old uniform away!' In view of her attachment to the uniformed father during the war, A. seems always to have felt that her attitude towards uniforms and military things was a hypocritical one. The uniform here obviously stands for the father, and it is interesting in connection with the coprophilic significance of the fetish that A. on several occasions likened his mother's attachment to his father to a woman who likes a scent which you can't bear; but she makes such a fuss about not having it that at last for the sake of peace you say: 'Have your beastly scent!'

Beginning about the age of 12, there developed a great conflict over the possibility of A. himself joining the O.T.C. The conscious attitude was one of horror at the idea and fear that the would be forced to join; and this was rationalised on the basis of pacifism; but unconsciously the determining phantasies were not so much purely aggressive ones as homosexual–sadistic. Being made a soldier meant being made into a woman, paradoxical though it may sound; or perhaps more accurately, being made into a suitable object for the sadistic sexual attentions of the father. The utmost horror was produced when his father actually suggested that it might not be a bad thing for him to join. This found its expression in the transference during a period when he was continually under the compulsion to ask whether I had ever been in an O.T.C.

A. managed to avoid joining the O.T.C., but he compromised by joining the scouts. One day he dressed himself in his scout uniform and tied himself up, but he did not know what to do next; this was at the age of 13 or 14. The idea of tying up had been anticipated at much earlier ages, when he had tied up dolls and also a dog, tying its legs to the legs of a step-ladder and thus stretching them apart.

An emission was consciously produced for the first time at the age of 17, when he dressed himself in a black mackintosh and chained himself to a wardrobe. The result was surprise to him. This experiment led on to more and more complicated and sadistically designed ones, with the use of wires, tight gagging, tying himself up in a sack, etc. He was just beginning to play with the idea of hanging and complete annihilation at the time when he was sent to Dr Eder for analysis. The further development of the fetishism consisted of various elaborations of similar themes – women, but also occasionally boys, in different varieties of uniform or mackintoshes, and latterly almost exclusively nurses in uniform. There was of course always a phantasy of a sado-masochistic kind woven round these figures; most commonly of an older woman humiliating and punishing a younger one. During the course of his analysis with Dr Eder he modified his technique by embodying his phantasies in drawings rather than carrying them out on his own person, though this also continued to some extent. This modification served several purposes – it made it possible for him to bring his masturbation into the analysis, as it were; it represented at a much more unconscious level an invitation to the analyst to treat him as the figures in the drawings were treated; and it also served the purpose of a further line of defence against the anxieties connected with his destructive phantasies – the fact that it was mere drawings that he was dealing with was a reassurance that it was neither his real parents nor himself that were being treated in this way.

When he came to me for treatment, A. was, as I have mentioned, in a very depressed and hypochondriacal state. This was closely connected with the death of Dr Eder. The hypochondria proved very refractory and continued through a large part of the analysis. Time does not permit me to go into it in any detail, but I should like to make a few remarks about it.

While introjective phantasies were obvious and were interpreted from the outset, it became more and more clear that a very important function of the hypochondriacal complaints was their use as a sadistic weapon against the parents, whom in fact he often reduced to a state of despair verging on breakdown. He used it particularly to disturb them at night. This activity often took the form of demanding that his father should examine him and find something, for example a positive Babinski. Although this 'something' that had to be found was ostensibly of a bad nature, it was evidently not entirely so, and in fact he often used terms of rather ecstatic admiration about his symptoms. They represented both a penis and a baby. His abdominal pains were labour pains, while his two legs with their twitching and inequality stood for the two parents in intercourse. I want to make it clear that I am not discounting the importance of the introjective mechanisms that were at work, which were very clear at times, as when he said that he felt his body was fragile, like china, and full of blocks of dead things. All I am suggesting is that in a case of hypochondria of this type, introjection is not the whole story, and that interpretation would be inadequate which left out of account the phantasies derived from the phallic level. I have felt for a long time that there are at least two types of hypochondria, the hysterical and the psychotic. I should regard this case as belonging to the hysterical group.

I should have mentioned earlier that A. was a medical student and when he came to me was just beginning his clinical studies. He was therefore able to elaborate his hypochondriacal ideas with a great wealth of detail, while at the same time he was not embarrassed by too exact a knowledge of clinical and pathological facts. Thus, his ideas about inequality of his legs, to which I have referred, were related to the idea of disseminated sclerosis, to which he clung for a long period. A similar fear was that of secondary carcinoma. In both cases the notion of an infinite and increasing number of bad things disseminated inside was of importance, and this was connected with fears about robbing his mother's inside and the difficulty of putting everything back in order. These phantasies came out in a large number of dreams, which led up to the dream of the attic. The principal object inside the mother towards which these attacks were directed turned out to be the father's penis, and the attacks were chiefly of an oral-sadistic kind. But I think it is a significant fact that it was just the penis against which they were directed. These phantasies were closely related to homosexual ones about sadistic attacks on his own inside by his father's penis, as in a dream about letting a man into the house, knowing the man was going to murder him. This theme appeared also in inverted form in the idea of a woman enticing a penis or a person inside with the object of destroying it there. At the same time he unconsciously regarded his own penis as a kind of breast, much sought after by women, whom he could nourish or frustrate at will, the latter much the more exciting phantasy.

This combination of the phallic and the oral found a pretty expression in a hypochondriacal preoccupation with his tongue which A. developed later. This symptom was connected not only with phantasies about the hidden female penis but also with oral sadistic phantasies. There were also anal elements – the tongue was dirty. I have to admit, indeed, that the picture I have given so far is misleading in that I have failed to bring out the quite prominent anal and urethral features of the case. They were very obvious and I could say a great deal about them if space allowed; but rightly

62

or wrongly I had the impression that they were of less fundamental importance, probably because they did not lend themselves so readily to assimilation with the rest of the material. Thus it is quite possible that I have unduly neglected them; but if so it was not for want of seeing them, for they were manifest on the surface. In connection with the anal material, however, just as with the oral, a close association with phantasies from the phallic level was not far to seek, in as much as the faeces nearly always represented a baby and were connected with a passive homosexual attitude to the father.

All this anal, urethral, and oral material linked up in an intimate way with the mackintosh fetish, for the mackintosh served as a protection for the mother against such assaults. Not only so; it also seemed to stand for the period of milk feeding, the rubber of the mackintosh being a substitute for the rubber teat. The fetish may thus be regarded, in Freud's phrase, as a memorial not only to castration fear but also to the trauma of weaning.

I pass on now to the other main aspect of the case which I wish to discuss: that is, to the difficulties A. encountered in his efforts to achieve a normal genital relationship. These difficulties may be for convenience divided into two groups: first a series of abortive and relatively short-lived attachments, with which I shall deal quite briefly, and secondly a love affair which occupied the whole of the last year of the analysis, and which still continues.

There do not seem to have been any really early attachments to girls. Up to near the time when his first analysis started, he was occupied principally with what he called the prince and princess phantasy, in which the prince represented himself. The main theme of this phantasy was misunderstanding, resulting in a quarrel and the separation of the prince and princess. This was the climax of the phantasy, and the subsequent reconciliation was relatively devoid of affect. These phantasies started at the age of 12, at a time when he had been left in a boarding school while his parents made a new home in London – an unhappy period which is associated in his mind with being forced into unpleasant and uncomfortable clothes, such as an Eton jacket and collar; it left its mark on his masturbation phantasies.

A. translated this phantasy almost word for word into reality in the course of his first attachment, which began about the age of 18. He seems to have chosen his partner with almost uncanny skill, and she played her frigid part to perfection. There were constant misunderstandings and quarrels, and she would allow no caress or show of affection, even in words. This type of relationship afforded A. so much satisfaction that he continued it over a long period until it reached the final conclusion of separation that was inherent in it. It is really inaccurate to say that it continued so long because of the satisfaction it afforded; it would be truer to say that he clung to this relationship because it gave him just the safeguards he needed; and one of the chief of these safeguards was just that he should not achieve satisfaction but on the contrary should be frustrated. This is a point to which I shall return later when discussing the last girl. I believe it may almost be described as the keynote of fetishism.

The next girl was semi-Asiatic, and the anal note was dominant. She did in the end come to mean to him merely faeces and he finally expelled her with real relish after having come into conflict with her father. He felt that he had killed her by this expulsion, but so far from being troubled with guilt about this, his feeling was one of annoyance when she gave signs of further life.

There followed a fellow medical student, but this attachment never proceeded far. Its end was interesting. He began one hour by saying that he felt marvellously better. Someone had told him that a lady had been ringing for him. At once he thought it was this girl, was overcome with emotion and had a mass peristalsis, as he put it. He then described his latest masturbation. The picture consisted of a nurse in frock and collar but without apron, cuffs or belt; there was also a fully-dressed nurse and a sister with flowing cap. This phantasy arose out of his excitement in seeing a nurse dressing at a window. It turned out that actually she was undressing, and this was a big disappointment, for the real excitement was in seeing the uniform put on, and the full phantasy would have been of a woman in a beautiful evening dress or nightdress being metamorphosed into a nurse in uniform. Here again we get the theme of satisfaction dependent on frustration, or rather a sort of partial frustration, for while the nurse is not the mother, still in phantasy she is the mother in disguise.

A. then told me that a friend to whom he had confided his passion said: 'Oh yes, she's quite a nice girl, but she does have such a B.O. (Body Odour).' All the other men agreed that the girl smelt. It was only then that A. realised that he had known all along, but didn't mind. The realisation that everyone thought this was a tremendous relief. It meant that a pretty girl could smell bad, that faeces could be good. I suggested that another factor in his feeling of relief was due to the consideration that no one would grudge him his girl or try to take her away – for the theme of having his love object taken away was always very strong and prominent in the transference, though in fact the result was generally engineered by himself. The following day he remarked casually that he had lost interest in this girl – so that again the girl became faeces, and as soon as he was conscious of this it was all over.

It was only three days later that he began to talk of a nurse he was working with who attracted him. He felt he wanted her to be in ordinary clothes and that all the details of uniform, collar stud, etc., which so excited him in his phantasies, repelled and sickened him in her. At the same time, he was continually getting erections when with her, a thing that had never before happened to him by reason of a girl's company. He said that in addition to all the agony from his symptoms there was excitement as well and a feeling of new possibilities in life.

A few days later A. took this nurse, whom I shall call B., to the pictures. He was not to have come to analysis the next day, but he rang up and made a special appointment, because, as he said, he had had such an experience last night as never before. B. was very friendly and cuddly and put her head on his arm. She was so warm, it really got ridiculous and he wanted to laugh. He felt uneasy because her conduct was so unrestrained. In brief, he had managed to get a girl who was warm instead of cold, because she satisfied his ascetic requirements through being a nurse, who was literally constrained by her uniform as well as her discipline. At this time his mother was in hospital, and he felt that she must be got rid of by death in order for him to have B. Later, following a reassuring visit to his mother and the realisation that she was not to be castrated or to die, he became depressed, feeling he had no love left for B., for he now felt he had the penis and no longer that she had something he had not. There was a constant recurrence of this anxiety lest he find B. empty and lose all love for her. What he liked most about her and what gave him most confidence was feeling that she was physically strong and so able to withstand his aggression; and on the other hand her warmth and responsiveness most roused his anxiety. He felt that if he was not thwarted and got all he wanted there would be nothing left. Here again we find this apotheosis of frustration which seems to me so characteristic of fetishism, and which brings it into such close relation to masochism. It results in many of the fetishist's aims being so to speak inverted, as I see it. For instance, his scopophilia is satisfied not by seeing the naked body, which repels him, but rather by the clothes which serve to conceal it and frustrate the primary impulse. For the pleasure in free bodily movement and the sadistic use of the musculature there is substituted pleasure in bonds and tight lacing. Manual masturbation is taboo, in the sense that it seems not to occur to him as a possibility; on the contrary, the hands are generally tied. It is therefore no surprise to find that the straightforward genital relationship is also intolerable. It appears to him as something disgusting and dangerous. The underlying phantasies were undoubtedly numerous and complicated, and they aroused powerful resistances which made this perhaps the most difficult part of the analysis. I must content myself with saying that they related chiefly to castration and to incorporation, and more specifically to incorporation by the woman involving castration of the man. Anal features were so strongly interwoven that it appeared likely that an important feature of the operative phantasy consisted of anal incorporation.

Homosexual phantasies, often quite conscious, were always in evidence.

One of his first dreams about B. was actually of this nature, representing her as taking the active role in anal intercourse with him and causing him to produce a dirty baby.

Another important aspect of his relation to her may be expressed by saying that it was an oral relation to the father's penis. This equation of B. with the penis came out in the most interesting way in connection with one of the masturbation drawings, which represented a cross with the figure of Christ on it. Another cross was marked on the ground, and B. was kneeling on this cross, tied up, and gazing at the crucifix. When A. gave me this drawing, the first thing I noticed was a remarkable hiatus in the figure of Christ, involving all that part in the vicinity of the genitals. The second point was that B.'s position on the other cross corresponded very closely to this gap, so that she appeared to represent a huge erect penis. The conscious idea was that B. was doing penance for having come to A. It appeared from the analysis of this drawing that the sexual object of the phantasy was not just the father's penis, but really the penis plus the mother, or the mother with the father's penis.

There were a number of phantasies of attacks on the interior of the mother's body with a view to finding the penis; and it was clear that these phantasies were motivated only partially by castration anxiety – another important factor was the phantasy of the penis as a source of food. At about this period, A. spontaneously underwent a period of abstinence from mastur- bation for the benefit of analysis. This led to great excitement during several of the analytic sessions, excitement felt largely in the mouth, and combined with phantasies of nurses in white, stiff, crackly uniform, and so on. The mackintosh was felt to be a protection against the dangers to the object inherent in these phantasies of oral aggression. Unless the woman was pro- tected in this way, he felt unable to imagine a breast except for eating, a vagina except to be ripped open, a woman's neck except to strangle her.

There is another leading feature of this case which I have not sufficiently emphasised, and that is the strong tendency towards the mechanism of the turning of the impulse against the self. This was most conspicuous through- out. Thus, though A. always referred to his phantasies as sadistic ones, they were at least as obviously masochistic, since he was clearly identified with the victim. The same thing applies to the uniform or mackintosh: it is not merely a covering and protection for the sexual object, it also serves the same purpose for himself. Perhaps the climax of all these phantasies as regards intensity of feeling was one which he had in the analysis during the period of abstinence; essentially it represented himself as a child in a grown-up mackintosh being copulated with in the most marvellous way by his father. A further elaboration of this phantasy was that when in the mackintosh he is really inside his mother's body and is identified with her, and that in this way his father indirectly copulated with him.

He said that the mackintosh is like a wall surrounding a town so that you can't see out. This wall is rotten at is base. He associated to this the idea of a penis dropping off, and faeces. He then had a picture of the anus and genitals, all very dark and shadowy. I interpreted that the rottenness at the base of the wall referred to the possibility of seeing up from underneath – there was much confirmatory material pointing in this direction. A. confirmed this by observing that the mackintosh must be completely buttoned up so that no clothes are visible and it is possible to imagine the body naked underneath, and also by the excitement he obtains by putting on the mackintosh over his naked body. This aspect of the matter is closely in line with Freud's theory about foot fetishism.

As the affair with B. continued, A.'s anxieties relating to his oral and phallic aggression became more acute. He felt that kissing her meant eating her up and feared her excessive kissing. He had by this time become intensely attracted by the idea of the naked female body. He had what he described as terrible erections, but said he 'couldn't press the point'. At last be bought a condom, but was much relieved at B.'s refusal of intercourse. He tried to escape from the situation by excessive masturbation.

One of his deepest fears was of eating up and destroying his object in attempting to gain excessive possession of it. There was also all along a strong reluctance to commit himself to any love object that was outside or separable from himself. The fetish helped him to avoid the dangers of being dependent on a woman – the danger first of the woman refusing, and secondly, of external forces taking her away. It appeared that the external force was not necessarily the father, but might be the mother herself, the 'woman' in this case being not the mother as a whole object, but her breast as a part-object. Owing to these fears, for him a goal attained was no satisfaction, but only the struggle for it; he said: 'It is like following the sun; you can never reach it, and if you did you would be burnt up.' For him, the *conditio sine qua non* for excitement was inaccessibility.

After some work on this material, A. made two or three abortive attempts at intercourse, but was unable to get or keep an erection at the appropriate moment, in spite of attempt to stimulate himself by phantasy. Once he said he didn't want to get inside B., and proceeded to bite his finger. This led him on to say that a woman in uniform results in masturbation and orgasm; a woman not in uniform has a quite different effect – she makes his mouth water, his teeth gnash, and he wants to eat her up.

Since the analysis was interrupted, his potency has steadily increased, though the old phantasies have not entirely disappeared.

It is impossible in the space at my disposal to give any more clinical matter or to touch on the many other interesting sides of the case, and I must now try briefly to sum up the points which seem to me to emerge.

First, this case once again proves abundantly the over-determination of the fetish. I think it also demonstrates beyond doubt the far-reaching importance of castration anxiety in this connection. Ample confirmation is provided also for Dr Payne's findings regarding the importance of sadism and of introjection-projection mechanisms.

Here, however, I should like to raise a point which has only to be mentioned to be obvious, and yet I feel it is sometimes neglected: the point namely that introjection need not be an essentially oral process, though I should imagine there must always be what one might describe as an oral flavour about it. Thus, I found again and again in this case that what appeared on the surface to be phantasies based on oral incorporative tendencies turned out to be on another level phantasies regarding phallic penetration, impregnation, etc. This is all so obvious that I feel ashamed to point it out; but I am not sure that it always gets the attention it deserves. There is a tendency, I think, to feel that the oral aspect is 'deeper' and therefore more important, which means presumably more active dynamically in the particular state we are dealing with; but this is surely by no means axiomatic. Although it is difficult to be sure of one's objectivity in judging such matters, I certainly gained the impression that the superficially obvious oral and anal features were often used as a disguise for more important underlying phallic anxieties; and yet I would not regard them as a mere disguise – I think they must have considerable significance in their own right. In other words, the fact that the disguise takes that particular form is by no means a matter of chance, but must be intimately connected with the nature of the phantasies that are being repressed and constitute in fact a kind of 'return of the repressed'.

That brings me to a second point which I feel is not only of theoretical but also of practical importance; I mean the problem of what factors are chiefly responsible for the occurrence of castration anxiety. Are we to regard it as the talion punishment for incestuous phallic wishes directed towards the mother, as Freud appears for the most part to do? It seemed clear to me, in this case at least, that one very important determinant is to be found in the oral aggressive impulses directed towards the father's penis incorporated in the mother. And yet it is castration anxiety that we are dealing with, not the trauma of weaning or something of that sort. If the oral and anal elements were the essential ones, it would be very difficult to account for the well-known clinical fact that fetishism is a phenomenon found almost exclusively in males.

I would stress the essential part played by masochism, and what I have referred to as the inversion of the sexual aim, for want of a better term. By this I mean that the aim of the component impulse seems to be frustration rather than satisfaction, and indeed a rather unsatisfactory kind of satisfaction is derived from frustration. Obviously this is closely related to masochism, if indeed it can be distinguished from it.

The homosexual element is also much in evidence in this case, which illustrates admirably Freud's statement that the patient is saved by his fetish from homosexuality, and it shows how narrow may be the margin.

Finally, reverting to the problem of phallic versus pregenital, I should like to make the following suggestion with regard to the aetiology of fetishism. May it not be that what we have actually to deal with is neither the one thing nor the other, but a combination of the two? I do not simply mean that I want to have it both ways – what I am suggesting is a specific constellation, to use Dr Glover's conception. I do feel that there are points about this case which give strong support to this view; in particular, the extraordinary compound (for it is much more than a mere mixture) of phallic, oral and anal aggressive and erotic phantasies.

To put it in another way, I would suggest that fetishism is the result of castration anxiety, but of a specific form of castration anxiety, a form produced by a strong admixture of certain oral and anal trends.

Notes

1 Read before the British Psycho-Analytical Society, 7 February 1940.
2 S.M. Payne (1939) 'Some Observations on the Ego Development of the Fetishist', *International Journal of Psycho-Analysis* 20: 161–70.

4

Notes on the analysis of sexual perversions[1]

In the 'Three Essays' Freud uttered a famous aphorism which is sometimes treated as though it epitomises all he has to say about the perversions. I refer to his statement that 'neuroses are, so to speak, the negative of perversions'. Now neurosis is, of course, in Freud's view, a compromise between a sexual impulse and its repudiation, and the statement, as it stands, suggests that the perversion represents the positive, unmodified sexual impulse, whose modification through defensive processes on the part of the ego gives rise to the neurosis. Thus it seems implied that in perversion we are dealing with an id activity, little interfered with by ego or superego. This at least is the interpretation put upon Freud's early discussion of perversion by many of the non-analytic critics. I need scarcely add that a general survey of Freud's writings on the perversions shows that this is a travesty of his view. In his discussions of homosexuality, of sado-masochism, of exhibitionism and voyeurism, and of fetishism Freud quite clearly credits the pervert with numerous other defence mechanisms besides regression, and obviously regards the ego as deeply involved in the process of perversion formation. One of the most interesting of these discussions is related to the splitting of the ego in fetishism, a splitting which is to be found, as he points out, not only in other perversions but in neuroses and psychoses as well.

The mechanism of splitting, both of the ego and of the object, has been discussed in detail by Melanie Klein; she relates it to denial, omnipotent idealisation, and annihilation. Although she has described these as schizoid mechanisms, she clearly does not mean that they are to be found only in schizophrenics, but rather that they are amongst the earliest and most fundamental of the defence mechanisms of the ego. I have no doubt myself that splitting of the object and of the ego, denial and omnipotent manipulations of the relation to objects play a leading part in perversion formation and help us to understand its relationship to psychosis. Mrs Klein suggests that in this early phase such mechanisms play a role similar to that of repression at a later stage. Here we have an important clue, I think, to the striking phenomenological differences between neurosis and perversion, which led Freud to say that the one is the negative of the other. In other words, we are dealing not with a contrast between defence and no defence, but between repressive defence and more primitive defence of a schizoid or splitting character.

Now the splitting mechanism, as described by Mrs Klein, is characteristic of an early stage of ego development, when ego organisation is still very imperfect and disintegration can easily take place. It is a stage when both libido and aggressivity are expressed predominantly in oral terms and when the breast is the object of both these instinctual impulses. The importance of the oral factor in various perversions has been increasingly stressed in more recent contributions. Indeed, this emphasis on the oral factor is to be found at least as early as 1921, in Sadger's *Geschlechtsverirrungen*.

On the other hand, if we turn to Fenichel's discussion of the perversions, we find the main emphasis consistently placed upon the castration complex, and this aetiological monotony has led to a good deal of criticism. No analyst experienced with perverts can doubt that the castration complex is in fact extraordinarily prominent in these patients. I suggested in my previous paper that we are dealing not with an either–or, that is, either with defence against castration anxiety or defence against some earlier, pregenital danger situation – but rather with a specific modification of castration anxiety, determined in its form by earlier, pregenital, and especially oral developments. Some such hypothesis seems to me inescapable if we are to do justice not only to the two classes of psycho-analytic experience just mentioned, but also to the well-known clinical fact that some perversions are extremely unequally distributed between the sexes. It is well known, for instance, that fetishism and genital exhibitionism are incomparably commoner in the male sex. If one lays all the aetiological emphasis on oral factors and on such primitive mechanisms as splitting of the ego and of the object, how is one to account for such a striking clinical finding? There is always a danger that the fascination of more recent discoveries may lead to the neglect of earlier, well-established findings. By standing on Freud's shoulders it may be possible for us sometimes to see further than he could; but if we abandon that position and rely on our own stature alone, our horizon is apt to become very limited.

Clinical material

Case A

This man came to me at the age of 30 with severe personality difficulties and gross sexual inhibition, his sexual life being confined to masturbation with sado-masochistic phantasies and shoe fetishism. He was extremely perturbed over the idea that he might be homosexual, and intensely afraid that everyone would suspect or find out his guilty sexual secrets.

This man illustrates in an extreme degree the splitting of the ego. He has two quite distinct personalities, which he calls upstairs and downstairs. Upstairs is a brisk man of the world, polite, considerate, and co-operative, capable of working out clever and successful systems of operation on the Stock Exchange, or of outstanding success in more academic fields. On the couch, however, it is mostly downstairs that is in operation. Downstairs is completely absorbed in the nursery situation, and for it everything is seen in these terms. Downstairs is a baby, and even speaks with a baby voice, entirely different from the Oxford tones of upstairs. Downstairs, in fact, takes to the transference situation like a duck to water, and intensely resents anything that interferes with its projections, as when the analyst shows signs of being a real person. Downstairs is ruthlessly aggressive and egocentric, but at the same time very timid, and analysis has to proceed with the patient holding the surgeon's hand, as he puts it. It is essential that the analyst be someone who can be ruthlessly attacked without showing signs of being hurt, and without hitting back. Hence I was for long identified with Golly, a plaything that was of great emotional significance to A., to whom he could confide his joys and sorrows, as well as make safe sexual experiments, such as rubbing him between the legs. Golly was a compromise between a living object and a completely inanimate one, such as a shoe.

Underlying this is the need to control the object fully, so that it can neither frustrate, nor cause guilt when sadistically attacked. This involves an avoidance of animate objects – A. felt he could not make any sexual approach to a girl unless she were anaesthetised. Thus in the transference the analyst must be completely passive and impersonal, and is practically never referred to as 'you', but in the third person, as 'the analyst'. There is, at the same time, an intense vigilance towards me, with the closest attention to the slightest sound I may make – coughs, lip movements, 'tummy rumbles' – all of which are at once interpreted as having reference to the patient, generally as indicating disapproval, and so as danger signals. This dual attitude comes out in the fact that although he sedulously avoids looking at me, he constantly tries to catch me unawares by coming early, and by approaching my door silently and without knocking. Here there is a clear relation to an early primal scene, and, as will appear later, it is really a third person, or father's penis inside mother, towards whom he is so vigilant and who threatens persecution. The primal scene seems to have occurred at the age of about two years, when his father came back from the war and usurped his place with his mother.

Shortly after this there occurred another experience, which he calls 'The Lady on the Lawn'. The details are not clear, but its essence must have been a sexual approach to the mother, modelled on what he supposed father to have done – this he conceived as a sadistic attack which mother at first resisted but later succumbed to and enjoyed. She was in fact frigid and regarded father as a sexual and even homicidal maniac, so the little boy's idea may be accurate enough. In the scene on the lawn, his approach to mother was rebuffed with horror and, I think, an implication that he was identified by this behaviour with the bad father. His further development seems to stem from this rebuff. It is characterised by splitting of the object. Mother becomes idealised and desexualised – a beautiful lady in the sky, cool, asexual, towards whom one must deny one's love. The sexual object undergoes various transformations. In part it becomes Golly, or a shoe – but a shoe in relation to a little boy, who is having it put on and laced up tightly. The further development has much reference to the father and to punishment and the typical sexual phantasy is that a little boy is being treated in this way by nurses or other hostile adults, who are talking over his head about him, saying what they are going to do to him, the climax being to take him up to Daddy's room, where he will he will be punished.

A further split in the object takes place between the idealised mother and the bad nurses. He wants to tell mother of his ill-treatment by the nurses, but fears to do so, for they are always standing by to contradict him, and will take a terrible revenge when they get him back in the nursery. In the transference this situation comes out repeatedly – he feels there is a third person in the room, so he cannot tell me anything directly, but only hint at it, or say the opposite. On several occasions he has felt so sure that there was someone listening that he has had to get up and look behind my screen. At a deeper level, this hostile, persecuting third person represents the father's penis inside the mother; a constantly recurring infantile phantasy or dream is of creeping up a tunnel under the bed, made of sheets; suddenly a terrifying figure like Punch appears, chases him and torments him by tickling – here again the homosexual persecution betrays a strong erotic component. Recently, he thought I avoided greeting him lest I betray by my voice that I was not really myself but a bad terrifying person inside me, masquerading in my external form.

Again, in the fourth year of analysis, there was a strong tendency to identification with the pregnant mother – he thought he was getting very fat, growing breasts and turning into a woman. His sister was born when he was two years old, and I think the scene on the lawn probably occurred during the pregnancy. Interpretations relating to this pregnancy have met with the most violent resistance.

The fragmentary material I have given will serve to illustrate the splitting mechanism, the withdrawal from personal objects, the denial of reality and the strong introjective and projective mechanisms. The characteristic feature, which brings this so near to psychosis, is his calm acceptance of these mechanisms and phantasies – so long as he is on the couch and 'downstairs' is in the ascendant, the ego does not resist these ideas. However, 'upstairs' is always there in the background to make sure that downstairs is safe, in or out of the analytic situation, and it seems to be this ego split, allowing a certain autonomy, and in case of danger even a degree of leadership to upstairs, that saves him from psychosis. At the same time, we have the splitting of the object, which occurs in more than one direction; there is the split into idealised, desexualised mother, versus sexual, sadistic, bad father and nurses, who are so dangerous, on the one hand, and the fetish class of objects on the other – Golly, shoes – with whom sexuality is permissible and safe. Indeed, it had not occurred to him till he was about twenty and read a book on sexual perversions that his peculiar feelings about shoes were anything but harmless. This illustrates the very important function of perversions in avoiding guilt feeling. Whatever form they may take, they are essentially *not* the guilty oedipal activity. In the case under discussion, sexuality and sadism is projected on to a conveniently well-adapted father figure, or on to wicked nurses. As far as the patient is concerned he can say 'I don't *do* anything, it is done *to* me – the shoe is put on, the laces are tightened, it grips me.' Essentially, this is the masochistic defence against guilt.

Case B

My second patient, a flagellant, is singularly free from sexual guilt, though he has many phantasies of being found out and publicly exposed. This guiltlessness is readily understandable where he is being tied up and beaten; but the mechanism seems to operate just as successfully when *he* does the beating. What becomes of guilt feelings in sadism? I am not sure that we have the answer to this question, but I suspect that again the splitting mechanism has something to do with it. My second patient was very conscious of the double life he led and chuckled inwardly to think what people would say if they only knew that this pillar of society, as he is to outward appearance, indulged in such outrageous behaviour. He himself, however, regarded his perversion as perfectly harmless, and insisted that most people just do not have 'the right idea' about it. That is, he and those like him abhor real cruelty, and enjoy themselves only if their partners are enjoying the complementary role as well. None the less, one of his more refined pleasures was to revisit a girl he had beaten and examine the weals. Thus here again there is a denial of reality in the sexual sphere, and assertion that pain is pleasurable and wounds, whether in oneself or another, something to gloat over.

In addition to this split in the ego, there was in this case an equally significant split in the object. By 'object' I do not mean the female partners of his flagellations, who were of little significance to him as people, but only as fellow-enthusiasts and necessary to the execution of his phantasies; these were always in some degree spoiled by the imperfections of reality. No, the real object seemed to be the instrument of whipping, and his attitude to whips was very similar to that of a fetishist to his fetish. He was fascinated by them, collected them, and gazed at them in shop windows. The point of interest here is that he had also a severe phobia of snakes, which was a real burden to him as it interfered seriously with his hobby of travelling. He frequently dreamt of them, typically that a snake suddenly confronted him in a passage. The connection between whips and snakes, and their common phallic significance had been entirely unconscious before analysis.

The oral factor showed itself in an eating disturbance and bouts of excessive drinking to the point of amnesia. He came to analysis regularly just five minutes late, repeating his behaviour at his mother's dining table.

In this case, too, there was a marked withdrawal from all emotional involvement with people; what he most wanted in the world was to be left alone with his hobbies. This led to a peculiar transference situation. He much appreciated me as the only person to whom he could talk freely; but at the same time the transference never developed into a personal relationship, and he did not expect any real help from the analysis, looking for his salvation to some external event which would free him from his daily tasks and enable him to carry out his phantasies undisturbed. The event he chiefly relied on to produce this happy result was the death of his widowed mother, to whom he was extremely strongly, but extremely ambivalently attached.

Case C

This is a case of shoe fetishism in a man of 30. The material was completely dominated by a powerful castration complex and a desperate defence against feminine identification. The mother was the prime castrator, who wanted both him and his one-year-younger brother to be girls. The brother independently developed a boot fetishism, but I was not able to examine him. The mother made a religion out of a dead and angelic older sister, whom the patient never saw. She kept a room always locked which contained a life-sized doll, and after her death it was found to contain an extraordinary hoard of useless articles, including 140 handbags. The analysis was regarded as a castration threat, which would completely remove the fetish, leaving him nothing. In the shoe, on the other hand, *he* gets part of the woman, instead of losing his penis, as in sexual intercourse.

His actual homosexual ideas, that is, of a man as sexual object, were firmly repressed and covered up by the intense emphasis on the castrating mother and his rage and aggressive phantasies towards her. The father appeared in the role of prohibitor both of sex and of aggression against the mother. He was the anal expert, and frequently interfered with the patient's bowels by purgatives, enemas and suppositories. C. had in his character a paranoid layer of mistrust of everyone and felt they were plotting against him. I think it was the stout defences against this paranoid–homosexual layer that led to the premature end of the analysis after two years – he left me to go and work with another father figure.

C. had a great fear of any close association with a woman, because he would identify with her and so become a woman. But also he resented the demand made of a man that he should be *active* in sexual intercourse. Moreover, a married man has to *feed* the woman. The fetish makes no such demands.

There were some very interesting phantasies in connection with his rage against the castrating mother. In one of these he penetrates her body with his penis; she then turns into a hairy gorilla-like creature with great teeth with which she bites off his female nipples – that is, a talion revenge for his oral attack on his mother's breast. In another phantasy he was made female through his body being penetrated *by breasts*. In a dream, he was doing an operation inside a woman's body, castrating her internal penis. In another access of rage against his mother, after penetrating her body, he tears her up from inside with his penis. His mother inculcated a fear of falling on something and being split open, especially in his testicles. He had a phantasy of his mother's shoe kicking him and splitting up his anus and rectum. He had many phantasies of tearing me to pieces. He blamed me because he is in pieces and I don't put him together again. This material was closely connected with the parturient mother, and with memories of seeing her urinating.

The configuration of the material at this point led me to a speculation about the phantasy associated with the split ego and split object. Is not the female genital the split object *par excellence*, and cannot the phantasy of a split ego arise from an identification with this split genital? I am aware that when we speak of splitting of the ego and of the object we are referring to mental mechanisms which we assume to underlie the phenomena, and that phantasies pertain to a different level of discourse – nevertheless, phantasies, our own no less than our patients', must always play a part in the way we conceptualise these underlying processes. It seems to me, therefore, that the phantasy of being oneself split in pieces just as the vulva is split may well be very relevant to the mental mechanism of splitting of the object and introjection of the split object, leading to splitting of the ego. It is implicit, of course, in such a phantasy of the vulva as a split object that it was once intact, and that the splitting is the result of a sadistic attack, whether by the father or by oneself. I shall return later to this subject when discussing castration anxiety in relation to the perversions.

Case D

In this man of 26, the presenting symptoms were manifest homosexuality in the form of adoration at a distance, together with marked ideas of reference in relation to this, reaching delusional intensity. In addition he had developed elaborate and bizarre masturbation techniques, often with a masochistic quality, such as pushing pencils up his urethra and umbrellas up his anus. In this case there was an obvious split in the ego similar in principle to that of A.; but here there was even more fear of the part identified with the id and its aggressiveness. This fear was largely projected on to me. On the one hand he blamed me for encouraging expression of the dangerous explosive part; on the other, he thought I was a timid, prim and conventional person, so that *he* had to keep control of the situation on either count. In this way there was repeated in the transference the central problem of his relationship to his mother. She, he was always convinced, whilst cold towards his father, was erotically attached to him – for instance, she would appear naked in his room as if by accident – and the whole onus of avoiding incest was borne by him alone. The mother was dangerous not only erotically but also aggressively, as a death-dealer. He thought she took pleasure in having animal pets killed; and she told her children that as she had given the children life she could also take it away. The boy took flight to his father, following a pattern laid down in his second year when his mother was pregnant. The resulting homosexuality led to further anxiety of a paranoid character. The persecutors were not, however, the homosexual object, but other men, or his mother, or other women. So here there is a split in the object of a homosexual – the erotic feelings being directed to an absurdly idealised homosexual object, worshipped at a distance, the aggressive feelings dealt with by projection leading to feelings of persecution by both men and women. The split in his ego became manifest in the transference. He felt that I sympathised only with the superficial intellectual side of him that talked to me, not with the feeling inside, which I feared. He identified himself with simple emotional natives, whilst I was a typical Englishman – that is, he exteriorised the split in himself by projecting half on to me. Conversely, he had projected all his erotic oedipal feeling on to his mother.

Oral-incorporative material was prominent, and was related to his persecutory preoccupations. He was very fond of eating, but he must not be watched, as this led to persecutory ideas. While travelling in a bus he had the phantasy that unless he kept his mouth open he would incorporate the bus conductor, who would have become very small, but would swell up inside and burst him. He dreamt of going into the Underground, which then disintegrated – he blamed me for encouraging him, in the analysis, to take the risk thus symbolised. He not only feared to incorporate me or my penis, but also feared I would incorporate him and then persecute him. For instance, I was supposed to have a dictaphone, so that after he had murdered me he would be convicted on the evidence so recorded. He also thought he heard me make movements sometimes which he believed were caused by my preparing a strait-jacket for him. There were frequent erotic phantasies about me, which also caused him much trouble, their repudiation being chiefly projected on to me.

It will be seen that this patient was very near to psychosis and actually over the border line from time to time, in my opinion. His paranoid anxiety in relation to me led him to break off treatment after a year; but he had enough insight for me to succeed in persuading him to continue with another analyst, with whom, however, the same story was repeated in some eighteen months.

Lack of space forbids me to quote more clinical material, apart from mentioning one patient seen twice in consultation at the Maudsley Hospital. This man had obsessive phantasies of hurting women, ultimately by biting into them, and an irresistible urge to photograph his wife partially or completely unclothed. Points of interest here were, first, a memory of being suckled and bathed by his mother – he was not weaned till the age of two – secondly a strong feeling of marvelling and envy at the structure and functions of a woman's body, and a desire to participate in his wife's experience of childbirth. He had a vivid childhood phantasy of being a surgeon to whom mothers brought their children, mostly little girls, in whom something had worn out, which he was to replace from his store of spare parts. We see here an omnipotent phantasy of being able to satisfy the woman's need for a penis; and on the other hand a strong wish to identify with the woman. I have no doubt that photography here signifies introjection.

Conclusions

To sum up, let me try to formulate some theoretical conclusions. First, I must repeat that the castration complex plays a leading part in every case, and that is to be taken for granted in connection with what follows. In the case of fetishism, for example, I believe that the fetish has relations to what Winnicott has described in a recent paper as transitional objects – those inanimate objects to which so many young children become inseparably attached in an affectionate way during the first year or so of life. But I think it is confusing the issue if we proceed to speak of these objects as fetishes. Fetishism, in my view, cannot arise until the phallic stage of the Oedipus complex has been reached; it occurs as a result of a partial regression, motivated primarily by castration anxiety. This partial regression reaches back to the oral-sadistic stage, and to the stage of ego development and object-relationship characterised by splitting of the ego and the object – the stage of normal development to which, I believe, Winnicott's transitional objects belong.

My analytic experience of the perversions has been weighted on the side of fetishism; but experience of other perversions leads me to believe that much of what is true of fetishism has a more general validity. Thus, there is always a strong castration complex leading to at least a partial abandonment of genital sexuality by way of a regression to pregenital levels. The relation to the castration complex accounts for the affinity to the neuroses, noted so early by Freud. The partial regression to oral and early anal levels corresponds to the clinical fact that perverts are not infrequently near to, or actually develop, psychosis. In so far as they do not actually do so, I wish to suggest that the reason is to be sought in their exploitation of the splitting mechanism, which permits them to remain in part at the phallic level, with a superficially normal relation to reality, whereas another part of the personality is virtually psychotic. It is in the fact that the first part remains to act as liaison officer with reality that prevents clinical psychosis.

Here I must explain what I have in mind by the term 'splitting mechanism'. No doubt there are numerous ways in which the ego and the object may be split, and the clinical result must depend on the nature of the split. Where both or all of the split-off parts of the ego are at a primitive level of object relationship, the split will lead to psychosis of a schizophrenic kind; thus, splitting *need* not preserve from psychosis. The particular kind of splitting I have in mind, however, is that to which Freud drew our attention in his 'Outline of Psycho-Analysis' and in his paper 'Splitting of the Ego in the Process of Defence'. Here, you will remember, Freud described how, in cases of fetishism, one part of the split ego retains a good relation to reality, whilst the other part, using the denial mechanism, clings to what is virtually a psychotic delusion. I suggest that it is this type of unequal split which is characteristic of perversion.

I should like to add that the anxiety connected with the female genital, which we call in brief 'castration anxiety', is not just castration anxiety if by this we refer merely to the shock of finding no penis and the classical conclusion following on this discovery. Much is contributed to the anxiety by the *latent* pregenital, sadistic factors which become *activated* only follow-ing the regression. It is in this connection that I think the term 'split object' has relevance to some of the sadistic phantasies that crystallize around the split female genital. Projected oral and anal sadism leads to the paranoid features which are so characteristic not only of homosexuals but of perverts in general. Sadism so endangers the object that it has to be protected in elaborate ways – by abandoning direct sexual demands on it, by substi-tuting a homosexual object, by limiting oneself to looking or being looked at; most exquisitely of all in fetishism, by substituting a inanimate object with which one can do anything without hurting the ultimate personal object; an object, moreover, which is always there, never frustrates and never retaliates; an object, too, for which one does not have to fight with the father. The pregenital sadistic aim has been especially stressed by Sylvia Payne.

In conclusion, I wish to suggest that what characterises perversion and makes it different from neurosis or psychosis is a special technique of exploiting the mechanism of splitting of the ego, by which the pervert avoids psychosis, since a part of his ego continues to accept reality and to behave fairly normally in the non-sexual sphere. The split allows his mind to function on two levels at once – the pregenital, oral-sadistic level corresponding to psychosis, and the phallic level, where his conscious mental content bears so much resemblance to the repressed content of the neurotic. This may explain why it has proved so difficult (as Glover pointed out) to place the perversions satisfactorily in a developmental series of psychopathological states.

Note

1 Paper read at the 17th International Psychoanalytical Congress, Amsterdam, 1951.

5

The general theory of sexual perversion[1]

The subject of perversion is one which has been by no means neglected by psycho-analysts, yet in view of the central importance given to it so early by Freud in the theory both of sexuality and of neurosis, it is perhaps surprising that even more attention has not been directed to it. One reason for this may be found, paradoxically enough, in the very fact that Freud wrote a masterpiece on the subject at such an early stage. His 'Three Essays on the Theory of Sexuality' (Freud, 1905), published exactly half a century ago, is an outstanding example of his genius, for in that work he had the insight to perceive clearly the intimate connection between the manifestations of early sexuality, of adult sexual perversions, and of neurosis and psychosis. I think the essence of the book may be expressed by saying that perversion represents the persistence into adult life of elements of infantile ('polymorph-perverse') sexual activity at the expense of adult genitality, these infantile striving having failed to undergo the normal transformations of puberty, and having failed also to succumb to the defence mechanisms that would have converted them into neurotic symptoms. Or, to use Freud's own famous phrase, 'neuroses are, so to say, the negative of perversions'. Thus, perversion is represented as the persistence of the infantile. Looked at from the point of view of the 'Three Essays', perversion is seen as a vicissitude of instinct, or to express it in later terminology, as an id phenomenon. In the 'Three Essays' Freud seems to regard it as a more or less direct manifestation of component sexual instincts, and therefore scarcely capable of further reduction.

It is this aspect of Freud's early formulation which I think may be responsible for the relative sparseness of psycho-analytic writings on the subject, for it conveys the impression that little more can be said; and perhaps even more important, it suggests that the therapeutic outlook is a gloomy one and hence tends to discourage clinical work with the perversions.

In his interesting book, *Sinn und Gehalt der Sexuellen Perversionen* (*Meaning and Content of the Sexual Perversions*) (Boss, 1947), Dr Medard Boss of Zurich bases his criticism of the psycho-analytic theory of perversion principally on this aspect of Freud's formulations – that is, on the concept of component instincts and of the possibility of a causal-genetic understanding in psychology. Or so, at least, I apprehend his criticism. Although he mentions later analytic work on the role of the ego, he concentrates in this connection chiefly on Reich, Schulz-Hencke, and Horney, and accordingly concludes that it is not possible to apply one line of criticism to such widely divergent views – a conclusion with which one can only agree. What Boss seems to overlook is that there has been a steady growth of psycho-analytic theory since 1905, theory of the ego as well as of the id – a development which was mainly due to Freud himself. We are not dealing with a situation of either/or – either id or ego – but with both interacting. This fact, however, is not apparent from a study of the 'Three Essays', which was written before ego-psychology existed except in the most rudimentary form. In spite of Freud's frequent additions and emendations in later editions, the book was left substantially in its original form, as a historical document. It is therefore necessary to look elsewhere if one wishes to appreciate the present-day status of the psycho-analytic theory of the perversions.

Only a few years after the publication of the 'Three Essays' it began to be recognised that sexual perversions might have to be regarded as defensive formations rather than simply as pieces of infantile sexuality that had evaded defence. This was implicit in Freud's 1910 paper on Leonardo (Freud, 1910). It first became fully explicit in 1919, in 'A Child is being Beaten' (Freud, 1919), where a particular perverse fantasy is unequivocally related to the Oedipus complex and to various forms of defence against it. In this paper Freud further suggests that it may be found that the relationship to the Oedipus complex has a more general validity for all sexual perversions.

I wish now to draw your attention particularly to a very important theoretical paper which appeared four years later, in 1923. I refer to Hanns Sachs's 'Zur Genese der Perversionen' ('On the Origin of Perversions') (Sachs, 1923), a paper which unfortunately has not been translated into English.[2] Here Sachs has undertaken the task of reconciling the viewpoint of the 'Three Essays' with the new ideas put forward by Freud in 'A Child is being Beaten'. The essential problem as he saw it at that time was the relation of perversion to the Oedipus complex, to the unconscious, and to repression. 'A Child is being Beaten' had shown that the component instinct is not continued through in a straight line to the perversion, but must first pass through the Oedipus complex and be deflected by it somewhat as a light ray is refracted by passing through a lens. Thus we find that perverse gratification is subject to quite narrow conditions which far exceed the demands of a simple component instinct. Moreover, these component instincts generally appear in the perversion only after an elaboration which has raised them to a higher level and made them capable of normal libidinal cathexis of an object, sometimes of the most refined kind. In view of the evident fact that perversion is only the conscious part of a much larger unconscious system, the statement that neurosis is the negative of perversion does not exhaust the subject. In neurosis the repressed phantasy breaks through only as an ego-dystonic symptom, whereas in perversion it remains capable of consciousness, being ego-syntonic and pleasurable; but apart from this difference in sign here is much similarity between the two, for both are mere residues of the great developmental process of infantile sexuality, the conscious representatives of unconscious instincts. Indeed, in some cases there is an alternation between neurotic phobia and perverse gratification, and Sachs observed such a change when in the course of analysis a phobia of beating gave way to sado-masochistic masturbation fantasies. I have myself observed two cases where whipping fantasies or practices were combined with an intense snake phobia.

Sachs saw drug addiction as something intermediate between perversion and neurosis, in that like perversion it is clearly a gratification, yet like neurosis it has ostensibly nothing to do with infantile sexuality. This relationship with drug addiction was, of course, worked out much more fully nine years later by Edward Glover (1932).

Sachs drew attention to the general finding in a perversion that in spite of the transformations it may go through in the course of development, one element remains constant, for example the idea of being beaten. This is seen particularly plainly in fetishism, where one piece of a repressed complex remains conscious, like a harmless screen memory, which hides the essential piece of infantile sexuality. Thus, he says, a perversion comes into being through the preservation in consciousness of a specially suitable piece of infantile experience, on to which the infantile pleasure is displaced.

Now this particular piece of experience must have some peculiar relationship with the ego, which allows it to escape repression – and this brings us to the kernel of Sachs's theory. He suggests that when there is a conflict involving a specially strongly developed component instinct, complete victory may be impossible for the ego, so that repression may be only partially successful; the ego then compromises by repressing the greater part at the expense of sanctioning and taking into itself the smaller part – that is, allowing conscious expression to the perverse phantasy. The mechanism of perversion seems to be this solution of division, whereby one piece of infantile sexuality enters the service of repression and so carries over pregenital pleasure into the ego, whilst the rest undergoes repression. 'A Child is being Beaten' illustrates how this mechanism is used especially to deal with the task of repressing the Oedipus complex, and Sachs proceeds to show that his hypothesis fits equally well the case of male homosexuality based on too strong fixation to the mother, where resolution is achieved only by sanctioning homosexual fixation, which is incorporated in the ego. Sachs emphasises, however, that what he has described is only the mechanism, not the dynamics of the instinctual victory. The component instinct involved owes its strength not to the alliance with the ego but to factors of constitution and experience which have caused it to develop more than normal strength.

I would remind you again of the date of this paper, 1923. Many of you may agree with me that Sachs has constructed here a remarkably firm and coherent foundation for the building up of a theory of perversion. Much remained to be added, of course, but I would suggest that it should be added to, rather than replace, Sach's formulation. These necessary additions include the part played by the superego, a concept just beginning to emerge in 1923; the central importance of castration anxiety; the role of aggressive impulses and of the death instinct and of the related anxieties, together with erotisation as a defence against anxiety; the role of denial and splitting of the ego and of the object in the defensive process; and the relation of perversion to reality sense and to psychosis.

Let us turn our attention first to the superego, since Sachs's theory is to an important extent one related to structure, and his structural formulation is clearly incomplete without reference to the superego. It is a remarkable fact that in Freud's later writings on the perversions – 'Fetishism' (1927). 'Splitting of the Ego in the Process of Defence' (1940b), and in the relevant chapter of his 'Outline of Psycho-Analysis' (1940a) – he nowhere mentions the superego. I wonder whether the explanation is to be sought in a persistence in Freud's mind of his original conception that neurosis is the negative of perversion, so that if the superego plays an essential part in the formation of neurosis, perhaps perversion comes about through the absence of superego activity. Be that as it may, this tendency to ignore the superego in perversion is evident also in many other psycho-analytic writings besides Freud's.

If we accept as generally valid Freud's suggestion in 'A Child is being Beaten' that perversion is an outcome of the Oedipus complex, then in so far as the superego is to be regarded as the heir of the Oedipus complex it would be natural to look for a particularly close relationship between perversion and superego. In fact, this has been fully recognised in the case of masochism, for example, in Nacht's monograph on the subject (1938).

And indeed, although the role of the superego in other perversions has been less explicitly emphasised, it is only fair to say that this has been done implicitly in a considerable number of more recent contributions which make it clear that perversion constitutes a defence not only against castration anxiety but also against guilt feelings. It is possible, of course, that much that was formerly expressed in superego terms is nowadays stated instead in terms of relationship with internal objects. In fact, in Sylvia Payne's 1939 paper she writes that 'The relationship of a man to his fetish is the same as his relationship to his internalised parents', and that 'The fetish therefore stands for part-objects which have been eaten, and also preserved. The internalised objects may have the significance of pre-genital superego formations.' She also describes how the defensive and protective function of the mackintosh fetish rests on its capacity to defend against sadistic attacks, especially those connected with excretory activities. That is, the fetish protects the 'good' object against the aggression which might destroy it. I have quoted this paper merely as one example of a number of contributions which touch on the superego. Many of these contributions refer, however, mainly to the pregenital type of superego, which is not universally acknowledged to deserve that name.

Recently there has been an interesting approach to an investigation of the role of the classical superego in perversion formation. I refer to the work of Melitta Sperling based on the simultaneous analysis of mother and child; of Otto Sperling on group perversion (1956); and of Kolb and Johnson (1955) on the attitudes to sexuality of the parents of adolescent perverts. These investigations have drawn our attention to the way in which a faulty superego may be developed when the parental model which is offered is one which prohibits normal heterosexuality above all else, and treats pregenital or perverse activities with relative leniency, or even encourages them, because they fulfil an unconscious perverse need in the parent, who is therefore unable to cope with the child's behaviour and his defective superego. This reminds one of Sadger's views of over thirty years ago about how women have no need of perversion because they have ample opportunity to gratify their pregenital sexuality in their relations with children (Sadger, 1921).

I should like to illustrate some of these points by a clinical example. The patient's sexual activity consists of male shoe fetishism, sado-masochistic fantasy, and masturbation. His mother was closely attached to her own dominating mother, who is said to have wrecked his parents' marriage. The mother was sexually frigid and regarded the father as a sexually perverted monster, implying also that all men were like that and that male sexuality was sadistic and disgusting. The primal scene was visualised in these terms, but with a horrified realisation that finally the mother succumbed and perhaps actually enjoyed it. The little boy had been breast-fed, then weaned and handed over to a series of nurses whom he felt to be sadistic. Approaches to his mother on an oral-breast level met with a relatively gentle rebuff. Later, however, a genital approach called forth an intense emotional reaction in her, a precipitate withdrawal, and an open equation of him with the unspeakable father. This episode proved to be the turning-point in my patient's development. The violently prohibiting and deeply injured mother was introjected and continued from then on to be felt as something inside his head, pinning him down with a finger-nail (it appears that in the oedipal scene she had pushed his head away). His sexual impulses continued active, but ever since then his preoccupation has been to find outlets for them which would not offend the mother or her internalised imago. When about seven years old he was caught by her masturbating, and this too was treated as an injury he had done her, making Mummy very sad, and he had to promise solemnly never to do it again. Needless to say, this promise has been broken on innumerable occasions, but honour is satisfied if it is only a 'little' masturbation, and especially if emission is avoided or is minimal. The positive side of the perversion, the shoes and sado-masochistic fantasies, are related to the father, whom he attempts to keep as a bad figure, but one for this very reason compatible with sexuality, especially when this can be disguised as a situation of punishment. I have picked out of these elements in a very complex case with a view to illustrating the importance in perversions of faulty superego formation arising from faulty sexual adjustment in the parents.

If we attempt now to amplify Sachs's formulation by allowing due importance to the superego, perhaps we might alter it to run something like this: a sexual perversion consists in the acceptance and adoption by the ego of a certain element or elements of infantile sexuality, the other elements (and in particular the oedipal wishes) being warded off by repression or other means. The reason for the ego's adoption of the chosen piece of infantile sexuality *may* lie in its innate or acquired strength which the ego is too weak to repress and which it therefore accepts in order to be the better armed with id energy to oppose the rest; but the dynamics and economics of the situation cannot be understood without reference to the superego. That is to say, the choice by the ego of the particular piece of infantile sexuality is dictated to an important extent by the ego's judgement of what will please, or at least pass relatively unchallenged by, parental imagos, eventually internalised, i.e. by superego formations. The attempt to please the superego is especially obvious in masochism, but it operates in other perversions also. This formulation must be understood to refer to pregenital archaic superego formations as well as to post-oedipal ones concerned with the supposed parental attitude to genital sexuality, so that the ego is coping also with reintrojections of projected pregenital id impulses; hence perversions can be seen to deal with the danger of destructive impulses directed towards the object, which threaten both the self and the object. The perversion thus preserves a modicum of sexual outlet and pleasure whilst at the same time it avoids the unpleasure of anxiety and guilt feelings that would otherwise arise.

Let us turn now to a consideration of castration anxiety, whose significance in the perversions was so much emphasised by Freud, and following him by Fenichel (1945). No one who has had much clinical experience with sexual perverts can fail to have been impressed by the way in which they are dominated by castration fear and defence against it. Differences of opinion arise only over the significance of this concentration of attention and fear on the penis, for it is open to different interpretations. Ever since the analysis of Little Hans Freud stressed the fateful conjunction for a little boy of an external castration threat for masturbation with the observation of female genitals, leading the boy to the conclusion that castration really may happen to him (Freud, 1909). Now few will be disposed to deny that such experiences may have an important crystallising effect and may give conscious form and expression to the fear; but as a full explanation for such a dominating and far-reaching anxiety Freud's theory seems to depend too much on accidental and external factors, too little on endopsychic ones. The problem was discussed very fully by Ernest Jones in his 1933 paper, 'The Phallic Phase', which I cannot attempt to summarise. He stresses the part played by sadistic projection, the genital sadism being derived from earlier oral sadism which, he says, may well be the root of male as well as of female homosexuality. Perhaps we may put it in the following way: the stumbling-block for the future male pervert comes in the oedipal situation when the sexual aim becomes an actively phallic one directed to the mother. Such active phallic function is necessarily combined with a certain amount of aggression, and in the pathological case which we are considering the sadism is of such a high intensity and so much reinforced by pre-existent oral and anal sadism that it gives rise to intense anxiety and the need to retreat from the situation. The essential point of controversy seems to be this: what are the main sources of this intense anxiety, and why is it experienced as a threat to the penis? The talion principle at once springs to mind; if the penis is the executive of the sadistic impulse, punishment will naturally fall on the penis, and if the father is regarded as the injured party, he will be the castrator. This is undoubtedly true at one level – the question is whether this is the level from which the anxiety is mainly derived. Bak (1953) has recently drawn attention to the conflict created by identification with the penisless mother, leading to a wish to give up the penis in order to maintain the identification and avoid the danger of separation from her;

this gives rise to the alternative danger of castration, and the dilemma may be solved by a fetishistic compromise, where the apparent insistence on the maternal phallus is really a protection against the id wish to shed the penis in order to maintain identity with the mother.

In Jones's view the boy fears castration as the consequence of his phallic impulse to penetrate into the mother's vagina, of which he has unconscious knowledge. The danger of the mother's vagina is due to the presence of the father's penis, and conflict arises when feminine wishes are developed or exploited to deal with this internal penis in the vagina, the reason for conflict being that such feminine wishes imply castration. Thus, there is a measure of agreement with Bak's viewpoint; but for Jones the phallic mother is really a combined parent figure, and we are dealing with a disguised triangular relationship, not just an alternating identification with two different mother-imagos. The ostensibly 'feminine' attitude to the father's penis inside the mother conceals oral and anal sadistic designs on it, phantasies of getting possession of it and destroying it. These sadistic wishes are displaced on the cavity supposed to contain the penis, so that penetration into the vagina exposes the boy's penis to as much danger as his father's penis would face if it entered the boy's sadistic mouth. If this view is accepted, then Jones is justified in claiming that oral sadism is at the root of excessive castration anxiety, and hence at the root of sexual perversions in so far as they are a defence against castration anxiety.

We can now perhaps add to our formulation that the force which drives the ego to the particular defensive manoeuvres that we have recognised as characteristic of perversion is fear, which takes the form of intense castration anxiety, and that the intensity of this anxiety in relation to penetrative phallic activity is due to sadistic components, ultimately of oral origin.

This brief discussion of the significance of castration anxiety has brought us naturally to the next topic, the role of aggressive impulse. I will not say the role of the death instinct, for that would raise a thorny theoretical problem, which I hope we can avoid. In his paper on 'Jealousy, Paranoia, and Homosexuality' (1922) Freud described a new mechanism in certain cases of homosexuality where the homosexual love relationship is based on a defence against earlier intense jealousy and hostility for rival brothers; and two years later in 'The Economic Problem in Masochism' (1924) he attempted to elucidate the problems of sadism and masochism in terms of the death instinct. It was more especially in England, however, largely owing to the influence of Melanie Klein's work, that specially strong emphasis began to be placed on the role of early aggressive impulse with its associated anxieties, and on the defence mechanisms of introjection and projection; this general tendency naturally showed itself also in writings on sexual perversion. This is true, for instance, of Edward Glover's paper 'The

Relation of Perversion Formation to the Development of Reality Sense' (1933), where he suggests that perversions may form a developmental series reflecting stages in the overcoming of anxiety concerning the individual's own body or external objects, and that they represent attempts at defence against introjection and projection anxieties by means of excessive libidinisation. Certain perversions are the negative of certain psychotic formations, and they 'help to patch over flaws in the development of reality sense'. Jones's paper 'The Phallic Phase', already mentioned, is also very relevant in this connection.

A further contribution to the role of aggression in homosexuality was made by Nunberg in 'Homosexuality, Magic and Aggression' (1938), where he describes a type of male homosexual whose aim represents a compromise between aggressive and libidinal impulses, expressed in the desire to possess strong men and thus become magically strong and potent, at the same time achieving revenge on the rejecting mother, restoring narcissism, and strengthening the weak ego. It will be noted that a similar concept of a destructive love, from which the object needs protection, is to be found in Payne's paper on fetishism (1939), though she lays more stress on its pregenital nature. Another, more recent, example is Bak's 1953 paper on fetishism in which he has stressed the danger of destruction of the object and the perverse defence against this. Indeed, the report of the discussion of perversions at a meeting of the American Psychoanalytic Association in 1953 (Arlow, 1954) states that the identification of narcissistic object choices as defences against destructive wishes appeared in almost every contribution.

Herbert Rosenfeld (1949) has brought forward clinical material to demonstrate how paranoid anxieties encourage the development of strong manifest or latent homosexuality as a defence, and how clinical paranoia may result when the homosexual defence fails. The idealised good father figure is used to deny the existence of the persecutor. Rosenfeld stresses the mechanism of projective identification in homosexuals, which he traces back to infantile impulses of forcing the self – not just the penis – into the mother.

These and similar contributions clearly show not only the importance of aggressive impulse and the defence against it in the aetiology of perversion, but also the closet relations that exist between perversion and psychosis, confirming Glover's statement (1933) that certain perversions are the negative of certain psychotic formations, libidinisation and idealisation of the object being exploited as a defence against aggression and its concomitant paranoid anxieties.

Another aspect of this relation to psychosis must now be considered, approaching the matter from the angle of the ego. I have in mind in the first place Freud's discussion of splitting the ego and the mechanism of denial of reality. For an understanding of the theoretical background we must take account of Freud's 1925 paper on 'Negation', which was further elaborated by Ferenczi in 'The Problem of the Acceptance of Unpleasant Ideas' (1926). The essence of negation is that the ego can by this means extend its boundaries in that it accepts what would otherwise remain repressed, with the proviso that this particular thing is consciously denied. Freud's 1927 discussion of fetishism gave a prominent position to this mechanism of negation, whereby the ego at once defends itself and enlarges itself. The boy's castration fear leads him to deny his perception that the female has no penis. This use of negation enables him to preserve his belief in the female phallus, yet at the same time he gives up the belief and constructs a compromise object, the fetish. The fetish represents the female phallus in which he can still believe and which now absorbs all the interest previously directed to the latter; at the same time he is aware of real female genitals and is left with an attitude of aversion to them. Freud remarks that such a dual attitude to unacceptable reality can occur in other non–psychotic conditions besides perversion.

Many years later, at the end of his life, Freud took up this problem again in 'An Outline of Psycho-Analysis' (1940a) and in 'Splitting of the Ego in the Process of Defence' (1940b). In psychosis, he says, there is not a complete withdrawal from reality but a split in the mind; if the stronger part is detached from reality then the necessary condition for psychosis is present. Such splits can be found also in fetishism and in neuroses, but in neuroses one of the contrary attitudes is repressed, so that there is no split in the *ego*. In fetishism, too, we can speak of a split in the ego only when the patient continues to dread castration despite his fetishistic denial of it. This means, I suppose, that if the fetishistic defence succeeds in warding off castration anxiety, the state of affairs resembles that in neurosis, where repression obviates any split in the ego.

In this discussion Freud concentrated his attention on what was happening in the ego. It is easy to see, however, that he could equally well have approached the matter in terms of the object, and have spoken of a splitting of the object in fetishism, the fetish representing one product of the split, the still dreaded female genital the other. Equally obviously, the one is a 'good' object, the other a 'bad' one in the sense of Melanie Klein. In fact, her paper on schizoid mechanisms (Klein, 1946) elaborated this concept of splitting of the object, and it seems reasonable to attempt to establish a connection between splitting of the ego and splitting of the object as defensive processes. It will be remembered that Rosenfeld (1949) drew attention to the role of projective identification in male homosexuality. Now, identification with the object would account for the coincidence of the two splitting processes, and it is a widely accepted fact that narcissistic object choice is characteristic of perversion in general, not only of homosexuality. This would be in agreement with Bak's formulation of fetishism (1953), with its alternating or simultaneous identification with the phallic or penisless mother. In my Amsterdam paper (Gillespie, 1952) I made an attempt to combine Freud's concept of splitting of the ego with Klein's splitting of the object, and I suggested that a successful exploitation of these mechanisms saves the pervert from psychosis; and that when the split in the ego fails to salvage a sufficiently important part of the ego for the service of reality adjustment, then psychosis is the result, a clinical outcome not unfamiliar in sexual perversions.

This discussion has been concerned essentially with perversion in the male, though no doubt much of it is relevant also to female perversion. I have avoided opening up the latter subject, partly because it is clinically much less important, partly because of our knowledge of it is so much scantier, and partly out of considerations of time.

I will now attempt the difficult task of summarising very briefly the principal points to which I have drawn your attention, and I must hope you will pardon the inevitably dogmatic formulation.

The raw materials of perversion are supplied by the constituent elements of infantile sexuality. A clinical perversion, however, is generally specialised in an elaborate way, leaving only one or two routes open for achieving sexual excitement, discharging sexual tension, and establishing a sexual object relationship. Such a perversion represents a defence against the Oedipus complex and castration anxiety. The defence involves a regression of libido and aggression to pregenital levels, so that there is an increase of sadism, leading to further anxiety and guilt feeling and defences against them designed to protect both the self and the object. Libidinisation of anxiety, guilt and pain is specially characteristic as a method of defence in perversion.

The ego's behaviour and defensive manoeuvres are no less important for an understanding of perversion than are the vicissitudes of instinct. The ego adopts a certain piece of infantile sexuality and is enabled in this way to ward off the rest. The ego is able to do this, first because the superego is specially tolerant of this particular form of sexuality, secondly because of a split in the ego and in the object such that an idealised object and a relatively anxiety-free and guilt-free part-ego are available for the purposes of a sexual relationship, which takes place, so to say, in an area where the writ of reality-testing does not run.

Notes

1 Contribution to the Panel on Perversions. Read at the 19th International Psycho-Analytical Congress, Geneva, 24–8 July 1955.
2 Sachs's paper is now available in translation – see references.

6

The structure and aetiology of sexual perversion

A rigid definition of the term 'sexual perversion' is probably best avoided, but I hope it will be agreed that it should imply persistent or habitual sexual behaviour of a certain type rather than mere isolated acts; that the behaviour should be accompanied by specifically sexual excitement; and that it should deviate from some standard of normal sexual conduct. Difficulties arise, however, when we proceed to any attempt to specify this standard of normality. Can there be any universal standard or should we think only in terms of a particular culture at a particular time? If the latter, are we to rely on a statistically defined standard of normality or on the moral code professed by the culture, which may deviate widely from the average actual behaviour of its members? Endless difficulties arise, which cannot be discussed here.

I wish to suggest that, despite its manifest-limitations, a biological standard has some real advantages. Inasmuch as the sexual instinct has the biological function of ensuring procreation and thus promoting survival of the species, it seems reasonable to designate as a perversion any way of sexual life which interferes seriously with the procreative function. The diagnosis of sexual perversion would then be based on the degree and exclusiveness of the sexual activity, no just on its quality. Such a concept of perversion has a universal validity, unlike the others. Nevertheless, I do not claim for it any status higher than that of a rough yardstick, for it ignores an essential aspect of human sexual life, namely, the psychological relation to the sexual object; it gives no weight to the ego's part in sexual life, normal or perverse, and evades the issue of love and the possibility that an essential element in perversion may be the failure to form a satisfactory loving relationship with a sexual object. However, since perversion shares these features with neurosis and psychosis, the biological concept may provide a valuable method of rough differentiation.

It must be assumed that every reader of this book is thoroughly familiar with Freud's original and classical contribution to the subject in 'Three

Essays on the Theory of Sexuality' (1905). I will merely state the essence of his concept at that time, namely, that perversion represents the persistence into adult life of elements of infantile ('polymorph-perverse') sexual activity at the expense of adult genitality, these infantile elements having failed to undergo the normal transformations of puberty and having failed also to succumb to the defence mechanisms that would have converted them into neurotic symptoms. Thus Freud arrived at the famous formulation that 'neuroses are, so to say, the negative of perversions', and perversion is represented as the mere persistence of the infantile, a kind of atavism of ontogenesis.

This concept of the nature of perversion is a good example of Freud's genius for grasping the connections between things which are not obviously related, in this case perversion, neurosis, and infantile sexuality. It is essential, however, to remember that Freud had already reached this point in his thinking by 1905 and that it was by no means his last word on the subject of perversion. His later work quite clearly implies a much less simple view, as is evident from his papers on homosexuality, sado-masochism, fetishism and other related topics. These later developments in Freud's theory of perversion have been obscured by the fact that, although subsequent editions of the 'Three Essays' contain numerous additions and some corrections, Freud left the main text essentially unaltered for the purpose of historical documentation. This has had one unfortunate consequence: less well-informed critics have been led to infer that his early views underwent no further development. I hope to show how far this inference is from the truth.

In his paper on Leonardo, written in 1910, Freud speaks of a fetish as constituting a substitute for the sorely missed penis of the woman; in the same paper, he describes a type of male homosexuality due to repression of attachment to the mother, followed by identification with her and object choice on a narcissistic basis; such homosexuals are running away from other women who might make them unfaithful to their mothers. These points of view show clearly that, by 1910, Freud had already recognised the *defensive* function of certain perversions.

The decisive change came with the paper, 'A Child is Being Beaten' (1919). Here Freud unequivocally relates a particular perverse phantasy to the Oedipus complex and to various forms of defence against it. Moreover, in his discussion he extends these ideas to perversion in general. All later psychoanalytic work on the perversions has been greatly influenced by this paper. Since its publication, perversion has been regarded in analytic writings as a complex psychic formation, expressing defence as well as impulse, and related to the same nuclear complex as neurosis; it is no longer just the raw material out of which a neurosis might have been made.

This new way of looking at sexual perversion was carefully worked out from the theoretical point of view by Sachs in his paper, 'Zur Genese der Perversionen' (1923). He picked out, as the most important problem about perversion, its relation to the Oedipus complex, to the unconscious and to repression. Freud had shown, in 'A Child is Being Beaten', that the component instinct does not continue in a straight line to perversion but must first go through the Oedipus complex as a light ray is refracted by a lens. This is consistent with the fact that perverse gratification is regularly bound to quite narrow conditions which far exceed the demands of a simple component instinct. Moreover, pregenital component instincts only exceptionally appear in the perversion in an objectless or auto-erotic form; mostly, they appear after an elaboration which has raised them to a higher level and made them capable of normal libidinal cathexis of an object, sometimes of the most refined kind. Freud's statement that neurosis is the negative of perversion does not exhaust the subject, for it is clear that perversion is only the conscious part of a much larger *unconscious* system. In neurosis, the repressed phantasy breaks through only as an ego-dystonic symptom, whereas, in perversion, it remains capable of consciousness, being ego-syntonic and pleasurable; apart from this difference, there is much similarity between the two: both are mere residues of the great developmental process of infantile sexuality, the conscious representations of unconscious instincts. Indeed, in some cases, there is an alternation between neurotic phobia and perverse gratification. Sachs observed such a change in the course of an analysis, a phobia of beating giving way to sado-masochistic masturbation phantasies. (I have myself observed two cases where whipping phantasies or practices were combined with an intense snake phobia.) Drug addiction seems to be intermediate between perversion and neurosis, being clearly a gratification, yet having ostensibly nothing to do with infantile sexuality. (The relation between perversion and drug addiction was later, in 1932, worked out more fully by Edward Glover.)

Just as in the beating phantasies discussed by Freud, only one constant element persists throughout, namely, the idea of being beaten, so in other perversions one element remains constant; it is seen with particular clarity in fetishism, where one bit of a repressed complex remains conscious, like a harmless screen memory which hides the essential piece of infantile sexuality. Thus a perversion comes into being through the preservation in consciousness of a specially suitable piece of infantile experience onto which the infantile pleasure is displaced. This piece of experience must have some peculiar relationship to the ego which allows it to escape repression. Sachs suggests that, when there is a conflict involving a specially strongly developed component instinct, complete victory may be impossible for the ego and repression may be only partially successful; the ego then has to be content with the compromise of repressing the greater part at the expense of sanctioning and taking into itself the smaller part. This solution by division, whereby one piece of infantile sexuality enters the service of repression and so carries out pregenital pleasure into the ego while the rest undergoes repression, *seems to be the mechanism of perversion.* (It should be noted that the idea of 'partial repression' had long ago been anticipated by Abraham (1910), following a suggestion of Freud's.) That this mechanism is used especially to deal with the task of repressing the Oedipus complex is well illustrated in 'A Child is Being Beaten'. Sachs shows that his hypothesis fits equally well the case of male homosexuality based on too strong fixation to the mother, resolution being achieved only by sanction of fixation to the man's own sex, this being incorporated in the ego. Summing up his argument, Sachs emphasises that what he has described is only the mechanism, not the dynamics, of the instinctual victory. The component instinct owes its strength not to the alliance with the ego but to factors of constitution or experience which have caused it to develop more than normal strength.

Up to this time, little attention had been paid to the part played in perversion formation by impulses of aggression and hostility. Freud's (1922) paper on 'Jealousy, Paranoia and Homosexuality' began to touch on this theme. The paranoiac was described as using his ambivalence as a means of defence against his homosexuality; but Freud also described a new mechanism in certain types of homosexuality whereby early intense jealousy and hostility for rival siblings yield to repression and transformation, so that the rivals become love objects the reverse process of that in persecutory paranoia. Further important theoretical developments came in Freud's (1924) paper, 'The Economic Problem in Masochism', where he tries to elucidate the problems of masochism and sadism in terms of the concept of the death instinct.

The importance in general psychopathology of aggression and of early anxieties and primitive defences against them began to be increasingly stressed, particularly in England, by Melanie Klein and those who were influenced by her work. This is reflected in Edward Glover's (1933) paper, 'The Relation of Perversion Formation to the Development of Reality Sense'. Stages in the development of reality sense, he says, should not be considered solely in terms of impulse or object but should be related to stages in the mastery of anxiety, in which the roles of libidinal and destructive impulses alternate. He suggests that perversions may form a developmental series reflecting stages in the overcoming of anxiety about the individual's own body or external objects. Certain perversions are the negative of certain psychotic formations. Perversions represent periodic attempts to protect against current introjection and projection anxieties by excessive libidinisation. When some form of infantile anxiety is reanimated in adult life, one way of dealing with the crisis is the reinforcement of primitive libidinisation systems, and this gives rise to a perversion. 'Perversions help to patch over flaws in the development of reality sense.'

Another aspect of the part played by aggression is brought out in Nunberg's (1938) paper, 'Homosexuality, Magic and Aggression'. He describes a new type of male homosexuality in which aggression is an integral part of the homosexual love; the aim represents a compromise between aggressive and libidinal impulses and consists of the desire to possess strong men and thus become magically strong and potent. The man is then revenged on women for his mother's rejection, thus restoring his narcissism and strengthening his weak ego.

However, 'A Child is Being Beaten' had drawn particular attention to the role of the Oedipus complex in perversion formation; Freud's (1927) paper 'Fetishism' reinforced this insight by its heavy emphasis on castration anxiety and the need for defence against the threat implied in the discovery of the missing penis of females. Fenichel, both in his original textbook (1931) and its later English version (1945), consolidated this view of aetiology for the perversions in general, and this led to an impression of monotony which was criticised by Glover (1933). Nevertheless, it has to be recognised that the castration complex seems to provide a satisfactory explanation for the clinical fact of the much greater incidence in males of perversion in general and of fetishism in particular, a fact which other aetiological formulations do little to explain; Fenichel (1934) answered Glover's criticism quite effectively in his paper, 'Defense against Anxiety, Particularly by Libidinization'.

The whole question of the psychological significance of the penis was evidently due for review and, in particular, the concept of the phallic phase introduced by Freud in 1923, the essence of which is that the absence of a penis means castration. This review took the form of a historic controversy between Freud and Ernest Jones. (See Freud, 1925c, 1931, and Jones, 1927, 1933.) In 'The Phallic Phase' (1933), Jones suggests that sexual inversion is, in essence, hostility to the rival parent which has been libidinised by appropriating the organs of the opposite sex, organs that have been made dangerous by sadistic projection. The genital sadism is derived from earlier oral sadism, which may well be the specific root of male as well as of female homosexuality.

Freud's (1925b) paper, 'Negation', and Ferenczi's (1926) paper, 'The Problem of the Acceptance of Unpleasant Ideas', give the theoretical background of ego psychology or Freud's later contributions on perversion, which were concerned largely with fetishism. Negation is a mechanism whereby the ego is able to extend its boundaries by accepting what would otherwise remain repressed, with the proviso that it be consciously denied. The mechanism of negation is given a central position in Freud's (1927) discussion of fetishism. Out of castration fear, the boy denies his perception that the female has no penis. Thus retaining his belief in the female phallus, he at the same time gives it up, constructing a compromise object, the fetish, which absorbs all the interest formerly belonging to the female phallus, leaving him with an aversion to real female genitals. This dual attitude to unacceptable reality, says Freud, can occur in other non-psychotic conditions apart from perversion.

Freud (1940a and 1940b) returned to this theme in his 'Outline of Psycho-Analysis', Chapter 8, and in 'Splitting of the Ego in the Defensive Process'. He states that, in psychosis, complete withdrawal from reality rarely if ever occurs; what occurs is a split in the mind, one part being detached from reality; if this part becomes the stronger, the necessary condition for psychosis is present. Such splits can also be found in fetishism and in neuroses. However, Freud goes on to say that we can speak of a split of the ego in fetishists only in cases where they continue to dread castration despite their fetishistic denial of it. Neuroses differ in that one of the contrary attitudes is repressed, so that there is no split in the ego. Freud himself was in some doubt whether this idea of a splitting of the ego was something new or something long known. It is interesting to note that in his (1894) paper, 'Neuro-Psychoses of Defence', he discusses 'splitting of consciousness' at some length; of course, this was a very long time before the concepts of the ego and of repression had been worked out.

Melanie Klein's (1946) paper, 'Notes on some Schizoid Mechanisms', inaugurated the discussion of what may be regarded as a related topic, namely splitting of the instinctual object. In my paper (1952) on the perversions, I attempted to combine the two concepts and to bring them into relation with the oral regression which has impressed so many psycho-analytic writers on the perversions. I suggested that strong castration anxiety leads to a partial regression to pregenital levels, thus accounting for the affinity of some perversions to psychosis. A successful perversion evades psychosis by means of a split in the ego, which leaves a relatively normal part capable of coping with external reality while allowing the regressed part to behave in the limited sexual sphere in a psychotic manner. This implies not merely a libidinal regression but also a regression of the ego and of its relations to objects, of the nature of its anxieties and of its means of defence against them. The ego regresses in part to a stage characterised not only by splitting of the ego but also by splitting of the object. The sexual object of the pervert represents the idealised 'good' object resulting from this split; the 'bad' object is dealt with in other ways, e.g., by denial, omnipotent annihilation, or phobic avoidance.

It may have been noted that little has been said about the superego in perversion, and, in fact, it is only recently that there has been much discussion on this point. If perversion is a regressive result of the Oedipus complex, and if the superego, as classically conceived, is the heir to the same complex, it would be natural to expect a close relationship between them. At the time when Sachs wrote his paper (1923), the concept of the superego was only beginning to emerge. Had he written later, he would no doubt have discussed how the ego is able to reconcile its manoeuvre of accepting and adopting as part of itself certain pregenital id impulses with its need to live at peace with the superego. It is true that not all perverts are free from feelings of guilt about their sexual activity, but they generally show much less guilt over their preferred piece of infantile sexuality than would a normal or neurotic person. This leads to the question whether we have to deal with a particular type of superego in the pervert, one which condones just that type of sexual activity rather than any other. If so, how is such a superego developed? May it not be the result of a type of parental attitude to sexuality which gives the impression that genital sexuality is the worst sin and certain pregenital activities are relatively harmless? My own clinical experience lends some support to such a view; it was advanced by several speakers at a symposium of the American Psychoanalytic Association, reported by Arlow (1954).

The foregoing makes no pretence of being a comprehensive critical review of psychoanalytic writings on the structure and aetiology of sexual perversion in general, and no attempt has been made in this chapter to deal with the special psychopathology of individual perversions. I have merely picked out a few of the contributions which seem to me typical and illuminating for the general theory. I shall now attempt to sum up briefly the main points which can be regarded as fairly widely accepted at the present time and, so far as possible, to integrate them.

1 The raw materials out of which a perversion is built are derived from the constituent elements of infantile sexuality.
2 While there may be a clinical condition of polymorphous–perverse sexuality based upon a mere persistence into adult life of infantile sexual elements, the usual clinical form of perversion is not of this kind. It is generally specialised in an elaborate way, so that only one or two circumscribed routes are available leading to the achievement of sexual excitation and the discharge of sexual tension.
3 Perversion in this latter sense is a psychic formation which arises as a method of dealing with the Oedipus complex and, in particular, with castration anxiety.
4 The method involves, in the first place, a regression to pregenital levels of instinctual development, both libidinal and aggressive, resulting in an increased sadism. This leads to anxiety and guilt, and the further development of the perversion is an attempt to cope with this anxiety and guilt, that is, to protect both the self and the object. Libidinisation of anxiety, guilt and pain is a specially characteristic method of defence in perversion.

5 Perversion cannot be understood merely as a vicissitude of instinct, as an id phenomenon. The ego is deeply involved. While an essential element in perversion is a libidinal regression, equally essential in determining a perverse outcome rather than a neurosis or a psychosis is the nature of the ego's defensive manoeuvres. The ego accepts the perversion and so allows a circumscribed outlet to sexuality. Having given this sop to Cerberus, the ego is then able to ward off the other elements of the Oedipus complex, as well as the predominantly sadistic regressive products of retreat from that complex. The ego achieves this result at the price of a permanent split in itself and a partial denial of reality. A more extensive (psychotic) denial of reality is at the same time avoided.

6 A full understanding of the aetiology of perversion would include not merely an explanation of its structure, how that structure came into being, and what mechanisms are responsible for it, but also an explanation of what determines this particular outcome rather than any other. This is, in general, a task which daunted Freud himself. Perhaps it is enough to say, with Sachs, that the dynamics of the instinctual victory which characterises perversion must be sought in the strength of the component instincts, and that this strength is derived from inherited constitutional factors combined with infantile experiences which favour the excessive development of such factors. Twin studies have provided some evidence of a hereditary element in homosexuality, while psychoanalytic work has shown how frequently early environmental factors are operative, such as an overseductive mother and a weak or absent father. I doubt if we are yet in a position to explain satisfactorily what determines the outcome of perversion rather than something else. I think it can be said, however, that we now have some understanding of the processes whereby a perversion comes into being.

7

The psychoanalytic theory of sexual deviation with special reference to fetishism

Historical development

An attempt will be made in this chapter to present as simply as possible the psycho-analytic theory of sexual deviation or perversion, with special reference to the case of fetishism. Before we go on to discuss this, it would be as well, I suppose, to consider for a moment what we mean when we talk of a sexual perversion. Evidently we are dealing with some kind of deviation from normal sexual behaviour, and this, of course, implies that we have some normal standard of comparison. However, this is by no means so obviously true as it may appear at first sight, for the fact is that there are wide variations of sexual behaviour even in one culture such as our own, and certainly some of these variations must be considered normal, otherwise we should find ourselves in the ridiculous position of postulating a normal standard which, in fact, is attained by only a small proportion of the population. Whatever criticism may be made of Kinsey's work in this field (Kinsey, Pomeroy, and Martin, 1948; Kinsey *et al.*, 1953), one of his merits is to have called attention to this wide variation, and to have demonstrated it in a fairly objective way.

Although it would be unwise to attempt any hard and fast definition, I think it is fair to say that we ought not to speak of a sexual perversion unless we are referring to an individual's habitual sexual behaviour rather than to some occasional manifestation or to mere fantasy. If we are biologically minded we might perhaps add that this habitual behaviour is such as to interfere seriously with the biological function of reproduction and family life, by which I mean the raising of children. Such a description lays stress more on the negative aspects of the behaviour than on its positive qualities, and so long as we are concerned with these conditions as psychopathological deviations rather than as mere personal peculiarities, this seems a reasonable attitude. In fact, as Freud more than once pointed out, the two features that justify us in regarding a given type of sexual behaviour as

101

pathological are, first, its persistent, repetitive quality, and secondly its exclusiveness and tendency to replace a loving sexual relationship with a mature person of the opposite sex.

At the same time, however, it must be admitted that any such attempts at definition in biological terms do much less than justice to the psychological complexities involved, and I hope that this will become clear in the course of my further remarks. With this provisional approach we are, it is true, in a position to study and classify the sexual perversions, as has been done by a number of older workers such as Krafft-Ebing (1893) and Havelock Ellis (1900). However, it is Freud's approach to the subject which I am mainly concerned to discuss, and the essence of his approach in this field, as in that of the neuroses, was to go beyond classification and to attempt to understand the origins and psychological meanings of these conditions.

Freud's first and most comprehensive approach to the subject of sexual perversions was made in 1905 in his 'Three Essays on the Theory of Sexuality'. The central discovery of Freud which is at the heart of the 'Three Essays' is of the intimate connection between infantile sexuality, neuroses, perversions, and the development of normal adult sexuality at and following puberty. The term 'infantile sexuality' refers to the sexual activities and fantasies which Freud discovered to be a regular phenomenon of the first four or five years of a child's life. Before Freud it had been widely assumed that sexual manifestations normally occur for the first time at puberty and take the form of an irresistible attraction to members of the opposite sex. This would imply that the sexual function was in an extreme degree innate or instinctual. Freud, despite his own assumption that sexuality is essentially based on instinct, saw clearly that the popular view of an instinctual onset of sexual activity at puberty simply did not correspond to the facts, and that a long and fateful history in childhood precedes and largely determines the outcome of the developments at puberty.

Infantile sexuality itself has an instinctual basis which the child brings with him in his inherited constitution: its unfolding is to some degree a matter of automatic maturation, and to this extent follows a preordained course. The common mistake of regarding sexual sensations and activities as identical with and limited to genital functioning will not stand up to critical examination even in the most 'normal' adult; in the child, of course, such an equation of 'sexual' with 'genital' is manifestly absurd. It has to be recognised that in everyone, but above all in the young child, sexual feelings may be associated with the stimulation and functioning of many parts of the body. Those parts which are especially prone to give rise to sexual feelings were described by Freud as erotogenic zones. Clearly the genital organs themselves are the most obvious example, but the mouth and the excretory organs are also very important in this connection, especially in the earliest years. Thus infantile sexuality is first predominantly associated with oral activities and pleasures, then increasingly dominated by interest and pleasure in excretory activities, and finally becomes more and more concentrated in the genital erotogenic zones. This is a matter of shifting emphasis, not the replacement of one zone by another; thus oral erotism persists throughout the later phases, and genital erotism is present from an early stage. In addition to the variations in emphasis due to the stage of maturation of the child at a given moment, and the variations due to the unique inherited constitution of the child, the particular form assumed by an individual child's sexuality is influenced also by environmental factors, that is, by his personal experiences, such as special difficulties at a particular stage. For instance, a child may have breast-feeding difficulties due to the mother's anatomical or psychological failure of adaptation to the infant's needs, or he may have a traumatic weaning; or his excretory function may be interfered with by frequent enemas; or he may be genitally seduced by a nurse. When such experiences occur in a child predisposed to over-react to them because of his constitution or because of the particular stage of development he has reached at the time of the experience, the result is likely to be a *fixation* at that specific phase of emotional development.

Since the concepts of fixation and regression play such an essential part in the psycho-analytic theory of sexual deviation, it may be advisable to examine them more closely at this point. First, we should note that 'fixation' refers to something relative rather than absolute; when we use the word to indicate a pathological process we should remember that we are dealing merely with an exaggeration of a normal phenomenon. For although there is a strong tendency towards growth, maturation and progressive development in the child, due to innate factors which normally are reinforced by environmental pressures (i.e. what is expected of the growing child by his parents and later his teachers as well as his contemporaries), nevertheless there is also in every child a conservative element, a reluctance to give up old ways and modes of gratification – in general, an unwillingness to grow up. We find this at all stages, from weaning through toilet training up to the Peter Pan type of problem. In cases where this general tendency is grossly exaggerated in some particular area, we can speak with justice of a pathological fixation; the fixation may be either to a special method of getting satisfaction, e.g. sucking, or to a particular object. Such a pathological fixation means that there is a greater or lesser failure of the subsequent developmental process, and an insecurity of such progress as is made.

The concept of *regression* is complementary to that of fixation, and it corresponds to a phenomenon that is very familiar clinically. It implies a developmental retreat, a going back to earlier emotional attitudes and types of behaviour. Such a retreat is apt to occur when any serious difficulties arise in a child's emotional life; a good example is seen in the case of a child in whom toilet training has been well established, who nevertheless starts to wet his bed again when faced with the crisis presented by the arrival of a new, rival baby. In cases of this kind, where current stress produces such a regressive retreat to an earlier stage of development, the stage retreated to is commonly determined by the presence of fixation points of the sort we have been considering. Freud compared them to towns that have been left occupied by garrisons in the wake of an advancing army; when the army gets into difficulties and has to retreat it is likely to withdraw to one of these garrison towns, which correspond to the fixation points.

Provided that the difficulties of early development are not too extreme, the child arrives by the age of 3 or 4 years at a stage when his psychosexual life is dominated by genital impulses and fantasies, and these are directed mainly towards his parents or parent-substitutes; in a normal family setting this results in some variety of the classical Oedipus complex. There are many reasons why these oedipal yearnings and rivalries in relation to the parents lead inevitably to intense conflict in the child's mind – conflict between impulses of love and hate; conflict between desire and fear of the consequences of his demands; and conflict in many other areas. Consequently the oedipal phase is a particularly difficult and complicated one, and a child who is predisposed by constitution or early experiences – a child, that is, who has acquired strong fixation points – is very liable to retreat from his oedipal problems by a process of regression, and thus to reactivate the earlier types of libidinal activity characteristic of the fixation, e.g. anal or oral.

As already mentioned, in the 'Three Essays' Freud made clear the intimate connection between sexual perversion, the sexuality of early childhood, the psychopathology of neurosis, and the development of adult sexuality following puberty. Put very briefly, the relationship is as follows. During the first few years of life the child normally undergoes a process of psychosexual development which differs in many ways from normal adult sexuality and, especially in its earlier phases, possesses a number of the characteristics which, when they occur in the adult, are regarded as perverse. Examples of this are the sexual use of non-genital parts of the body, pleasure in display of or looking at forbidden parts or excretory processes, pleasure in inflicting pain, etc. There is a gradual increase in genital interests, which culminates in the oedipal stage of development. This is followed by the rather puzzling 'latency period', when there is a recession of sexual activity, during which 'shades of the prison-house begin to close upon the growing boy'; a period when the instinctual impulses become bridled by increasing conformity to outside pressures and inner defences against impulse. The onset of puberty upsets the equilibrium established in the latency period through a biologically determined increase of the instinctual forces, aggressive as well as sexual. The stormy period of adolescence normally leads to transformations of psychosexuality of such a kind that the sexual impulse becomes concentrated in a heterosexual, genital drive directed towards non-incestuous objects. The numerous elements of earlier, 'infantile' sexuality which do not fit into this pattern are dealt with in various ways which lead either to their suppression or to their transformation into forms which are no longer overtly sexual. This is brought about by processes such as the reaction formations which constitute important elements in character development (sadistic impulses, for example, becoming replaced by attitudes of kindness and pity), and sublimations, in which primitive sexual impulses are diverted into non-sexual and socially acceptable channels (sexual curiosity, for instance, being converted into scientific curiosity).

Such is the model of *normal heterosexual development*; and both psychoneurosis and sexual perversion can be seen as different types of failure of this normal development. Freud had already shown in the years before he wrote the 'Three Essays on the Theory of Sexuality' that the *neurotic symptom* is based on elements of childhood sexuality which are unacceptable to other parts of the personality and therefore give rise to conflict in the mind; the symptom in fact is a compromise which gives expression both to the underlying sexual impulse and to the forces which are concerned to ward it off. It is therefore the expression of an unsuccessful effort at defence against some part of infantile sexuality; whereas, as we have seen, in a normal development these impulses are dealt with more successfully.

The concept of sexual perversion that emerged from the 'Three Essays' may be expressed by saying that perversion represents the persistence into adult life of elements of infantile sexual activity; this persistence of childish sexuality takes place at the expense of adult genitality, the impairment of which is an essential feature of true perversion. Thus there has been a failure of the normal transformations of puberty which should produce such modifications of the infantile sexual urges and such emphasis on heterosexual genital ones as to produce normal adult sexuality.

However, in the case of sexual perversion another possible outcome besides the healthy one has failed to occur – that is, the pathological outcome of neurosis. We may say, therefore, that not only have the infantile sexual strivings failed to undergo the normal transformations of puberty; they have also failed to succumb to the defence mechanisms that would have converted them into neurotic symptoms. In cases of neurosis where this does happen, it does so likewise at the expense of adult sexuality, and the neurotic symptoms are in part a substitute for adult sexuality.

It becomes clear, then, that perversion and neurosis share the important feature of replacing adult sexuality, at least to some degree; but on the other hand, they seem to be diametrically opposite in another respect, namely that the perversion is *not*, and the neurosis *is*, the outcome of the action of defence mechanisms on infantile sexuality. Freud expressed this opposition very vividly and memorably when he said in the 'Three Essays' that neuroses are, so to say, the negative of perversions. This formulation implies that perversion has to be seen as the persistence of the infantile, and Freud's acute antithesis of neurosis and perversion suggests that whereas in neurosis the infantile sexual elements are persistent but converted by defence mechanisms into neurotic symptoms, in perversion, on the other hand, they merely persist in an unmodified form. The emphasis would be on fixation, rather than on a defensive regression, and perversion would have to be regarded as a vicissitude of instinct, as essentially an id phenomenon.

Now I have laboured this point, not because I want to drive it home – far from it. My reason for doing so is that these formulations of Freud's, arrived at as early as 1905, have had an enormous influence, both inside and outside psycho-analytic circles, in building up what is in some essential ways a quite false picture of the psycho-analytic theory of sexual perversion which has gradually emerged since 1905, largely as a result of Freud's own work. An aphorism such as Freud's about neurosis being the negative of perversion has the merit of enshrining a piece of truth in a memorable way. The trouble is that it can seldom cover the *whole* truth, and this is certainly the case here. For while it is important to recognise the *differences* between perversion and neurosis, it is equally important to remain alive to certain essential features they have in common. One of these common features is already apparent from the 'Three Essays', namely that each of them is to be regarded as an imperfect or abnormal outcome of psychosexual development.

However, the parallel is closer than this very general statement implies. Not very long after the first publication of the 'Three Essays' in 1905, it became gradually recognised in psycho-analytic writings that perversion could *not* be regarded simply as a persistence of the infantile with no attempt whatever at defence manoeuvres. It is true that the defence of repression was conspicuous by its apparent absence the defence so characteristic of the hysterical neuroses on which Freud's early studies and theories were largely based; but when Freud discussed certain aspects of homosexuality in his 1910 paper on Leonardo da Vinci, he implicitly assumed that defensive mechanisms were at work.

This defensive view of perversion, which brings it so close to neurosis in an essential respect, came right out into the open in 1919 with Freud's paper entitled 'A Child is Being Beaten'. In this paper he discussed in detail a particular sado-masochistic fantasy which he had come across in a number of patients. His analysis related it not merely to infantile sexuality, but much more specifically to the Oedipus complex. He found that it was the outcome of various forms of defence against the oedipal conflicts, including both repression – for much of the underlying basis had become inaccessible to conscious awareness – and also the mechanism of regression from the genital level where the conflict originated to the anal–sadistic level on which the fantasy was expressed. Freud further suggested in this paper that the findings he had reached in this limited field might have a much wider validity, and might, in fact, apply to sexual perversions in general. This is indeed what has been abundantly confirmed by later analytic work.

It will be seen that the theoretical standpoint had by now changed in a very important way, and it was no longer possible to see perversion and neurosis as poles apart, the one simply the negative of the other. The two extremes, in fact, meet in the Oedipus complex.

The theoretical position was much clarified in 1923 by Hanns Sachs in a paper which took as its starting point the work of Freud that I have just referred to. He pointed out that it had become evident that overt perversion or perverse fantasy represents only the conscious part of a much larger unconscious system, just as this is true of a neurotic symptom. Both are mere residues of the great developmental process of infantile sexuality, the conscious representatives of unconscious instincts. Sachs drew attention to the interesting cases where there is an alternation in the same patient between a neurotic phobia and a perverse gratification. In other cases, the two may exist side by side, the patient being unaware of any relationship, though this may be obvious to the trained observer. For example, I have observed two cases where whipping fantasies or actual flagellation were combined with an intense snake phobia (both whip and snake being clear phallic symbols.)

If there is not the antithetical difference between perversion and neurosis that Freud at first seemed to imply, what then is the essential difference? Clinically we may say that in neurosis the repressed fantasy breaks through to conscious expression only in the form of a symptom unwelcome to the ego typically accompanied by neurotic suffering, whereas in perversion the fantasy remains conscious, being welcome to the ego and pleasurable. The difference seems to be the one of ego attitude and positive or negative emotional sign, rather than a difference of content.

The question that now arises is this: how is it possible, in cases of perversion, for the ego to take this tolerant and welcoming attitude to elements of primitive sexuality which other individuals find it necessary to deal with so sternly, either by the formation of neurotic symptoms or by the normal transformations of adolescence? Sachs approached this problem first by pointing out that, in spite of the changes a perversion may go through in the course of development, in general one element remains constant – for example, in the fantasy discussed by Freud, the idea of being beaten. In other words, perverts have a strong tendency to specialisation. This is seen particularly plainly in cases of fetishism, where one piece of a repressed complex remains conscious, like a harmless screen memory which hides the essential piece of infantile sexuality. Thus a perversion comes into being through the preservation in consciousness of a specially suitable piece of infantile experience, on to which the rest of the infantile sexual pleasure is displaced.

The problem can now be formulated in this way: what is the peculiar relationship between the ego and this particular piece of childhood sexuality which makes it possible to avoid repressing it, and allows it to come to consciousness and even to overt expression in sexual activity? The answer that Sachs suggested is that in these cases the ego is dealing with a specially strongly developed component part of the sexual instinct, a part so strong that the ego is unable to repress it completely. The most that the ego can manage is a compromise; it represses the greater part at the expense of sanctioning the smaller part, and actually adopting it as part of its own organisation. By this compromise, this partial capitulation, the ego is then in a stronger position to fend off the remaining infantile sexual demands. The mechanism of perversion seems to be this solution of division, whereby one piece of infantile sexuality (the core of the perversion) enters the service of repression – changes sides, as it were – and so carries over pregenital pleasure into the ego, whilst the rest of infantile sexuality undergoes repression. This, as Sachs says, is the mechanism by which the perversion is produced; but a further essential factor, which I have already mentioned, is the circumstance that the ego has to deal with a specially strongly developed component instinct. This means that Freud's original formulation in the 'Three Essays' remains valid, but to it there needs to be added the description we have just considered of the defensive mechanism employed by the ego – a defensive mechanism characteristic of sexual perversion, and different from those characteristic of the neuroses.

Now just as Freud's formulation of 1905 required important additions and modifications of the kind we have been considering, in the same way we must remember that the formulation of Sachs dates from the year 1923. Since that time many further additions have been made to psycho-analytic theory, and some of these are highly relevant to the theory of sexual perversion.

The concept of the superego was just beginning to emerge in 1923, and it is clear that any formulation would be incomplete from the point of view of later theory if it failed to take cognisance of the superego. It will be remembered that Freud had found that the beating fantasies were the outcome of various forms of defence against oedipal conflicts. Now the superego, as originally described by Freud, is to be regarded as the heir of the Oedipus complex, and it therefore seems reasonable to look for a particularly close relationship between perversion and the superego, since both can be regarded as some sort of a solution to the Oedipus complex. It is perhaps in masochism that the role of the superego and of the problem of dealing with guilt feelings is most obvious, but it has become clear that an important function of perversion in general is to deal with guilt feelings. A number of American analysts (Johnson and Szurek, 1952; Kolb and Johnson, 1955; Sperling, 1956) have studied the sexual attitudes of the parents of perverts, and have shown how a faulty superego may be developed on the basis of the parental model. The kind of parental model that is likely to be found in cases of sexual perversion in the child is one which prohibits normal heterosexuality above all else, and treats pregenital and perverse activities with relative leniency, or even encourages them, because they fulfil an unconscious perverse need in the parent. The parent is therefore unable to cope with the child's behaviour and with his defective superego.

If we attempt now to amplify Sachs's formulation by allowing due importance to the superego, perhaps we might alter it to run something like this: a sexual perversion consists in the acceptance and adoption by the ego of a certain element or elements of infantile sexuality, the other elements (and in particular the oedipal wishes) being warded off by repression or other means. The reason for the ego's adoption of the chosen piece of infantile sexuality *may* lie in its innate or acquired strength which the ego is too weak to repress and which it therefore accepts in order to be better armed with id energy to oppose the rest; but the dynamics and economics of the situation cannot be understood without reference to the superego. That is to say, the choice by the ego of the particular piece of infantile sexuality is dictated to an important extent by the ego's judgement of what will please, or at least pass relatively unchallenged by, parental imagos, eventually internalised, i.e. by superego formations. The attempt to please the superego is especially obvious in masochism, but it operates in other perversions also. This formulation must be understood to refer to pregenital archaic superego formations as well as to the post-oedipal ones concerned with the supposed parental attitude to genital sexuality; hence perversions can be seen to deal with the danger of destructive impulses directed towards the object, which threatens both the self and the object. The perversion thus provides a modicum of sexual outlet and pleasure, whilst at the same time it avoids the un-pleasure of anxiety and guilt feelings that would otherwise arise.

Another area which needs amplification is that of castration anxiety, whose significance in the perversions was much emphasised by Freud. The clinical facts are not in doubt, in that perverts are certainly dominated by castration fear and their defence against it, but differences of opinion have arisen among analysts over the significance of these phenomena, which are open to different interpretations. There has been an increasing stress on the importance of aggressive wishes and sadism, by which one means a compound of aggressive with libidinal impulses. Without going into this complicated subject in any detail, we may at this point add to our formulation that fear is the force which drives the ego to the defensive manoeuvres that we have recognised as characteristic of perversion. This fear commonly takes the form of intense castration anxiety, and the intensity of the anxiety, related as it is to penetrative phallic activity, is largely due to sadistic components which, in the last analysis, can be traced back to origins in the oral stage of development connected with aggressive biting.

The importance of aggression has become increasingly recognised in the last few decades, and it has important further connections with our subject. For example, Freud (1922) described a mechanism in certain cases of homosexuality where the homosexual relationship represents a defence against an earlier state of affairs when the individual felt intense jealousy and hostility towards rival brothers. The role of the primitive mechanisms of introjection and projection has been much emphasised, especially in this country, and the influence of Melanie Klein's work has been strong in this area. Edward Glover, in 1933, suggested that perversions may form a developmental series reflecting stages in the overcoming of anxiety concerning the individual's own body or external objects, and he suggested that they represent attempts at defence by means of excessive libidinisation against anxiety connected with introjection and projection. These primitive mechanisms are related to psychotic formations, and Glover suggested that certain perversions, have to be regarded not so much as the negative of neuroses, but of psychoses, and that, as he put it, they help to patch over flaws in the development of reality sense.

The important additions to Freud's early formulations which we have been considering are largely connected with the greatly increased interest in the ego and its activities which analysts have shown in the last two or three decades. Another aspect of this must now be mentioned. I refer to what Freud (1925b, 1927, 1940b) called splitting of the ego, which he related to the mechanism of negation or denial. This differs in an essential way from repression, besides also resembling it. In repression an unwelcome piece of reality, such as an unpleasant memory, is banished from consciousness – so far as the ego is concerned, it has ceased to exist. In the case of negation, the unwelcome piece of reality is admitted to consciousness, but at the same time it is consciously denied.

Let us take for an example the case of fetishism, where the erotic feelings are attached, not to the genital aspect of a member of the opposite sex, but to some non-genital part of the body or some article of clothing, in which

sadistically attacked without danger of retaliation or of guilt feelings. Hence his pronounced preference for inanimate objects, of which the prototype in childhood was a much-loved doll.

The background to his development and the dominating figures of his inner world consisted of a frigid mother and a father whom she openly regarded as a sadistic monster, together with a succession of nurses who were likewise regarded by the boy as sadistic. His early sexual overtures to his mother were rebuffed by her with horror and an equation of the boy with his unspeakable father. His further psychosexual development was dominated by the need to satisfy all these nursery figures, and it necessitated much splitting both of his ego and of his objects. The mother was idealised and desexualised, and all active heterosexual impulses were inhibited. The bad father and nurses were appeased by masochistic submission, and sexual feeling was displaced on to inanimate objects, especially shoes.

It took a long time to work through this patient's problems but eventually he was able to court and marry a woman of about his own age, and before the analysis ended she had produced a son and heir, greatly to his satisfaction.

The theory of fetishism

There are a number of reasons why fetishism is one of the most psychologically interesting perversions. In the first place, although it sometimes takes strange forms, in essence it is no more than a caricature of certain important features of normal sexual love. We customarily take it for granted there should be a certain amount, and even a high degree, of selectiveness in choosing a sexual partner. Many factors enter here but specific physical characteristics are commonly sought. Indeed, we should be apt to regard as less than human anyone whose sexual choice demanded no more than that the object should be in possession of genital organs of the opposite sex – yet any such more selective demand contains in it a principle which, when pushed to an extreme and elaborately developed, is what we see in cases of clinical fetishism. This principle consists in the displacement of erotic feelings from the genitals of the love object on to some other part of the body, or on to some peculiarity of the body, e.g. being one-legged, or on to something more or less closely related to the body, especially various articles of clothing.

In its minor form, which as we have seen merges into normal sexual behaviour, fetishism consists in a demand that the sexual object shall have certain well-defined physical characteristics, or shall wear certain specific kinds of clothing. Here the human sexual object is still of some importance. In the major form of fetishism the process is pushed a stage further; now

112

the longing for the fetish, e.g. a shoe, a mackintosh, furs, etc., actually takes the place of the normal sexual aim of genital union. The fetish, in fact, may finally become completely detached from any human object, and possession of and play with this inanimate object may become the fetishist's exclusive sexual activity.

The love which is thus felt for an inanimate object in the severer forms of fetishism has an interesting parallel in the development of many young children – the phenomenon which Winnicott described in 1953 when he introduced the useful term 'transitional object'. He meant by this the attachment that so many infants develop towards some specific inanimate object – a shawl, it may be – from which they will in no circumstances be parted and which must remain unchanged (e.g. it may not be washed). It may be regarded as a development out of such activities as thumb-sucking, which involve the self-comforting use of a part of the infant's own body (auto-erotism) – a development in the direction of going out to the external world for satisfaction. It is doubtful whether, from the infant's point of view, such transitional objects are felt as part of himself, or as a special external object, part of the not-me world. Probably it is a half-way house, hence Winnicott's use of the term transitional.

It is important, however, not to confuse 'transitional objects' with fetishes. The former originate at an early stage of development, closely related to the breast or bottle-feeding situation. Whilst no doubt sexual in the wider sense, they are not specifically related to genital organs or functions. They are found in both sexes, whereas one of the most striking features of fetishism is its great rarity in the female. It may well be true in some cases that what is ultimately chosen as a fetish may have featured in that individual's early life as a transitional object; but a great deal must happen if the one is to be converted into the other. A fetish, as we shall see, is a product essentially of the genital phase of development, even if it has to be regarded as a kind of retreat from that phase. Such a retreat or regression leads to the reanimation of many earlier phases of experience, and it may well often happen that an old preoccupation with a transitional object of infancy becomes revived in this way so that a new, genital, significance is now attached to an object which originally had a different meaning for the child.

It was Binet who first suggested, in 1887, that fetishism results from an experience, normally in childhood, in which sexual excitement became aroused in some special circumstance which then remains permanently associated with such excitement – no doubt his theory would later have been described in terms of conditioning. Freud at first confirmed this finding of Binet but later pointed out that the initial occurrence of sexual excitement in these particular circumstances itself requires explanation and that, in reality, behind this first recollection of the fetish's appearance there lies an earlier forgotten phase of sexual development. Freud further drew attention to the symbolic connection which sometimes accounts for the significance of the fetish, as in the case of the foot, the shoe, or fur, all well-known symbols of male and female sexual organs. The importance that many fetishists attach to the smell of the object is also related to the delight of young children in what later, through repression, come to be felt as unpleasant smells. By the time he came to write a short paper in 1927 devoted to the subject of fetishism, Freud had evidently reached the conclusion that there was one factor in the aetiology of fetishism which was the paramount and essential one – namely the fear of castration and the inability to tolerate the knowledge that human beings exist who do not posses a penis, beings who would, therefore, in the little boy's view, have to be regarded as having been castrated. This leads to an inability to accept the female genital as a fact of nature, and all the more to accept it as a sexually stimulating and desirable thing. Such feelings, of course, can readily lead to a homosexual development; the *sine qua non* for a male homosexual is that his sexual partner must be possessed of a penis, and indeed some male homosexuals can be not inaccurately described as penis fetishists.

However, the true fetishist avoids homosexuality just by the creation of his fetish, for the fetish represents the sorely missed penis of the woman, who can then be accepted without too much castration anxiety, provided the reassuring fetish is present. Nevertheless, as we have seen, in the severest cases the fetishist dispenses with the woman entirely. The castration fear implies, of course, that the boy has either perceived a female genital or in some other way become aware of its nature, hence a belief in the female phallus involves a denial of an actual perception. From then on, therefore, the child is entertaining two contradictory ideas in his mind at the same time – or rather his ego deals with this dilemma by the creation of a compromise, the fetish, which is something that really exists and can be seen and touched, unlike the female phallus, and yet something which stands for the latter and so asserts its existence and allays castration anxiety. The fetish remains as the sign of triumph over the castration threat and spares the fetishist any need to become homosexual by making the female into a tolerable sexual object. The denial of real perception which is the basis of this mechanism is in some ways reminiscent of what happens in psychotic denial of reality; but in the case of the fetishist it is only one current of the mental life that behaves in this way; the sexual life is split off from the rest, which may be quite well adjusted to reality. Thus Freud came to attach much importance to a defensive splitting of the ego in the aetiology of fetishism.

Having thus picked out these vitally important essential mechanisms and fantasies, Freud seems to have somewhat lost interest in some of those other aspects of fetishism to which he himself had earlier drawn attention.

Freud laid great weight on the way in which powerful castration anxiety might be produced in a boy by threats of castration in connection with masturbation followed by the opportunity to observe female genitals; this sequence had the effect of convincing the boy that the threat of castration was no idle one but corresponded to something which had actually happened to others, and therefore might really happen to him. However, important as this may be in certain cases, one may well doubt whether it is the whole story. Before such a perception of female genitals can constitute a threat, it is evidently necessary that the little boy should identify himself with the girl or woman, at least to some extent. In Fenichel's 1930 paper on the closely related subject of transvestitism he attempts to show that the transvestite combines the defensive manoeuvres of the fetishist with those of the homosexual. The latter has dealt with his possessive love for his mother by instead identifying himself with her, whilst the fetishist has not accepted the woman's lack of a penis. The male transvestite, says Fenichel, always in his fantasies conceives the woman as equipped with a penis in order to allay his castration anxiety; and besides this he has identified himself with this phallic woman. It seems, however, that this double defence that Fenichel describes in transvestitism may be found also in cases that are clinically fetishism, not transvestitism. Two such cases were described in 1936 by Kronengold and Sterba; in these cases the fetishistic act represented a passive feminine masochistic identification with the suffering mother, and the fetish was her phallus.

In a case that I myself described in 1940, feminine identification, more or less conscious, was very prominent, and to my mind was an essential factor in causing the woman's lack of a penis to be apprehended as a castration threat. With it went a passive homosexual attitude to the father, together with the secondary defences introduced to deal with the anxiety aroused by this situation. My patient's masturbation fantasies combined fetishistic with masochistic (disguised as sadistic) ones, much as in the case I described earlier in this chapter. The fetish here consisted of uniforms and mackintoshes which the patient either gazed at on real women, or wore himself, or he made drawings or simply fantasies of women wearing them. The sado-masochistic part considered in the woman being forced to wear the uniform, which was regarded as a humiliation, and this was often represented as the punishment for some offence against the 'persecutor', who was generally an older woman. Great stress was laid on the tight parts of the uniform: collar, belt, cuffs; but in addition there was much tying up, gagging and so on. He often tied himself up and put on mackintoshes and uniforms in order to masturbate; and, apart from this, there was no doubt that he identified himself in the other fantasies with the 'persecuted' woman. In fact at one stage of his development it was always a boy, not a woman, who was victimised.

The importance of identification in fetishism was brought out very clearly by Bak in 1953. He showed that there was a double concept of the mother, both as possessing and as not possessing a penis. The boy identified himself sometimes with the phallic mother, sometimes with the non-phallic one, and sometimes with both simultaneously; and these different identifications correspond to the 'split of the ego' described by Freud. The identification with the penisless mother leads to the wish to give up his own penis, and this leads to a sharp conflict with the narcissistic pride in it and wish to retain it. Both the dangers that threaten the boy, separation from his mother and castration, are warded off by the fetishistic compromise. The insistence on the existence of the mother's penis is really a protection against the unconscious wish to shed the penis in order to maintain identity with the mother.

In a series of papers, Phyllis Greenacre (1953, 1955, 1960) has made a number of important contributions to the subject of fetishism. These relate first to the problem of anxiety and to the conditions in early infantile life which tend to produce excessive predisposition to anxiety, conditions such as marked disturbances in the mother, for example. Further, gross disturbances in function of the child, resulting from anatomical anomalies or focal illness, may result in displacements and accentuations of libidinal functioning, leading to special forms of deprivation or gratification which make for later complications, by contributing to the formation of fixations. A common early disturbing experience which she found consisted of exposure to scenes of birth, miscarriage or menstrual bleeding which accentuated the tendency to regard the mother's genital area as something damaged (castrated). Such factors as these are likely to produce a faulty development of the child's image of his own body, which makes him peculiarly vulnerable to later stimuli such as seeing the female genital area during latency or puberty. The fetish then comes in as a restitutive attempt to restore the integrity of the mother's body and so of his own. There is also more or less interference with the satisfactory development of personal (object) relationships.

The special relationship of the fetishist to his object is indeed of crucial importance and a number of factors enter into it besides those already mentioned. As we have seen, there is a flight to a varying degree from a complete flesh and blood object to a part of it, or to some related inanimate thing. The substitute object, the fetish, has a number of other important advantages apart from preserving the fetishist from castration anxiety. These are mainly related to his concern to preserve undamaged the original oedipal love object, the mother. The anxieties of the Oedipus complex lead to a considerable amount of libidinal regression, that is, to a retreat to earlier, more infantile forms of sexuality of the types associated with the feeding and excretory processes (oral and anal stages of development). No doubt it is characteristic of the fetishist that he has formed fixations at these early stages (cf. for instance Greenacre's work). A prominent feature of these pregenital forms of sexuality is that they contain a strong aggressive element, which fuses with the libidinal impulses to produce sadism. In this way the sexual object is felt to be threatened by such sadistic impulses, and it therefore needs to be protected. An example of such pregenital attacks would be destruction by dangerous urine, and a mackintosh fetish can be seen to have a protective function in this connection. In a much more general way, however, the transfer of interest from the human object to the fetish spares the former, and enables the object to be approached both libidinally and aggressively with much less danger either of rejection or of retaliation. The function of fetishism as a means of protecting the primary object – ultimately the mother – from sadistic attacks which would threaten her total destruction was especially stressed by Sylvia Payne in her paper of 1939.

General summary of psycho-analytic theory of perversion

The essence of the theory is still to be found in Freud's 'Three Essays on the Theory of Sexuality'. It is impossible to begin to understand sexual perversions without a knowledge of infantile sexuality, of its peculiar features, its development and vicissitudes, and of the transformations which it normally goes through at puberty before emerging as adult sexuality.

Nevertheless, what we encounter clinically in cases of perversion is by no means, or only rarely, a simple continuation into adult life of all the elements of infantile sexuality. On the contrary, most clinical perversions are highly specialised and specific; that is, only very limited ways remain open to the adult pervert for achieving sexual excitement, discharging sexual tension and establishing a sexual object relationship. A clinical perversion of this kind has a very obvious defensive function, with the aim of warding off anxieties concerned with the Oedipus complex, and especially castration anxiety. It is, therefore, in the nature of a compromise between instinctual impulse and ego defence, and in this way closely resembles a neurotic symptom.

The defences adopted in perversion involve regressions of various kinds – regression of libido to pregenital levels, and regression too in the aggressive impulse: together this leads to an increase in sadism, which gives rise to further anxieties specific to the dangers both to the object and to the self which are inherent in sadism, and to consequent defences designed to ensure the safety of both.

The behaviour of the ego in perversion is especially characteristic; instead of an attitude of hostility to the instincts, dictated by superego pressure (as in neurosis), the ego adopts as its own one particular piece of infantile sexuality, and this helps it to oppose the rest. The result depends also on a superego which is tolerant of this specific aspect of sexuality. Splits in the ego and in the object make possible attitudes to reality, confined to the sexual area, which, if more widespread, would lead to a psychosis.

8

Contribution to symposium on homosexuality[1]

The subject of homosexuality is so vast and many-sided and affects so many areas of human life, both pathological and otherwise, that it is difficult to address an International Congress briefly on this theme. On reflection it occurred to me that there may be a way in which I can drastically limit the field of my discussion, and yet at the same time leave room to consider some of the more interesting and challenging issues emerging at the present time in relation to homosexuality. It may be remembered that at the Geneva Congress of 1955, as contributor to a panel, I attempted to outline the general theory of sexual perversion (Gillespie, 1956a). In spite of its inevitable incompleteness, this presentation did not appear to arouse much adverse criticism, and I have therefore ventured to assume that it represents a fair statement of the views of many psycho-analysts. It was not, of course, within the scope of that paper on the general theory of perversions to deal in detail with any particular perversion. I thought, therefore, that for the purposes of this year's Symposium on homosexuality it might be interesting to review some of our knowledge and theories relating to homosexuality and to enquire whether or not they can be accommodated easily and naturally in our general theory of sexual perversion. Should the answer be that they are not compatible with the general theory, then we should need to consider two possibilities: first, that something is radically wrong with the general theory as I have formulated it; or alternatively that homosexuality is a different kind of state or behaviour-pattern from the other conditions that we consider to be sexual perversions. Were we to reach the second conclusion, then the old distinction which was once drawn between 'perversion' and 'inversion' might be justified. A third possibility must by no means be ignored, namely that what we call 'homosexuality' may be very far from homogeneous, so that *some* of the manifestations we include under this label may be properly classified with the perversions, others not.

The hypothesis that homosexuality is not a homogeneous category is, of course, very familiar to psycho-analysts: the clearest early statement of the idea was made by Ferenczi (1914). It will be recalled that Ferenczi proposed to replace the term 'homosexual' by 'homoerotic', and to distinguish clearly between 'subject homoerotics' and 'object homoerotics'. It is remarkable that although many, including Freud himself, recognised that 'homoerotic' is a better name than 'homosexual', the former has never been widely adopted, even in psycho-analytic circles. I have little doubt that a cogent reason for this is the great importance that was always attached by Freud to the concept of bisexuality, with its biological rather than purely psychological implications. I shall return to this theme later. As to the distinction between subject and object homoerotics, the difficulty is that although the distinction is a valid one, it is valid for types of behaviour and fantasy, but is not in general valid for individuals, as Freud (1905) pointed out: that is, a single individual is very liable to show both kinds of behaviour at different times or simultaneously. Nevertheless, the possibility remains that what we call homosexuals are made up of more than one group, and that these groups differ from each other in a fundamental way. As I hope to show later, this hypothesis of heterogeneity receives support from a quarter entirely remote from psycho-analysis, namely from studies in human genetics.

In order to recall the main points that were stressed in my Geneva paper (Gillespie, 1956a) I will repeat the summary with which it ended.

The raw materials of perversion are supplied by the constituent elements of infantile sexuality. A clinical perversion, however, is generally specialised in an elaborate way, leaving only one or two routes open for achieving sexual excitement, discharging sexual tensions, and establishing a sexual object relationship. Such a perversion represents a defence against the Oedipus complex and castration anxiety. The defence involves a regression of libido and aggression to pregenital levels, so that there is an increase of sadism, leading to further anxiety and guilt feeling and defences against them designed to protect both the self and the object. Libidinisation of anxiety, guilt, and pain is specially characteristic as a method of defence in perversion.

The ego's behaviour and defensive manoeuvres are no less important for an understanding of perversion than are the vicissitudes of instinct. The ego adopts a certain piece of infantile sexuality and is enabled in this way to ward off the rest. The ego is able to do this, first because the superego is specially tolerant of this particular form of sexuality, secondly because of a split in the ego and in the object such that an idealised object and a relatively anxiety-free and guilt-free part-ego are available for the purposes of a sexual relationship, which takes place, so to say, in an area where the writ of reality-testing does not run.

Let us consider now some of the ways in which homosexuality may be considered to differ radically from the perversions in general. Beginning with the data of animal behaviour, as described, for instance, by Beach (1949), we find good evidence of homosexual behaviour amongst animals, and by no means always *faute de mieux*. Freud's (1905) refutation of the popular misconception that the sexual instinct is 'revealed in the manifestations of an irresistible attraction exercised by one sex upon the other' applies in the animal world as well as the human. The other anomalies of object choice which Freud mentions in the 'Three Essays', namely relations with immature persons and with animals of another species, have likewise been authoritatively described in the animal world. Various anomalies of sexual aim have also been frequently reported. It would seem, therefore, that comparisons with animal behaviour give little justification for regarding homosexuality as unique among the perversions. In any case, of course, it is highly questionable whether these animal activities have more than a superficial resemblance to the clinical perversions with which we are concerned.

Another possible distinguishing feature is to be sought in the social sphere. As we all know, certain civilisations, notably the classical Greek one, have not only condoned but even idealised homosexuality. And in many societies, such as our own, there is a distinct homosexual subculture with its own manners and linguistic jargon, so that it is possible for homosexual people to move in an artificial society where their behaviour is in conformity with the mores rather than in conflict with them. I do not think that this can be said of any other perversion. A sado-masochistic patient, a flagellant, bemoaned this fact and envied the way in which the path of the homosexual is made smooth for him. In this social aspect of homosexuality we have, I believe, one respect in which it may really be set apart from other perversions. It must be added, however, that in general this is true of male rather than of female homosexuality, even if the story of Lesbos shows that there are exceptions to the rule. Otto Sperling's (1956) work on group perversions may be a useful pointer to the further understanding of these social aspects of homosexuality; he emphasises the role of the perverted leader in conformity with Freud's theory of group psychology. Such a theory is clearly one which stresses the importance of the superego in its post- rather than pre-oedipal forms; and the same may be said of the work of Adelaide Johnson (Kolb and Johnson, 1955) and her co-workers. All this fits in very well with our general formulation, as I pointed out at Geneva, and introduces no difference in principle between homosexuality and other perversions, even though there are certain specific

121

features of homosexuality, such as its socially cohesive quality when aim–inhibited, which lead to social consequences not found in other forms of perversion.

Yet another area in which we might have to recognise a difference between homosexuality and other perversions is that of the hereditary element. In the 'Three Essays' Freud's (1905) conclusion was

> that there is indeed something innate lying behind the perversions [and of course he included homosexuality], but that it is something innate in *everyone*, though as a disposition it may vary in its intensity and may be increased by the influences of actual life. What is in question are the innate constitutional roots of the sexual instinct.

Now I think it must be admitted that we still know very little about the inherited aspects of these innate constitutional roots, although we know more and more about the variations in their intensity and the effects on them of the influences of actual life, particularly infantile life. But we are faced with a certain very striking claim in relation to the importance of heredity in overt male homosexuality. I refer to the often–quoted work of Kallman (1952a, 1952b) on homosexual twins. He reported in 1952 on the identical twin brothers of 37 out of 40 male homosexuals; of these 37 twins every one was at least 3 on Kinsey's scale, 28 of the 37 scoring Kinsey 5 or 6; whereas of 45 non–identical homosexual twins 26 twin brothers were traced, and only 3 of these 26 scored as much as Kinsey 3. The concordance in the identical wins was so perfect that it must have been embarrassing to Kallman – certainly such a result must be very unusual if not unique in psychiatric genetics. All that Kallman claimed that his result showed was that the inherited factor renders the individual particularly prone to a homosexual outcome. No one seems to have arrived at a satisfactory explanation of the result of this research. It has to be noted that it is excessively difficult to obtain a sample of this size, and Kallman's cases were highly selected for other things besides homosexuality – they were mostly criminal or otherwise abnormal. It may be that this is a factor in producing a result which runs counter to so much that we believe we know about the importance of non–hereditary factors in the aetiology of homosexuality. So far as I am aware, no similar hereditary study has been done on any other perversions, and clearly it would be extremely difficult to collect a large enough series of twins.

Besides Kallman's work, Eliot Slater (1962) has reported significant findings in another investigation of homosexuals which has genetic implications. He has shown that homosexuals tend to be born late in the sibship order, that is, in the second rather than in the first half of their families; and accordingly the age of the mother at their births tends to be higher than the average. It is well known that this is the case with mongols, but the degree of the shift is not so great in the case of homosexuals. Having regard also to a high variance, this research suggests that homosexuals are a heterogeneous group, one part of which might be accounted for by a chromosomal anomaly such as may be associated with late maternal age. The hypothesis not only leaves room for social and psychological factors in the aetiology of the total heterogeneous group, but actually seems to require some such supplementary hypothesis. This is the work to which I referred earlier in connection with the hypothesis that homosexuality is heterogeneous; I believe it merits our serious attention.

Anyone considering the status of homosexuality as one among many perversions, or alternatively as a condition different in quality from the perversions, is bound to give very careful attention to the concept of universal human bisexuality, as understood by Freud; for if, as Freud repeatedly stated, homosexual behaviour is a manifestation of the fundamental bisexuality of every human being, then it may well be essentially different from perversions. Such a view seems to be implicit, for example, when Freud expresses the opinion that a heterosexual development requires just as much explanation as a homosexual one; and that in principle the prospects for converting a confirmed homosexual into a heterosexual are not different from those of changing a heterosexual into a homosexual. Such remarks seem to show that Freud regarded the heterosexual outcome as a precarious one.

Freud's concept of bisexuality was partly based on biological and anatomical considerations, and on the existence of physical hermaphroditism; that is, there are in every individual anatomical traces of the sexual organs of the other sex, and in certain abnormal cases these mixed sexual characteristics are present in a gross and exaggerated degree. Following Krafft-Ebing and others, Freud concluded that there must be a corresponding state of affairs in the psychological sphere; that is, in every individual there must be present at least some rudimentary psychological characteristics of the other sex, and in some individuals a great deal of such inverted or homosexual characteristics. At the same time, however, we must recall that Freud was always very hard put to it to say just what is masculine and what feminine in psychological behaviour, the distinction tending always to turn into the essentially different distinction between active and passive.

Now what we are discussing here is the hypothesis of some sort of fundamental psychological bisexuality corresponding to, in the sense of being equally intrinsic with, the biological bisexuality which Freud, I think, believed he could safely assume. We are not discussing other things, such as identifications – probably no one would deny that practically every individual must make identifications with persons of both sexes and with the functions they perform in society, including their sexual functions, and that as a result of such identifications any individual may in a sense be described as having bisexual characteristics. Neither are we concerned here with the clinical use of the term 'bisexual' to describe someone who actually or potentially has sexual relations with individuals of both sexes. No, what we are talking about is a much more fundamental, perhaps even somewhat metaphysical idea, comparable to the Eros–Thanatos dichotomy – in other words, I suggest, one of those polarities characteristic of Freud's thinking. It was natural for Freud to accept the idea of biological bisexuality, for it was widely entertained at the time. However, it seems certain that there was another very cogent reason why he attached so much weight to the concept of bisexuality. It was one of the cornerstones of Wilhelm Fliess's theories, and became one of the bonds between the two men. The fact that the idea of a universal human bisexual constitution was communicated by Fliess to Freud and not originated by Freud was the source of a remarkable lapse of memory on Freud's part, recorded by him (1901) in 'The Psychopathology of Everyday Life'. Eventually, the theory of bisexuality became the occasion of the final estrangement (Jones, 1953), for Fliess accused Freud of having betrayed his secret 'discovery', the essence of which was the bisexual nature of each living cell. All in all, then, this must have been a theme of great emotional significance for Freud, and it seems conceivable that there is here a cause for the tenacity with which he clung to the concept.

Recent discoveries have demonstrated something that has a bearing on Fliess's secret 'discovery' of the bisexuality of every cell, something that at the same time represents in a sense just the reverse of what Fliess believed. I refer to nuclear or chromosomal sex, and the fact that it is now possible to demonstrate sexual differences between the somatic cells of individuals, differences corresponding in general to the manifest maleness or femaleness of the individual. In this manner, another dimension has been added to our concept of sexual differences – people may be said to be either male or female through and through in a way which I do not think we fully recognised before. This is surely a strong argument against the bisexual hypothesis in the sense that Freud meant it.

I need not remind you, however, that the process of sexual differentiation is far more complex than this. What seems most relevant at this point of my argument is the fact that an individual's genetic or chromosomal sex – the sex that the dealer of his chromosomes intended him to have, so to speak – is not necessarily the same as the type of sexual characteristics which he ultimately shows. Here, surely, was the discovery that seemed to lend colour at last to the far-fetched talk about 'a feminine brain in a masculine body', the 'third sex', and so on.

The notion that homosexuals are an 'intersex' seemed at one time to be strongly supported by the work of T. Lang (1940), who showed in a very large series of male homosexuals that there was an abnormal sibling sex ratio; that is, there were many more brothers and fewer sisters in their families than would be expected theoretically. This could be explained if the supposedly male homosexuals were in fact *genetically* females. However, more recent research has repeatedly shown that male homosexuals have *male* nuclear or chromosomal sex, so that Lang's theory is not tenable. But the *fact* of the abnormal sibling sex ratio has been confirmed by several subsequent investigators and needs another explanation. The one that must surely occur to a psychoanalyst is that the possession of brothers, and the consequent need to deal with problems of rivalry and hatred, is an important factor in the aetiology of a large number of cases of male homosexuality; if this is true (and we have Freud's (1922) word for it apart from our own clinical experience), then a man with brothers is more likely to develop homosexuality than one who has none. Thus Lang's result could be anticipated on psycho-analytic theory – though not, be it noted, on any theory that attaches significance only to the early mother–child relationship.

The whole theory of bisexuality, biological as well as psycho-analytical, was vigorously attacked many years ago by Rado; nothing, I believe, has emerged to refute his powerful arguments. Accordingly, should anyone wish to accord a special place to homosexuality, outside the perversions, on the ground that it is based on a fundamental biological and psychological characteristic, bisexuality, I for one would energetically repudiate any such claim.

When the term 'bisexuality' is used clinically it obviously bears a quite different connotation and refers to something whose reality is not in question. Weissman (1962) has recently made an interesting approach to the subject of overt male bisexuality. He distinguishes two types; first, where passive homosexual wishes are *regressions* from the oedipal level, and second, where they originate in pre-oedipal identification. The first type is similar to normal male bisexuality, and these are mainly overt hetero-sexuals, whose homosexuality can be considered as a part of oedipal bisexuality. The other type are predominantly overt homosexuals, and their heterosexual activity can be regarded as pseudo-heterosexuality aris-ing from superego and ego-ideal demands in a pre-oedipally determined homosexual. The psychosexual development of such cases is basically that of the perverse overt homosexual; they achieve heterosexual activity with the help of fetishistic mechanisms; that is, the female is treated as a fetish representing the phallus, with which her whole body is equated, and an ego split occurs during intercourse. Paternal superego demands for mascu-linity are satisfied in this way. The reason I have picked out this paper for discussion, although it deals with bisexuality rather than homosexuality as such, is that it brings into clear focus some important aspects of the psychopathology of homosexuality. It presents us with the notion that some forms of heterosexual behaviour are in a sense spurious and represent defensive activities on the part of an essential homosexual; whereas some homosexual activities are equally spurious, and are the defences of an essential heterosexual. For our present purposes we can ignore the overt heterosexual activities; we then find that we must distinguish between two kinds of overt homosexual behaviour. One is the behaviour so to say natural to the individual because of a pre-oedipal fixation; the other is defensive, being a regressive defence against oedipal problems. It will readily be seen that such a formulation is very relevant to my chosen theme; for the second type of defensive homosexuality fits admirably into the general theory of sexual perversion, whereas the other type, postulated as due to a pre-oedipal fixation, perhaps does not fit in. Furthermore, if the suspicion I have mentioned is correct, that there are at least two essentially different kinds of homosexuality, may not we have here a key to the understanding of the difference?

To my mind a central theoretical problem, now as forty years ago (Sachs, 1923), concerns the relative importance of the Oedipus complex and castration anxiety on the one hand, and the pre-oedipal factors on the other. Expressed in different terms, is it a three-body or a two-body relationship that is mainly involved? Thus the problem I have chosen as my theme can be reworded in this way: is homosexuality necessarily the outcome of an attempt to deal with the Oedipus complex, exploiting a particular piece of infantile sexuality for this purpose; or can it be better understood as a direct outcome of the pre-oedipal mother–child relationship?

It seems to be among the best established analytic findings that in homosexuality of *both* sexes the mother-relationship is a vitally important one. In the case of *female* homosexuality, so much less studied than the male, this was clearly brought out by Helene Deutsch (1933); yet she also discussed at length the role of the father-relationship and of regression from the Oedipus complex in the history of female homosexuals. She had seen a few quite special cases which suggested that the libido had always known only one object, the mother, but these were cases of general psychic infantilism with diffuse anxieties and perversions. Thus, Deutsch's (1933) views about typical female homosexuality seem to be entirely consistent with the general theory, based on Freud and Sachs, that the relation to the Oedipus complex is essential to the typical perversion. The same may be said of Jones's (1927) paper on female sexuality; despite his stress on oral and sadistic factors in lesbians, his view was an oedipal one.

Bergler was unequivocally on the other side. *Consciously*, he says, lesbians dramatise a husband–wife relationship, but this is a disguise; unconsciously they are enacting a child–mother relationship, with the unconscious fantasy of the masochistically ill-treated child and the cruel, denying mother. The masochistic conflict, originating in infancy, after various elaborations and defences against superego reproaches, results finally in the homosexual defence of pseudo-love; the core of the homosexual 'solution' is the elaboration of masochistic vicissitudes stemming from the first months. Thus it is very doubtful whether Bergler's view is compatible with the general theory; yet it is supported by much familiar and clinical experience.

The subject of overt female homosexuality was discussed recently at a meeting of the American Psychoanalytic Association, reported by Socarides (1962). Weiss expounded his strong support for the bisexual theory and his concept of the 'egotising' of either masculine or feminine tendencies, so that normally what is egotised corresponds to the anatomical sex, and the other tendency is gratified, *vicariously* in a heterosexual object; failing this, the ego feels physically mutilated. Weiss stressed the need for a homosexual woman to solve her oedipal problem before she can be helped by analysis. Personally, I could accept this ingenious formulation, provided it is understood that when we speak of bisexuality in this connection we are not referring so much to a fundamental biological fact as to the plasticity of social roles open to an individual; the acceptance of a role is what I understand by Weiss's term 'egotise'. At the same meeting, Kestenberg stated that the homosexual woman has renounced her oedipal father and her desire for a child and instead plays out a *mother–child* relationship with female partners or 'life dolls'. Both Weiss's and Kestenberg's views seem to be consistent with the general theory – female homosexuality represents a regression from and a defence against the Oedipus complex.

Reverting to Bergler's theories, originally developed in collaboration with Eidelberg (1933) in connection with the male breast complex, we must note that his view of male homosexuality is in many ways similar to his view of lesbianism. Male homosexuality is one of the abnormal solutions of the conflict over weaning; furiously disappointed with the breast, the boy discards the whole sex responsible, concentrating instead on his own penis. This is a cover for the pursuit of the disappointing breast, and so the homosexual lives according to what Bergler (1951) describes as the 'mechanism of orality'. It is not this mechanism, however, that makes the homosexual, but his narcissistic structure, which renders weaning so severe a blow to his illusion of omnipotence. The penis serves as a narcissistic recompense. Here, as with Bergler's discussion of lesbianism, one can readily recognise much of what he describes in one's own clinical material; and again if one accepts Bergler's explanation of the clinical facts one is faced with the difficulty of reconciling such a theory with the concept that perversion is necessarily involved with the Oedipus complex.

The type of view which I have illustrated by Bergler's work has something in common with that of Melanie Klein and her followers. Klein did not herself write much about the clinical perversions, though she clearly attached the greatest importance to the developing child's ability to pass successfully through predominantly homosexual phases in his or her development, this being in her view an essential background for a sound heterosexual development. Her ideas have been applied in the sphere of clinical homosexuality by Rosenfeld and Thorner. Rosenfeld (1949) is principally concerned with the relationship between *overt* male homosexuality and paranoia, homosexuality being a frequent defence against paranoid anxieties and anal sadistic tendencies. He suggests that besides identification with the mother and narcissistic object choice a frequent source of narcissistic homosexual attraction is the projection of parts of the self, particularly the penis, into another man; that is, projective identification. Thorner (1949) likewise stresses persecutory anxieties in the aetiology of male homosexuality; his patient externalised his internal persecutors and projected his anxieties into them in their role of sexual partners.

As in the case of Bergler's views, it seems difficult to reconcile these Kleinian theories of homosexuality with the general formula for perversion; that is, the Oedipus complex does not clearly come into the picture. But perhaps this merely reflects the ambiguous status of the Oedipus complex in current Kleinian theory. I think it would be going too far to say that the findings we have been discussing are incompatible with our formula, but it is also not at all obvious how they can be integrated.

There are many other important contributions to our subject which I should have liked to touch upon, such as Bychowski's formulations in terms of introjects; but the time has come when I must attempt to sum up.

I have posed a question about the status of homosexuality as a perversion; the most relevant non-analytic data are the outcome of genetic studies relating to the hereditary factor. Although their exact significance is still obscure they should make us wary of accepting uncritically the proposition that homosexuality is simply a perversion like any other. It would, however, be unwise to argue that homosexuality occupies a special place because it is based on universal constitutional bisexuality, more evenly balanced in some than in others.

Psycho-analytic work on homosexuality in both sexes has on the whole related it to the Oedipus complex and to regressive defences against oedipal anxieties; but for many years there have been powerful psycho-analytic arguments stressing the essential importance of pre-oedipal fantasies rather than the oedipal castration threat – in particular oral fixations relating to the mother, her breast, and the trauma of weaning. It has been suggested that there are two types of homosexual activity, the one based on a pre-oedipal fixation of this kind, the other arising as a regressive defence in the face of oedipal problems. If this is accepted, then the second type clearly conforms to the general theory of perversion, but the first type perhaps does not.

Freud's third type of male homosexuality, based on brother rivalry, may be more important than is sometimes implicitly assumed, and again this should remind us that homosexuality is probably heterogeneous in its nature and aetiology. Short of prolonged analysis, we still find it hard to make a sure diagnosis between the different types, and I suspect that just as with Ferenczi's subject homoerotics and object homoerotics it will be found that there is much overlapping. One would expect differences between the types in prognosis and in response to treatment. There is much scope here for important clinical research.

Note

1 Read at the 23rd International Psychoanalytical Congress, Stockholm, July–August 1963.

9

Concepts of vaginal orgasm[1]

On this special occasion in the history of the *International Journal of Psycho-Analysis* there are few psychoanalysts still active among us who have been subscribers ever since Volume 1 appeared. My own regular subscription began with Volume 13, which contained the translation of Freud's paper, 'Female Sexuality' (Freud, 1931).

If one takes a remote bird's-eye view of the most obvious changes in the climate of psychoanalytic interest and opinion that have made themselves felt in the pages of the *Journal*, and elsewhere, over these 38 years, one may think perhaps of the controversy between Freud and Jones over female psychosexual development; the full unfolding of the Kleinian theory and its applications, with its stress on the earliest stages and the most primitive fantasies and relationships to breast and to mother, together with the prolonged controversy resulting therefrom; and the development of the structural theory from the basis laid down by Freud, a development which owes much to Anna Freud. The further extension of ego psychology initiated by Hartmann before he left Vienna and greatly elaborated in America by himself and others is less adequately represented in the *Journal*, since much of this work was published elsewhere.

However, these main streams by no means constitute the whole of psychoanalytic progress over the years, even if they are the most purely psychoanalytic. Technical progress in extra-analytic fields has revealed various facts highly relevant to psychoanalysis, though unknown at the time of Freud's work. I am thinking in particular of recent work on sleep and dreaming which should take us back to reconsider *The Interpretation of Dreams* and the 'Project' that preceded it; and I think also of the remarkable findings resulting from Masters and Johnson's researches into the anatomy and physiology of the human sexual response, as well as the detailed and complex knowledge that has been accumulating recently of the process of sexual differentiation in the human embryo; this latter should lead to a fuller understanding of the meaning of bisexuality than was possible in Freud's time.

The last two subjects were recently presented to psychoanalysts (not without a certain bias, to be sure) by Mary Jane Sherfey and following this they were discussed at length at a meeting of the American Psychoanalytic Association, reported in its journal (Sherfey, 1966); they were brought especially to the attention of the British Psycho-Analytical Society in February 1969, by Drs Rey and Pines. This is the area in which the discoveries of Masters and Johnson most obviously call for a reconsideration if not a revision of traditional psychoanalytic theory and attitudes; here we have a good example of how we may profitably take up again an issue which was debated many years ago at the highest level in the pages of this *Journal*.

I wish to comment only on one limited part of Freud's (1931b) paper, 'Female Sexuality', the part to which Masters and Johnson's work is particularly relevant; the latter provides certain hitherto unknown facts which may possibly call for some modifications in Freud's formulations concerning female libidinal development. I refer to Freud's view that the female must not only change the sex of her love object, but must also overcome an initial phallic stage of development in which the leading erotogenic zone is the clitoris and the aim an active one directed towards the mother in the first instance; she must, said Freud, substitute the vagina for the clitoris as the leading zone, and must accept a passive aim in place of her original active one. This can be accomplished successfully in such a way as to produce a truly mature woman only if she can succeed in overcoming the very strong earlier attachment to the clitoral[2] zone with its active aim, a task which many women fail to accomplish satisfactorily.

This view of the relation between clitoris and vagina and of the difficult task of making the transfer had been reached by Freud at least as early as 1897, when he wrote about it to Fliess (Freud, 1950b), bringing it into relation with the abandonment of other, earlier, sexual zones, i.e. pre-genital ones. Even more relevant is a passage in 'Three Essays on the Theory of Sexuality' (Freud, 1905). After speaking of 'pubertal repression' in women Freud writes:

> When at last the sex act is permitted and the clitoris itself becomes excited, it still retains a function: the task, namely, of transmitting the excitation to the adjacent female sexual parts, just as – to use a simile – pine shavings can be kindled in order to set a log of harder wood on fire.

The following passage (especially when one recalls subsequent formulations) seems to indicate that this piece of insight, with its remarkable foreshadowing of the findings of Masters and Johnson, quickly became converted for Freud into the idea that the 'transfer of excitation' from clitoris to vagina implied a developmental process in which the clitoris should normally *give up its excitability* in favour of the vagina, and that its failure to do so in less normal cases is associated with anaesthesia of 'the vaginal orifice'.

One of the outstanding features of Masters and Johnson's researches is that they have literally thrown light in dark places, namely on the processes that occur in the female genitalia during sexual activity, using colour cinematography with the help of special apparatus. For my present purpose I will pick out only one or two of their findings; my references will be to Sherfey's (1966) paper and its quotations, since this may be more accessible than the Masters and Johnson monograph (1966).

First, then, Masters and Johnson state (Sherfey, p. 66):

> From an anatomic point of view, there is absolutely no difference in the response of the pelvic viscera to effective sexual stimulation, regardless of whether stimulation occurs as a result of clitoral area manipulation, natural or artificial coition, or, for that matter from breast stimulation alone . . . . The female's physiologic responses to effective sexual stimulation . . . develop with consistency regardless of the source of the psychic or physical sexual stimulation.

It should be carefully noted, of course, that it does not follow from this that the *psychological* response is necessarily uniform.

Secondly, as regards orgasm, Masters states (Sherfey, p. 69):

> the female responds to sexual stimulation . . . in a manner essentially akin to the localized congestive reaction which accompanies erection in the male penis . . . . [And] actual orgasmic experiences are initiated in both sexes by similar muscle components.

Finally, let us look at the role of the clitoris as elucidated by Masters and Johnson. As Sherfey remarks (p. 74):

> One of the most significant findings of Masters and Johnson is the fact that the clitoral glans is kept in a state of continuous stimulation throughout intravaginal coition even though it is not being touched and appears to have vanished.

owing to erection and retraction into the swollen prepuce. Masters and Johnson state (Sherfey, p. 74):

> A mechanical traction develops on both sides of the clitoral hood subsequent to penile distension of the vaginal outlet. With penile thrusts, the entire clitoral body is pulled towards the pudendum by traction exerted on the wings of the minor labial hood.
>
> When the penile shaft is withdrawn during active coition, traction on the clitoral hood is somewhat relieved and the body and glans

return to the normal pudendal overhang positioning . . . . This rhythmic movement of the clitoral body in conjunction with intra-vaginal thrusting and withdrawal of the penis develops significant secondary tension levels. It should be emphasized that this same type of secondary clitoral stimulation occurs in every coital position, when there is full penetration of the vaginal barrel by the erect penis.

Sherfey goes on (p. 78):

Furthermore, it is also obvious why the thrusting movements of the penis will necessarily create simultaneous stimulation of the lower third of the vagina, labia minora, and clitoral shaft and glans as an integrated, inseparable functioning unit with the glans being the most important and, in by far the majority of instances, the indispensable initiator of the orgasmic reaction. With these observations, the evidence seems overwhelming: *it is a physical impossibility to separate the clitoral from the vaginal orgasm as demanded by psychoanalytic theory.*

Now, if we accept these findings and statements, what becomes of the supposed distinction between clitoral and vaginal orgasm, and the value judgement which sets so many sophisticated Western women in pursuit of the elusive 'vaginal orgasm'? It seems probable that we must agree that an orgasm is an orgasm, and that one differs from another not in kind but in degree or completeness, or in the emotional satisfaction that accompanies it.

I wish to propose that in future if and when the term 'vaginal orgasm' is used we should no longer think of this as something excluding an out-grown clitoral erotogenicity; the term should instead be used exclusively to denote an orgasm that is *brought about* by thrusting movements in the vaginal barrel, whether or not such movements are indirectly producing excitation of the clitoris. The term 'clitoral orgasm' would then denote *orgasm produced by local stimulation* in the vicinity of the clitoris, not by thrusting movements in the vagina.

Having in this way eliminated the probably misleading idea that female maturity necessitates an outgrowing or 'repression' (to use Freud's early description) of clitoral erotogenicity, we can proceed to consider what obstacles actually stand in the way of vaginal orgasms as defined above; and here we shall find ourselves on familiar psychoanalytic ground and shall be concerned with many psychological problems, such as fear of penetration or invasion, problems of penis envy, masculine identification, and count-less others. But one bogey will be out of the way, and I believe this will be a real advance in the psychoanalytic understanding of female sexuality.

I should like to suggest further that, in view of what we have learned from Masters and Johnson, we should reconsider very carefully the question whether clitoral excitation is necessarily associated with the urge to penetrate and act the male; may not clitoral excitation on the contrary lead to the wish *to be penetrated* in order to satisfy its proper erotic aim in the physiological manner that has been described? In the former case, penis envy indeed seems an inevitable and therefore normal consequence of anatomy; but in the latter case *penis desire*, i.e. the desire to be penetrated and so stimulated both vaginally and clitorally, is the outcome to be expected in a normal female psychosexual development.

Finally, it should be said that an incomparably fuller discussion of the problems of female sexuality is to be found in the *Journal of the American Psychoanalytic Association* of July 1968. In particular, the semantic ambiguities in current uses of the term 'vaginal orgasm' are considered in great detail in an admirable paper by Glenn and Kaplan. My excuse for the present publication is that there may be an advantage in picking out one particular theme for discussion from among the very complex issues that face us in the study of female sexuality, if in this way one particular tree may be clearly visualised and distinguished from the wood. I make no apology for the symbolism.

Notes

1 Paper given for the 50th Anniversary of the *International Journal of Psycho-Analysis*.
2 I am aware that the correct form is 'clitoridal', but this is so clumsy and unpronounceable that I prefer to be incorrect.

10

Woman and her discontents: a reassessment of Freud's views on female sexuality

The vast dimensions of the subject of female sexuality have obliged me to limit my field rather carefully. I have therefore taken as my starting point Freud's own views on female sexuality. As we all know, Freud was a true scientist and his career was a voyage of discovery, during which new vistas kept presenting themselves; and so, of course, we have to reckon with Freud's changing views, for some of them were altered quite radically in his later years. Some, however, were retained relatively unchanged, and it is these steadfastly held opinions that led to a controversy, which became particularly lively in the 1920s. The opposition was led largely by women analysts, but they had the powerful support of Ernest Jones. This controversy is part of the intellectual environment in which Melanie Klein's lines of thought and clinical activity took shape, and so one begins to appreciate how far-reaching have been its consequences.

I have attempted to discover some of the germs of Freud's views on female sexuality by scrutinising his early published works and the correspondence with Fliess. The first important statements emerged in 1894–95, in Draft G of the Fliess papers (Freud, 1950a) and in the paper on anxiety neurosis published on 15 January 1895 (Freud, 1895). Draft G is remarkable for the so-called sexual diagram; the same ideas are presented purely verbally in the 1895 paper, where Freud makes it quite clear that his view of the sexual process applies, in the first instance, to men. I will quote:

> In the sexually mature male organism sexual excitation is produced – probably continuously – and periodically becomes a stimulus to the psyche. . . . This somatic excitation is manifested as a pressure on the walls of the seminal vesicles, which are lined with nerve endings; thus this visceral excitation will develop continuously, but it will have to reach a certain height before it is able to overcome the resistance of the intervening path of conduction to the cerebral cortex and express itself as a psychical stimulus. When this has happened, however, the

group of sexual ideas which is present in the psyche becomes supplied with energy and there comes into being the psychical state of libidinal tension which brings with it an urge to remove that tension. A psychical unloading of this kind is only possible by means of what I shall call *specific* or *adequate* action. This adequate action consists, for the male sexual instinct, in a complicated spinal reflex act which brings about the unloading of the nerve-endings, and in all the psychical preparations which have to be made in order to set off that reflex. Anything other than the adequate action would be fruitless, for once the somatic sexual excitation has reached threshold value it is turned continuously into psychical excitation, and something must positively take place which will free the nerve-endings from the load of pressure on them – which will, accordingly, remove the whole of the existing somatic excitation and allow the subcortical path of conduction to re-establish its resistance.

(pp. 108–9)

This view seems to depend on a close analogy with that other vesicle, the urinary bladder; in principle the difference would reside in the more complicated specific action required in the sexual act.

Freud goes on to say:

in essentials this formula is applicable to women as well, in spite of the confusion introduced into the problem by all the artificial retarding and stunting of the female sexual instinct . . . Where women are concerned, however, we are not in a position to say what the process analogous to the relaxation of the seminal vesicles may be.

(p. 109)

Freud's inability to discover a female analogue to the seminal vesicles is surely damaging to the theory. Another point to which I would draw attention, however, is his remark about the 'artificial retarding and stunting of the . . . sexual instinct', for it shows how much, at this early date, Freud was alive to the importance of social factors in producing effects that might be mistakenly attributed to inherent differences between the sexes. Similar remarks can be found in other parts of his early writings. For example, in Draft G he writes:

Women become anaesthetic more easily because their whole up-bringing works in the direction of not awakening somatic sexual excitation, but of changing all excitations which might otherwise have that effect into psychical stimuli . . . This is necessary because, if there were a vigorous somatic sexual excitation, the psychical sexual group would soon acquire such strength intermittently that, as in the case of men, it would bring the sexual object into a favourable position by means of a specific reaction. But women are required to leave out the arc of the specific reaction; instead, permanent specific actions are required of them which entice the male into the specific action.

(p. 204)

Note the word 'required'. I think that what Freud says here about the 'permanent specific actions' required of women which entice the male into the specific action is particularly interesting in connection with fairly recent work by one of our British colleagues, Dr Michael, whose investigations of rhesus monkeys (Michael, 1968) have shown that the male's sexual activity or lack of it varies, not with his own hormonal state but with that of his female partner. Considerations like this, which in a way Freud had anticipated by more than a half-century, just as he anticipated the discovery of sexual hormones themselves – such considerations should make one suspicious of formulations which ascribe sexual activity to the male and passivity to the female, a trap which Freud continually found himself escaping by a hairsbreadth.

Already in 1897 (Freud, 1950b) Freud's exposition of the origins of repression foreshadowed the views about the role of the clitoris which were to play so important a part in his theory. The 'something organic' in repression is a question of the abandonment of former sexual zones, i.e. the regions of the anus and of the mouth and throat, which originally instigate something analogous to the later release of sexuality. Memories of excitations of these abandoned sexual zones, thanks to 'deferred action' (i.e. the intensification due to sexual maturing) – such memories give rise not to libido but to un-pleasure, analogous to disgust – 'just as we turn away our sense organ . . . [from a stinking object] in disgust, so do our preconsciousness and our conscious sense turn away from the memory. This is *repression*' (p. 269). If psychically bound this leads to rejection (*Verwerfung*), the affective basis for morality, shame, etc. Disgust appears earlier in little girls than in boys, but the main distinction emerges at puberty, when a further sexual zone is (wholly or in part) extinguished in females which persists in males, that is, the region of the clitoris. 'Hence the flood of shame . . . till the new, vaginal, zone is awakened.'

It was, of course, in the 'Three Essays', published eight years later (Freud, 1905), that Freud elaborated all this more fully. He writes there:

If we are to understand how a little girl turns into a woman, we must follow the further vicissitudes of this excitability of the clitoris. Puberty, which brings about so great an accession of libido in boys, is marked in girls by a fresh wave of *repression*, in which it is precisely clitoridal sexuality that is affected. What is thus overtaken by repression is a piece of masculine sexuality . . . When at last the sexual

137

act is permitted and the clitoris itself becomes excited, it still retains a function: the task, namely, of transmitting the excitation to the adjacent female sexual parts, just as – to use a simile – pine shavings can be kindled in order to set a log of harder wood on fire . . . When erotogenic susceptibility to stimulation has been successfully transferred by a woman from the clitoris to the vaginal orifice, it implies that she has adopted a new leading zone for the purposes of her later sexual activity . . . The fact that women change their leading erotogenic zone in this way, together with the wave of repression at puberty, which, as it were, puts aside their childish masculinity, are the chief determinants of the greater proneness of women to neurosis and especially to hysteria. These determinants, therefore, are intimately related to the essence of femininity.

(pp. 220–1)

I hope you will forgive me if I now make a jump forward of seventy years. The subject will be the same, but the approach that of observation and physiological enquiry, which by 1965 had caught up with the Freud of 1895. I am referring to the clinical researches of Masters and Johnson (1966). This work has, I believe, aroused criticism and resistance in many people, sometimes rationalised as disapproval of scientific scopophilia. Sexual matters continue to be in some ways taboo, despite all appearances to the contrary, and for my part I see Masters and Johnson's bold and direct approach to the subject of human sexual activity as something quite analogous to Freud's own attitude in defying Victorian convention by handling these matters verbally with patients; and so I experience some of the hostile criticism of Masters and Johnson as *déjà vu*. What they have described are facts, unless the contrary is proved by further research; the theories that may be built on these facts are, of course, an entirely different matter; they have been used, for example, by Sherfey (1966) to support an extreme feminist point of view.

At this point I am not discussing feminism but the significance of clitoris and vagina in female sexuality. With the help of special apparatus Masters and Johnson were able to make direct observations on the changes in the female genitalia during sexual activity. These showed that: 'The female's physiologic responses to effective sexual stimulation . . . develop with consistency, regardless of the source of the psychic or physical sexual stimulation.' But note carefully that they are speaking of physiological, not psychological responses. They also observe that actual orgasmic experiences are initiated in both sexes by similar muscle components. As regards the clitoris during intravaginal coitus, it is kept in a state of continuous stimulation through the transmitted effect of alternate penile thrust and withdrawal even though, as Sherfey says, it is not being touched and appears to have vanished, owing to its erection and retraction into the swollen clitoral hood. Sherfey adds:

> Furthermore, it is also obvious why the thrusting movements of the penis will necessarily create simultaneous stimulation of the lower third of the vagina, labia minora, and clitoral shaft and glans as an integrated, inseparable functioning unit with the glans being the most important and, in far the majority of instances, the indispensable initiator of the orgasmic reaction.
>
> (Sherfey, 1966, p. 78)

With this last remark in mind, namely, that the glans of the clitoris is generally the indispensable initiator of orgasm, let us return to the 'Three Essays' and note that Freud had expressed just the same thought when he wrote of: 'transmitting the excitation to the adjacent female sexual parts, just as . . . pine shavings can be kindled in order to set a log of harder wood on fire'. But there is a vital difference, and I suspect that it is betrayed by Freud's phrase 'the adjacent *female* sexual parts' (my italics) – does not this mean, even if unintentionally, that the clitoris is *not* a female sexual part, and that it must therefore be given up? Does not Freud's theory of the pseudo-male clitoris which has to be given up imply an insistence that the female *must* be castrated – it is 'required of her', to use his phrase? After all, this female castration is actually practised in certain cultures. If I may be permitted to misquote Scripture: From her that hath not shall be taken away even that which she hath. And so Freud, having expressed so beautifully, by his simile of kindling, this true insight into the function of the clitoris, at once extends his concept in a different direction – mistakenly, I submit. He assumes that the transfer of excitation from the clitoris to the adjacent sexual parts is not merely a matter of topography but one of maturational development. He says:

> before this transference can be effected, a certain interval of time must elapse, during which the young woman is anaesthetic. This anaesthesia may become permanent if the clitoridal zone refuses to abandon its excitability . . . They are anaesthetic at the vaginal orifice but are by no means incapable of excitement originating in the clitoris or even in other zones.
>
> (p. 221)

And from this there arises the unrealistic and idealised concept of vaginal orgasm, about which I have written elsewhere (Gillespie, 1969).

With the knowledge at his disposal at the turn of the century, to say nothing of the paternalistic cultural background against which he was working, combined with Victorian prudery, the amazing thing is not Freud's erroneous conclusion but the fact that he was able to achieve so much insight into female sexuality. Often, over the years, he expressed the difficulty he found in exploring this 'dark continent'. It is a corner of precisely this darkness on which Masters and Johnson have been able to throw some light, in a highly literal sense, with their illuminated phallus and colour cinematography.

Freud did not make public any comprehensive revision of his views until the appearance of his very important paper on 'Some Psychical Consequences of the Anatomical Distinction between the Sexes' (Freud, 1925c), although already in 'The Sexual Theories of Children' (Freud, 1908) he is speaking of the castration complex and female penis envy, one of the main themes of the later paper. Now the visual discovery of the penis begins to assume a leading place. 'She has seen it [the penis] and knows that she is without it and wants to have it. Here what has been named the masculinity complex of women branches off' (Freud, 1925c, pp. 252–3). And Freud explains how the hope of obtaining a penis may persist indefinitely and account for strange actions; or its absence may be disavowed and so she may behave as though she were a man. Alternatively, she remains aware of the wound to her narcissism and develops a sense of inferiority, which she may extend to womankind in general, in this way showing at least one male characteristic. She becomes in general more prone to jealousy than a man. Her loving relationship with her mother becomes loosened, for she holds her mother responsible for her inferior equipment. She also turns against masturbation for the same narcissistic reason. But through the equation 'penis–child' she is able to give up the wish for a penis of her own; with the wish for a child in view she takes her father as a love object and her mother becomes the object of her jealousy. So she reaches her Oedipus complex in this roundabout way and has 'turned into a little woman' – *faute de mieux*, one feels obliged to add. To quote again: '*Whereas in boys the Oedipus complex is destroyed by the castration complex, in girls it is made possible and led up to by the castration complex*' (p. 256, Freud's italics). Ideally, in the boy, the Oedipus complex exists no longer, the superego has become its heir. So what of the female superego? Freud says:

> I cannot evade the notion (though I hesitate to give it expression) that for women the level of what is ethically normal is different from what it is in men. Their super-ego is never so inexorable, so impersonal, so independent of its emotional origins as we require it to be in men . . . We must not allow ourselves to be deflected from such conclusions by the denials of the feminists.
>
> (pp. 257, 258)

Of course the feminists and their latter-day counterparts of the women's liberation movement have done much more than deny Freud's conclusions;

they have counter-attacked vigorously and denounced Freud as a male chauvinist. But what should concern us is not whether Freud's views give offence – this they have always done in one way or another – but whether they are correct. The essential point concerns the nature of femininity. Is it something natural to the female child, or is it something that she has to learn to accept, after failing to achieve a more desirable condition? And if it is true that many females in our culture are reluctant to accept their role as feminine women, is this because that role is inherently unattractive for anatomical and physiological as well as for psychological reasons; or is it because society, dominated by men as the feminists maintain, has decreed that the feminine role is to be weak, submissive and enslaved? The feminists would say that Freud, with his scientific authority, has supported powerfully the male chauvinistic forces from which liberation must be achieved. Some of his remarks can easily be used to support this view of his attitude to female development and its deviations from *his* idea of the normal or desirable. For example, in his last comments on the subject (Freud, 1940a), he says: 'It does little harm to a woman if she remains in her feminine Oedipus attitude . . . She will choose her husband for his paternal characteristics and be ready to recognize his authority' (p. 194). How very convenient for a paternalistic husband, one can hear the feminists say.

For the present let us postpone any attempt to assess Freud's attitude and alleged anti-female prejudice and let us consider briefly some of the criticisms and attempted rebuttals of Freud's views that have been made by other psychoanalysts, mostly women. Perhaps the most outspoken, and one of the earliest, was Karen Horney (1926, 1932, 1933). For her, the 'undiscovered' vagina is the denied vagina; vaginal erotism is primary and not a derivative of oral erotism (in this she opposes the views of both Helene Deutsch and Melanie Klein). It is only anxiety that prevents the seeking of pleasure in the vagina – anxiety connected with the size of the father's penis, with observations of female vulnerability, and with injury caused by masturbation, either physically or in fantasy. Ernest Jones (1933) repeatedly cites Horney with approval and explicitly endorses her concept of the denied vagina. Of course Jones's paper covers a very much wider field and is greatly influenced by the views of Melanie Klein. It is a masterly piece of work and cannot readily be summarised.

No doubt it is equally impossible to summarise Klein's views; but they have been so influential and are in important respects so much at variance with Freud's earlier views that some attempt should be made to compare the two. Klein's conception of female sexual development was clearly formulated already in 1932 and, so far as I know, never fundamentally changed. She agrees with Freud to the extent that the girl wants to have a penis and hates her mother for not giving her one. What she wants, however, is not to be masculine through possessing a penis of her own, but to incorporate her father's penis as an oral object to replace the disappointing mother's breast. So far from being an outcome of her castration complex, this wish is the result of her dominant feminine instinctual components and the most fundamental expression of her oedipal tendencies, for these are orally rooted. Here Klein differs from Horney, who believed in *primary* early vaginal erotism. Although Helene Deutsch also held that the father's penis as an object derives from the mother's breast, she believed that all this, together with the emergence of the vagina, occurs only at sexual maturity. Klein disagrees with Freud's view that the girl's sexuality is essentially masculine and clitoris-oriented until puberty. She holds that after an initial breast-dominated phase common to both sexes, the boy passes next through a feminine phase with an oral-sucking fixation on the father's penis, just like the girl. So – it is the boy who is feminine, not the girl who is masculine!

According to Klein, the clitoris overshadows the vagina in early sexuality because of the girl's fears concerning the inside of her body, for she unconsciously knows of the vagina. In this area Klein is very much in agreement with Horney. Klein, however, adds that although clitoral masturbation fantasies are at first largely pregenital, the later fantasies centred on the father's penis assume a genital and vaginal character and thus, *to begin with*, take a feminine direction – 'being often accompanied, it would seem, by vaginal sensations'. Here I would remind you of Masters and Johnson and of Sherfey, who stress the integral nature of the clitoral-vaginal complex of organs. It was not possible for Freud to know of this, and I believe this led him to a false antithesis between clitoris and vagina.

Klein agrees with Freud that there is a difference between the girl's superego and the boy's, but for her the difference is of another kind. The impulsion to introject the paternal imago, represented by the father's penis, is much stronger in the girl because vaginal introjection is added to oral introjection, and so she is more at the mercy of a very potent superego. Later on, in coitus, she attempts to introject a 'good' penis to counteract the introjected 'bad' penis. She is thus more dependent on her objects, and this dependence is increased by her lack of a penis of her own.

In 'Female Sexuality' (1931a) Freud criticised some of the views I have been discussing, but strangely failed (as Strachey points out) to take note of the fact that these writers were in part reacting to his own paper (Freud, 1925c) on the anatomical distinction. By this time he has discovered the intensity and long duration of the little girl's attachment to her mother, so that the pre-oedipal phase in females gains a new importance; he freely admits his inability to see his way through any case completely, and likewise the possibility that women analysts may have the advantage of him here. However, he still feels justified in assuming that for many years the vagina is virtually non-existent and may not produce any sensations before puberty – and from this there follows the theory of two phases, first masculine, then feminine. He also notes that the clitoris, with its virile character, continues to function in later life in some obscure way. Some of this obscurity has now, I think, been removed by Masters and Johnson. Essentially, then, Freud holds fast to his theory of a normal masculine phase based on the clitoral zone, and a consequent feeling of being a castrated creature when this phase has to be abandoned, and the superior male organ has to be acknowledged. But the girl rebels against this and may develop a feeling of general revulsion against sexuality, or she may cling assertively to her masculinity, or thirdly, by a circuitous route she may arrive at the normal female attitude, taking her father as her object. Her Oedipus complex, having been created, not destroyed, by the castration fantasy, itself escapes destruction. The pre-oedipal attachment to the mother is far more important in women than in men, and their struggles with their husbands essentially repeat the struggle with the mother rather than with the father. The girl emerges from the phase of mother-attachment with the reproach, not only that the mother did not give her a penis, but also that she did not give her enough milk.

It may perhaps be agreed that in this paper on female sexuality Freud is feeling his own way rather than accepting uncritically what was being urged by his analytic opponents. Nevertheless, a few of these independent conclusions do seem to show Freud moving slightly closer to them – for example, the enormous importance for the girl of the initial relationship with her mother, and the possibly equivalent reproaches that she was not given a penis and was not given enough milk, which surely suggests that behind all the fuss about the penis there lies an earlier concern with the breast. It is interesting to note, in passing, that Freud resisted the tempt-ation to conclude that the girl's strong ambivalence towards her mother is due to her inability to direct her hostility on to her father, as the boy does, for he says that this conclusion would be premature before we have studied the pre-oedipal stage in boys – something which he does not seem to have accomplished subsequently. This is hard to reconcile with his statements about the greater obscurity of female sexual development. In the 'New Introductory Lecture on Femininity' (1933) Freud expresses himself more confidently in that he simply inculpates the castration complex for the girl's specific and greater hostility to the mother, as well as for her greater proneness to envy and jealousy. In general, this lecture recapitulates earlier formulations, and the same may be said of Chapter 7 in 'An Outline of Psycho-Analysis' (Freud, 1940a).

The need for limitation has led me to exclude two very important subjects from my discussion of Freud's views – namely narcissism and masochism. To discuss them adequately would require at least two further papers. I have also been unable to consider properly the very interesting and thought-provoking contributions of our French colleagues (Chasseguet-Smirgel, 1964), for example Grunberger's point that, since the origin of narcissism is to be found in the mother's love for her baby, the fact that, as he alleges, every mother is ambivalent towards her girl baby helps to account for female complaints about being a woman, and for women being narcissistic before all else. Chasseguet-Smirgel herself also stresses the narcissistic wound inflicted on the little girl by an omnipotent mother, and her inability to overcome this as the boy does with the help of his penis; so that penis envy really arises out of the need to cope with the omnipotent mother. Turok stresses the anal level of the conflict with the mother, who takes control of the girl's sphincter and demands possession of her stool. I think Turok would probably agree that what this stands for is the girl's internal, female sexual world. Penis envy is a manifestation of repression of the true underlying anal conflict, and the idealised penis represents the value of what she has lost all hope of having in herself, namely female genital maturity.

Before returning to Freud for a final attempt to bring together and review his theories, I want to say a few words on a phylogenetic theme; my attention was drawn to it first by David Attenborough's television programme on courtship and mating among animals. It was a beautiful and remarkable film, and it aroused in me the thought – how is it that we can observe and have rather intimate knowledge of the sexual lives and practices of so many species of land and aquatic animals, in such striking contrast to the little that we really know and have observed in the case of the human animal? And in view of this discrepancy how can one despise and condemn the attempts, however imperfect, of researchers like Masters and Johnson? One of the pictures that specially intrigued me was that of a male and a female fish expelling their sexual products into the same piece of water, first one, then immediately the other, in each case with what *could* be interpreted as orgastic wrigglings. Then, whilst I was preparing this paper, I received a reprint from Werner Kemper of Berlin of a paper (Kemper, 1965) with a title that could be translated 'New Contributions from Phylogenetics to Female Bio-psychology'. To my delight, he describes there this very phenomenon of fish reproduction, including the 'convulsive movements of manifestly [*offensichtlich*] orgastic nature'. Kemper's thesis is that there are four other important reasons, besides those listed by Freud, why female sexual development is so much more complicated and leads so much more frequently to dissatisfaction than is the case in the male. These are phylogenetic in nature, and the first of the four is illustrated by the fishes mentioned above, together with the well-authenticated assumption that life – and so our ancestors – began in the sea (and of course Kemper is well acquainted with Ferenczi's 'Thalassa'). The point is that the female fish appears to enjoy an orgasm in no way different from the male's; in each case it is a matter of orgastic pleasure in the act of expulsion of a bodily product (*Ausstossungslust*). The male creature, who now appears as the arch-conservative, has had the good fortune to be able to preserve this way of sexual life right through his development into a land animal, a viviparous mammal, and finally man himself; but not so the female, who has been 'required' (if I may use Freud's word in this connection) by the process of evolution to develop a vagina and uterus of her cloaca, and to get what sexual pleasure she can from taking the male's sexual product into it in the service of internal impregnation. Hers is the plastic, adaptive sex, but she has been obliged to give up the pleasure that her fish-ancestress had shared with her male partner. Is it too fanciful to suggest that the lack of female orgasm, which is, I believe, the rule in most mammals, can be understood in this sense; and to suggest that the human female, in our day at least, has learned again how to have an orgasm with the aid of just those muscle groups that go into action during male orgasm? And I would add too that the fact that nearly simultaneous orgasm is generally an essential factor in producing ultimate pleasure could readily be seen as a reflection of the fact that, in the case of fishes, near-synchronicity is of the essence, for without this condition fertilisation will not occur. The suggestion arising from all these ideas is that woman's dissatisfaction with her role is rooted a great deal more deeply than mere envy of the male's possession of imposing external genitalia. As Decter (1973) has convincingly argued, the extreme exponents of women's liberation are going far beyond the demand for a fair deal from men; they are demanding to be liberated from that unfair share in the reproductive process which evolution has imposed on the female of the viviparous species.

If we return now to Freud's early formulations, we can see that from the beginning he perceived that human society as we know it has imposed various requirements on the female, such as the demand that she leave out the arc of the male specific reaction and develop instead permanent specific enticing actions calculated to induce the specific reaction in the male. He also observed that frigidity often depends on a woman's marrying without love; that is, on social pressure.

A little later, however, he began to stress the overriding importance of the clitoris in childhood sexuality, which he declared to be masculine in both sexes. In this case it is inevitable that the little girl should compare herself unfavourably to the male, with very damaging consequences to her narcissism. Thus, behind the social factors which he had earlier recognised, he felt sure from this point onwards that there is an unavoidable problem for the female based on the slogan that anatomy is destiny, and he held fast to this conviction to the end. Despite Freud's belief in the essentially masculine (i.e. phallic and active) nature of the little girl's sexual strivings, he admitted that she shows characteristics that are clearly feminine. This is a point that has been emphasised by a number of analytic critics of his theory, beginning perhaps with Horney. However, when we take into account the more recent work such as the observations of Stoller (1969) on transsexualism and related problems, it becomes clear that in this area we need to be very cautious in coming to firm conclusions, since gender identity is independent of genetic sex; indeed even the anatomical sex does not necessarily correspond to the genetic constitution, and without the appropriate hormonal influence at a certain stage of embryonic development the genetic male will develop into a female, though the genetic female continues as such with or without the appropriate hormones. Thus we cannot confidently draw any conclusions about the significance of so-called feminine behaviour in little girls, since the type of behaviour that a child exhibits is determined to such an important degree by what is expected of it by parents who assume, or who wish, its sex to be this or that.

A striking change was introduced into Freud's thinking when, with his recognition of the vital importance of early attachment to the mother and its difference in the two sexes, he abandoned the notion of parallelism between male and female development. Nevertheless, he clung persistently to his conviction of the crucial influence of the girl's traumatic discovery of the penis, just as he continued to stress the boy's traumatic discovery of the no-penis. In both sexes these discoveries belied the initial assumption that everyone is like oneself anatomically. Freud seems not to have considered seriously the possibility that the occurrence of such sudden traumatic discoveries might depend on current conventions of child rearing. Nowadays it can seldom happen that a child is prevented from seeing the bodies of children of the opposite sex – a prohibition that was common in Freud's time and indeed in my own. It would be interesting to hear the comments of child analysts on this point.

At one place (1933, Lecture 33), Freud admits that some may accuse him of an *idée fixe* in believing in the influence of lack of a penis on the configuration of femininity. You may well ask – am I making this accusation? If you insist that I answer yes or no I should find myself in difficulty. It does seem to me that Freud overemphasised the traumatic effect resulting from the visual impression of the unfamiliar genitals of the other sex, and I cannot help comparing Freud's unshakable belief in this idea with his earlier traumatic theory of neurosis, produced by sexual seduction. It was many years before he recognised this error, and many more years before he admitted it publicly. Is it not possible that his theory of a castration complex resulting from a traumatic visual experience is a kind of residue from the neurosis theory, something that he clung to as if it were a treasure saved from the wreckage?

Why indeed should the little girl be so disturbed and so overcome by inextinguishable envy at the mere sight of an unexpected excrescence on the little boy's body? If it were a matter of witnessing an adult erection, that would be different, but this is not what Freud had in mind. Surely we must agree that the girl's reaction is not the result merely of recognising that he has something that she does not possess, but much more the result of her fantasies about it, based, on the most obvious and superficial level, on its urinary capacities, which would seem to offer more ego control and narcissistic gratification in the function. I would agree that the problem of where the female is hiding her penis is a big one for the boy, and I would suggest that this teasing conundrum constitutes an important ingredient in the impression of female insincerity and the dark obscurity in which she hides her sexuality; when Freud speaks of these things one senses a certain feeling of frustration and annoyance. When the clitoris is finally discovered as the answer to the problem, its diminutive size and lack of any obvious function lead naturally to the view that it is merely a vestigial penis, and that the girl's valuation of it shows that she is trying, in a pitifully inadequate way, to be a boy. The boy – and in this context I suggest that Freud had retained some of his boyishness, just like the rest of us chauvinist males – the boy in this way has his revenge for the female's insincere concealment – a concealment compounded of anatomy and prudery.

But the essence of the matter is that even if one admits the justice of these criticisms, Freud was in a much deeper sense right, if it be conceded that when he talks of the penis he is no more talking simply of a concrete anatomical organ than is Melanie Klein when she talks of the breast. I know that when one feels tempted to say that the penis stands for many less concrete things, rather than the other way round, one is in danger of going the way of Jung. Nevertheless, I think one is justified in saying that the anatomical difference between the sexes is important not so much for itself but because it is the outward and visible sign of the vastly more extensive differences in the reproductive roles which evolution has decreed shall be allotted to men and to women. Whatever psychological significance, if any, one may be prepared to attach to the contrast between a female fish and a woman, it cannot be denied that the evolutionary process that has produced the mammals has called for a profound internalisation of female sexuality, and that this has had very far-reaching psychological consequences, some of which take the form of resentment and dissatisfaction with the female role. Other consequences, of course, are of an opposite kind and can afford intense satisfactions which men cannot share except by identification and empathy. There is clearly a difference of opinion in analytic circles between those who would agree with Freud that the girl who settles for femininity does so only because she gives up the hopeless struggle to be a man, and others who hold that femininity is a primary thing, but has to be abandoned for a time out of fear of the mother, and that the girl's masculine clitoral sexuality is temporarily substituted for it. But it seems to me that the meaning of the clitoris is still somewhat obscure, for Masters and Johnson have demonstrated that it plays an important part in normal female sexual excitement and orgasm. Does this mean that Freud was mistaken in assuming that the clitoris is necessarily associated with masculine, penetrative strivings? Is it not possible that its excitement leads normally to the wish to be penetrated vaginally, so producing further stimulation of the clitoris as well as of the vagina? This is one of the many questions that I must leave unanswered.

Papers
B: The forces of life and death

11

Extrasensory elements in dream interpretation[1]

On a Wednesday morning recently, as I was travelling by car to the Maudsley Hospital on my regular route, I found myself in a serious traffic holdup at Vauxhall Bridge, which delayed me some ten minutes. I decided that next day I would take a different route, over Lambeth Bridge – a route I knew but abandoned years ago in favour of the better Vauxhall one. So next morning I made for Lambeth Bridge. As I turned the corner into Horseferry Road I noticed the street name, and it occurred to me, for the first time, I think, that at one time there must have been a ferry for horses where the Lambeth Bridge now stands. There was no obstruction on this route, and I thought no more about the matter. I knew that one of my patients works near Horseferry Road, and I may have thought of this, but do not remember doing so.

Next day, that is, on Friday, this patient a woman whom I shall call A., began her session with a dream, as follows:

> I was in the Horseferry Road; there was a hospital on one side of the road, a church on the other. The church had an awning in front of it, and there were crowds on both sides of the awning – evidently a wedding was going on. I crossed the road to the other side to get a better view, but some women there told me I was wrong to do so, and so I crossed back again. There was a woman in a long blue dress down to her ankles, and a hat, all very frilly and old-fashioned.

She brought numerous associations to the dream, both that day and the next, Saturday. The first association was to the Horseferry Road – namely that she was in it on the day before the dream – in the afternoon, I discovered later, whereas I was there in the morning – and at some time during the day, she does not know when, the thought crossed her mind, that there must once have been a horse ferry there. This immediate association was what caused me to prick up my ears and begin to wonder whether there was something more here than mere coincidence.

151

Further associations had to do with her work, and led to a fantasy of sailing down the river in a barge, as in olden times.

The wedding led her to think of the silver wedding of the Queen (the King was not mentioned), and of the fact that on the day of the anniversary (Monday of the same week) she had been held up in a crowd near Baker Street, and had had a close-up view of the King and Queen. She made a big point of the fact that all this was involuntary, that is, she would never have watched the procession deliberately. While waiting in the crowd, she very much hoped she would not be seen by me doing anything so vulgar – she feared this might happen because of the proximity of the Institute of Psycho-Analysis.

One of the women in the dream who made her recross the road was a woman she knows who told her recently about an internal, gynaecological, operation she was going to have. This association reminded her that on the day before the dream she had been thinking about all her illnesses, including a roughness of the skin in a very awkward place that she can see only with a mirror, i.e., near the genitals. It will be remembered that this woman with the gynaecological complaint was on the hospital side of the road.

There were several other associations to crossing the road; one of these had a slightly occult flavour, and concerned a relative who had died crossing the road.

Near the end of the hour, when she seemed to have come to the end of her associations, I asked her whether by any chance she had seen me in the Horseferry Road on Thursday. She said no, was I there? I then informed her of the relevant facts – namely, that I had driven through it owing to the previous hold-up at Vauxhall Bridge, and had had just the same thought about the name as she had. She responded immediately to this information by recalling that on the evening before the dream, that is, on the day we had both had the horse ferry thought, while at the cinema with a friend, for no reason she can think of, she suddenly remembered how she had once dreamed of the 'title' of a play I had seen. This is a reference to the other striking extrasensory experience I have had with this patient, to which I shall refer presently. Note that she had this apparently quite disconnected thought *before* she had even dreamed of the Horseferry Road, let alone had the dream analysed.

The effect of my communication was dramatic – she seemed overwhelmed at the sudden way in which the transference situation had become real to her, said she felt very queer and asked if she could go at once. It was in any case time, and I raised no objection; I doubt whether she would have stayed if I had. Few things have brought this unusually sticky and resistant analysis more thoroughly to life. She brings many dreams, and there have been many transference interpretations, but never with so marked a reaction.

152

Another fact that should be noted is that in the earlier part of this hour A. had felt and expressed resentment against me for my remarks, which she regarded as interference with her associations.

It is no part of my purpose to present a full analysis of this dream, which would involve an extensive discussion of the case as a whole. I will merely draw attention to the obvious scopophilic and exhibitionistic components and to the hints at a primal scene, a theme on which we had been working for a considerable time. I suspect that all this is intimately related to the phenomenon of extrasensory perception in this particular patient.

Next day, A. began by bringing another dream, this time about a small low cupboard, and a dispute between her and a friend as to where it should be placed – the latter shifted it to the left and A. moved it back again into the corner. This apparently repeats one of the themes of the Horseferry Road dream, and it reminded her of various incidents of being shut up in cupboards. She became silent. I said, 'Well?' and this, she said, led her to think of the previous day's experience. She suggested it was as if she were prenatally attached to me, that is, inside the cupboard. This, of course, also links up with the gynaecologically affected friend. Further association to her friend of the new dream led to an incident she had resented because it involved an interference with her private affairs and an assumption that members of her family should know her whereabouts. I interpreted that she felt the apparently telepathic experience of yesterday was a similar unwarranted interference – there were numerous pointers in this direction, including the idea that it was equivalent to an exploration of her body and her private parts. She agreed, but pointed out that it was really she who was interfering with me, namely by telepathically perceiving that I was in Horseferry Road.

Let us turn now to the earlier apparently telepathic experience which A. had recalled the evening before the Horseferry Road dream. This occurred in May 1947. One day she brought two dreams. The first was an anxiety dream about pursuit by a fugitive criminal and hiding from him behind a lavatory door. The second dream started with a photograph of a little girl who, she thought, looked like herself as a little girl. She said, however, in the dream, 'That's not Douglas Home, that's a little girl.' Someone else said, 'No, it isn't Douglas Home, it is –' and mentioned the name of a comedian which A. could not remember. Next day, however, she remembered it was George Formby, and added that another comedian is called Douglas Byng; she has never seen him, but her mother was fond of him; he was vulgar, and A. repeated one of his jokes which related to urination. The dream continued along different lines, which are not relevant to the present topic.

A. had no association at all to Douglas Home – she has known only one Douglas, and told a long and apparently irrelevant story about him. I

153

pressed for further associations to Douglas Home, and asked her if she knew who he is. She did not, so I supplied the information that he is the author of the prison play *Now Barabbas*, adding that I had seen it the night before she had her dream – in fact, it had made a considerable impression on me. She had not seen the play, but had several times thought of going, and recalled reading about it in *Picture Post*, and in fact remembered many details she had read there. She incredulously raised the possibility of telepathy, adding 'That would make things *too* complicated!'

It will be noted that the first dream of this night also dealt with a criminal, which is further evidence, I think, of unconscious knowledge of what had been occupying my thoughts the previous evening. When she raised the subject again that day, I pointed out that this telepathic business involved getting to know about me and my private life, so that it may be significant that Douglas Home's first name, William, was omitted in the dream – to me, the man's name was William Douglas Home, the last part being regarded as double-barrelled. The name Home also may be significant in this connection.

On the last evening of my Easter holiday in 1946 I was reading Elizabeth Bowen's book of short stories, *The Demon Lover*. One of these stories made a particularly strong impression on me, the one entitled 'The Inherited Clock'. The interest in this story focuses upon an old-fashioned clock in a glass case, to which clock much fear and superstition is attached in the family. The story verges on the occult, but it can also be regarded as an essay in psychopathology, for the heroine of the story, to whom the clock is bequeathed, knows vaguely that her fear of the clock has to do with some incident in her childhood whose memory she is unable to recapture. The story is an eerie one, well calculated to stimulate a dream, but so far as I know, I did not dream that night.

Next morning, however, a young man, B., in the second month of his analysis, came for his first session after the eleven-day break. He started straight away with an involved dream, which was evidently connected with the frustration of the holiday and consequent feelings of aggression. At the end of the dream Socrates, or some similar person, appeared. Someone had sent him a Golden Boy – it appeared that this was a statuette – and as a result of this, Socrates died of fear. In the next scene, B. was having a discussion about this with Dr Ernest Jones (who had sent him to me for analysis) and myself, and B. put forward the theory that it was not the Golden Boy that was responsible for Socrates' death from fear, but another gift which had accompanied the statuette – namely a Victorian clock, under a glass case, which produced death through the idea of the seconds of life ticking away. I should mention that in Elizabeth Bowen's story it turns out that the childhood incident consisted of the little girl

154

having interfered with the works of the clock by sticking her finger in, thus making it stop.

I asked B. if he had read the story, but he said no, and had few associations to this part of the dream — mainly the idea of clocking in, which evidently related to the return of analysis. His other associations related chiefly to aggression. Golden Boy, as he told me, is the story of a violinist boxer who is in conflict about hurting his hands boxing, and who kills a man. I must mention also that homosexuality is the main theme of B.'s analysis. I had the impression that the part about the clock did not fit quite naturally into the dream — it was almost like an afterthought, and seemed to be a device for taking part in a professional consultation between Jones, and myself, in which B. was able to show off his cleverness. In this way, it shows scopophilic and exhibitionistic tendencies, as in the case of A.

The last example I wish to quote occurred with an unmarried woman in her thirties, C. This example is more complicated in that it involved a dream of my own as well as the patient's. From my point of view, the matter began with my having a dream of a kind calculated to arouse an analyst's interest and indeed concern. The dream, which followed intercourse, was as follows: I had two stumps and two artificial legs. One foot hurt in its shoe, and I thought in the dream, 'Of course, it must be a phantom limb.' As I was not myself in analysis, there was no opportunity of analysing the dream properly, but I had some associations to it. One of my colleagues has such an artificial leg, and it may be that I had been thinking about it the previous day. But the most significant associations had to do with another patient, D. This man is a typical shoe fetishist, in whom the castration theme is extremely pronounced; from childhood he has had many fantasies about amputation of limbs associated with the sexually exciting idea of the female shoe, which has to be very tight as well as high-heeled. On the day before my dream his thoughts had been quietly revolving around the subject of the fetish, and in the course of this he recalled that when he was a boy a schoolmaster friend of the family recounted the story of Cinderella, with a great deal of emphasis on the cruel amputations carried out on the toes and heels of the ugly sisters so that they could get their feet into the glass slipper. On the next day, the day after my dream, he talked about kicking his brother, and recalled a cover memory he has often referred to, about a certain castle with dark underground tunnels in which a terrifying man lived who had no legs. This memory, as I have said, had been mentioned before, and could very well have come to my mind as a result of the material of the previous day — indeed it is possible D. may have mentioned it the previous day, though I have no note to that effect.

I think it will be agreed that the material relating to D., together with my one-legged colleague, goes a long way to account for the details of my dream, though not for my unconscious motive in dreaming it. The part about the phantom limb looks like a good piece of rational thinking in the dream; but in view of what followed, I wonder whether the word 'phantom' did not have another significance.

On the day after my dream, and the hour after D. had been talking about the legless man in the tunnel, my female patient C. began her session by saying that she felt terrible yesterday. She said that I had passed her in Paddington Street in my car, and she was terrified I would see her (which I had not, to my knowledge, done). There followed some discussion of what this meant in terms of her need for a cleavage between her external and her internal life.

She then told what she described as an extraordinary supernatural dream, terms she has never used at any other time. In the first part, she was in a shaft full of moving staircases, going up and down. Mostly, she was going down, but every now and then she was suddenly wafted up – a frightening but exciting feeling which she feels vaguely is related to sex. There was also a pair of very thin stockings, which were likewise floating up and down, and she was trying vainly to get hold of them, because they were hers. Her only association to stockings was that she has a pair with ladders, which had concerned her last night.

The second part of the dream was as follows. She was going to analysis, but it was in a place with gardens, trees and shrubs. There was a stall in the road with vegetables, and she wanted to buy a lettuce. A man was on a platform selling vegetables and daffodils, talking to a woman who was buying. At first, she thought he was sitting cross-legged, tailor-fashion, but (and at this point I had a strong feeling that I knew exactly what was coming, which proved correct) but then she realised that he had only two stumps, his legs being cut off above the knee and the stumps showing through what was left of his trousers. The stumps looked peculiar, as though they were sewn up with black thread, as material might be. The man lifted up a cabbage, and she was surprised to see under it two corn cobs. These were green, like everything else on the stall, including the daffodils, and the general impression was one of unripeness.

There were few associations to this dream. She felt she must have seen someone yesterday with stumps, but could not recall doing so (remember she had seen me and that had upset her). The meaning of greenness was not clear from the associations, but taking it along with the sexual symbolism of the dream I think we may reasonably guess that it has to do with her virginity and her conflict about whether she should retain it. But the dream becomes very much more comprehensible when taken in conjunction with my own dream of the same night, and the intercourse which preceded it. It seems as if having seen me in the street had had the significance of a primal scene, and she reacted in her dream as if she had seen me that night, not that day. Her dream begins with an elaborate symbolisation of intercourse, followed by a symbolisation of castration (her stockings floating in the air and being unable to get hold of them); the ladders in the stockings suggest intercourse again; then we have the quest for the lettuce (i.e., let us have intercourse), followed by a very unambiguous castration scene, and then a display of the male genitals (the cabbage and corn cobs). It will be seen that the main underlying themes here are very similar to those in the case of A.'s Horseferry Road dream. In C.'s case, I made no mention of my own part in the experience, and apart from her reference to the dream being supernatural, nothing was said by either of us about the extrasensory elements. This is a technical point to which I shall return later.

So much for the clinical material. Since I resumed analytic practice some two and a half years ago, I have had one or two other less striking experiences of a similar kind, but I have mentioned all the outstanding ones. Throughout his period, I have been analysing four to five patients at a time. It will therefore be seen that in my experience such incidents are by no means common; and, like others, I have been tempted to treat them as a nine-days' wonder and then forget about them. But there are cogent reasons, I think, why one should not allow this to happen. Analysts should be the last people to reject unwelcome new facts just because they are unwelcome. It was Freud's fearless pursuit of the truth, no matter where this might lead him, which, to me at least, has always seemed the most essential characteristic of true psychoanalytic research. In this matter of telepathy, Freud (1925a) has set us an example of cautious open-mindedness which we should do well to follow. I should like to quote a few sentences he wrote:

> I have often had an impression, in the course of experiments in my private circle, that strongly emotionally coloured recollections can be successfully transferred without much difficulty. If one then proceeds to submit to an analytical examination the associations of the person to whom the thoughts have been transferred, correspondences often come to light which would otherwise have remained undiscovered. On the basis of much experience I am inclined to draw the conclusion that thought transference of this kind comes about particularly easily at the moment at which an idea emerges from the unconscious, or, in theoretical terms, when it passes over from the 'primary process' to the 'secondary process'.
> In spite of the caution which is prescribed by the importance,

novelty and obscurity of the subject, I feel that I should not be justified in holding back any longer these considerations upon the problem of telepathy. All of this has only this much to do with dreams: if there are such things as telepathic messages, the possibility cannot be dismissed of their reaching someone during sleep and being received by him in a dream. Indeed, on the analogy of other perceptual and intellectual material, the further possibility arises that telepathic messages received in the course of the day may only be dealt with during a dream of the following night. There would then be nothing contradictory in the material that had been telepathically communicated being modified and transformed in the dream like any other material. It would be satisfactory if with the help of psychoanalysis we could obtain further and better authenticated knowledge of telepathy.

But it is particulary the recent extraordinarily detailed and convincing work of Jule Eisenbud (1946, 1947), published in the *Psychoanalytic Quarterly*, that has encouraged me to bring forward my own relatively very modest contribution. Eisenbud has initiated something quite new in the technique of dream interpretation – something which can hardly fail to make one shrink from the complications involved, just as my patient A. did. But it is clear that we are not entitled to shrink from facts because they are inconvenient. Only if the alleged facts can be shown not to be facts are we at liberty to disregard them, and we are far from being able to do this, I think.

At this point I should like to dispose of one possible misapprehension. I have not brought forward my clinical experiences in order to prove the existence of telepathy, but merely to show that if one assumes the possibility of telepathy or allied phenomena transcending the hitherto recognised laws of physiological and psychological functioning, then certain dreams can be shown to have a new meaning which would otherwise not have appeared. Sometimes, perhaps, it is only in this way that a given dream can be seen to have significance at all. The new meaning is usually to be found in the sphere of the transference. It follows that valuable material for analysis is likely to be lost if this aspect of dream interpretation is neglected.

It is on this account that I have devoted most time to A.'s Horseferry Road dream. It would perhaps be less impressive than the others if it were my aim to convey conviction of the reality of such experiences; but I have chosen to concentrate chiefly on this dream because it is the example which best demonstrates the point I am really trying to make, namely, that attention to extrasensory elements may, in certain cases, be essential to an adequate dream interpretation. It is also the most recent example, and this led to my taking its analysis along these lines much more seriously than I had done in the earlier cases.

As regards the proof of the existence of telepathic phenomena, that must come from quite different sources which are capable of rigid scientific, i.e., statistical control. I think it is fair to say that in the opinion of practically all competent observers who have really studied the subject, overwhelming proof has already been provided in such work as that of Rhine in America, and Carington, Soal, Tyrrell and others in this country. In psychoanalysis I doubt whether we shall ever be in the position, as these workers are, of being able to say: 'The chances against such-and-such a phenomenon being due to mere chance are a million to one.' Our results are more qualitative than quantitative, and from our point of view it is the pragmatic test that counts. The question we have to ask is: does the assumption of a telepathic process in particular cases lead us to a deeper or more coherent understanding of what is going on in a particular patient, and more especially, does it lead to a better understanding of the transference situation? From my own experience, I would say yes. In the case of Eisenbud's experiences, there can be no doubt at all that if he dismissed the telepathic hypothesis as impossible, a great deal of the significance of his clinical material would be lost.

That brings me to a difficult technical point. Should the analyst keep this better understanding to himself, or should he communicate it to his patient, and if so, how? It will be observed that I did not do this in the last case. This was partly because it was the first example I had come across, and I did not know of Eisenbud's work; but even now I should be very reluctant to tell a patient of my dream, as opposed to factual information such as that relating to the Horseferry Road, Douglas Home, or the Inherited Clock. But this may be another prejudice which one will have to overcome. The point in favour of making such communications to the patient is, of course, that without them he cannot be in a position to understand the full significance of his own dream. The technical problem is analogous to that of the interpretation of symbols, but is much complicated by the transference implications. As far as I know, Freud never retracted from the position that when the patient's associations to fail to provide the symbolic interpretation, the analyst must provide it for him. I know that modern practice runs counter to this, but I cannot help thinking that the reason we can often dispense with providing such interpretations is that most of our patients nowadays are themselves quite conversant with the common meanings of symbols, owing to the popularisation of psychoanalysis.

As this is meant to be a short communication, I must refrain from expanding many fascinating aspects of this subject. To me, it brings home remarkably vividly the reality of unconsciousness mental processes and the fact that there is a qualitative difference between unconscious and conscious processes. We are accustomed to the idea that the essential work of

159

analysis proceeds by the analyst's unconscious making contact with that of the patient; but this has customarily been taken to involve the mediation of the ordinary senses and the use of verbal and other physical means of communication. The facts of telepathy open up quite new possibilities of a much more direct means of communication between one unconscious and another. This is surely of the greatest significance for both our theory and our practice.

Another sphere that should be considered carefully from this point of view is that of the parent–child relationship. Clinically, one is frequently struck by the way in which a child seems to be influenced by a parent's fears, preoccupations, neurotic attitudes, and so on. Have we not perhaps too easily assumed that this occurs always by way of the parent's actual behaviour? Some cases I have come across seem difficult to explain on this hypothesis. Mrs Burlingham (1935) published some very interesting obser-vations on this subject and remarked: 'The power of unconscious forces is especially marked in the interplay between parent and child. It is so subtle and uncanny that it seems at times to approach the supernatural.' I think also that the phenomena we are discussing may be found to have much to do with the state of primary identification.

The indications seem to be that telepathic communication is a primitive, atavistic affair, which has been largely replaced by the more exact and refined method of communication by word and gesture. One would therefore naturally look for it in states of regression such as schizophrenia. May it not be that the so-called delusions of the schizophrenic – ideas of passivity and of influence, etc. – are based on a core of actual telepathic experiences? And could not the uncanny ability of the paranoid patient to understand the unconscious hostile motives of others have a similar basis? Since writing this paper, I have found that Ehrenwald (1947) has worked out this hypothesis in some detail.

It may be that telepathic occurrences are infrequent in analysis, or it may be that we nearly always overlook them. Be that as it may, if they occur at all, in or out of analysis, the theoretical consequences are immense. From this point of view, their rarity is of no more significance than the littleness of the proverbial servant-girl's baby. If their occurrence be admitted, we are forced to revise one of the most fundamental points of view of present-day psychiatry, that of psychosomatic unity, and we are faced again with all the difficulties of body–mind dualism and interactionism. Carington (1946) has put forward a theory of mind designed to cover the known facts of telepathy. It is based on associationism of the Wundtian variety, and seems to neglect the emotional factor almost entirely. Essenti-ally, the theory is that of a common subconscious, in which associations formed in one mind automatically become operative in all other minds. The theory is attractive in its simplicity and in the boldness with which it cuts the Gordian knot; but its neglect of all but the cognitive side of experience will not commend it to psychoanalysts, who should be in a position to advance a more satisfactory theory, once they become convinced that the facts are such as to demand a fundamental revision of some of our present points of view.

Note

1 This paper, based on clinical material collected between 1946 and 1948, was read as a 'Short Communication' to the British Psycho-Analytical Society in the latter year, and no material alterations have been made. I delayed publication in order to add further relevant observations which I hoped to make; but in the three years that elapsed I had no similar experiences that seemed worth putting on record. It is true that there were a few suggestive occurrences, but they could all be fairly easily dismissed by a sceptic. This negative fact is worth noting, since it seems to be characteristic of extrasensory phenomena that they come and go unpredictably. Hence it is rather easy to turn one's back on them, and it is unlikely that I should have published this paper had not Dr Devereux persuaded me. At the same time, the three years of apparent extrasensory inactivity must not be ignored in any assessment of the practical importance of the subject for the psychoanalyst.

12

Aggression and instinct theory[1]

When asked at rather short notice to write a paper on aggression for the forthcoming Congress I felt at first reluctant to undertake the task; but a vague feeling that there was something I wanted to say about the theory of aggression led me finally to accept. What later facilitated the expression of that unformulated feeling was a paper presented in July 1970 to the British Psycho-Analytical Society by Professor J.O. Wisdom (interested readers will find a general exposition in Wisdom (1969)); his theme was the important part played by *Weltanschauung* in scientific theories generally, and in the theories of psychoanalysis in particular. Freud stated more than once that psychoanalysis has no *Weltanschauung*; or alternatively that it simply shares that of science. Now one of Wisdom's main points is that there *is* no one scientific *Weltanschauung*, and that scientists deceive themselves if they believe that their theories are independent of an implicitly accepted *Weltanschauung*, which cannot be confirmed or refuted by any kind of testing, as can the other parts of their scientific theories. To cite one of Wisdom's examples, the two current and opposed astronomical theories of the origin of the universe appear to be espoused by their respective proponents in accordance with their belief or non-belief in God. The two psychoanalytic theories with which Wisdom mainly concerned himself were on the one hand Freud's libido theory, and on the other hand the theories which base themselves fundamentally on object relationship, such as Fairbairn's, but, in Wisdom's view, Melanie Klein's theory as well.

Now our main subject at the coming Congress is aggression, not libido; but clearly neither can be considered in isolation from the other. The importance of aggression was, of course, implicit in Freud's earlier work, but his conclusion that he had much underestimated it seems to have taken shape during the years of World War I that immediately preceded his writing of 'Beyond the Pleasure Principle' (Freud, 1920). No doubt psychoanalysts everywhere were deeply interested in Freud's new point of view and in his revised classification of instincts which gave equal status to aggression and libido, even if many found it difficult or impossible to follow Freud all the way in his concept of the death instinct. The new ideas were, I believe, adopted with more enthusiasm in some areas than in others. It was only when I came to London from Vienna in 1932 that I discovered what a transformation had affected psychoanalysis, especially perhaps in England. Crudely expressed, it seemed that the major emphasis was now on aggression and the analysis of the negative transference; libidinal impulses were on the whole good and could be left to look after themselves, provided 'the negative' was properly analysed. Civilisation depended on the taming of aggression rather than on the sublimation of sexuality.

I have made the tentative suggestion, soon to be modified, that our greatly increased interest in aggression originated with the startling new ideas that Freud first communicated in 'Beyond the Pleasure Principle'. They were, of course, further elaborated, especially in 'The Ego and the Id' (Freud, 1923a) and in 'Civilization and its Discounts' (Freud, 1930). These developments contained much else besides the recognition of the immense importance of aggression in human life. From the point of view of theory, I would pick out especially the principle that instincts serve the tendency to reinstate a former condition – a principle with which we have become familiar in two other guises: the principle of homeostasis, and the theory of cybernetics and feedback mechanisms. This, I suppose, is the essence of what Freud described as being beyond or more fundamental than the pleasure principle. It was Freud's bold generalisation of this new principle that seemed to justify his introduction of the death instinct, since it was based on the assumption that all organic life originated from inorganic matter. Unfortunately he confused the issue by invoking the second law of thermodynamics; apart from various other considerations, this is irrelevant to the point at issue, since it applies only to a closed system, whereas it is one of the characteristics of a living system that it is precisely *not* closed.

Now I am well aware that all this is very familiar to my readers and has often been argued before. I want to follow a somewhat different line by suggesting that the real beginning of the new development in Freud's thinking should be recognised not in 'Beyond the Pleasure Principle' but in his introduction of the concept of narcissism between 1910 and 1914, and especially in the paper he devoted to this subject (Freud, 1914). The discovery that the ego is cathected with libido (i.e. is taken as, or instead of, an object of love) to Freud's mind evidently nullified his previous classification of instincts under the two headings of ego instincts and sexual ones. It seems almost certain that his concern about the need for a modification of his instinct theory was much influenced by the pressure being exerted on him during the years we are considering by Jung in favour of an all-embracing libido synonymous with mental energy in general. At the same time Freud had to make it clear that he disagreed fundamentally with Adler's ego-oriented views, based as these were on a theory of social motivation rather than on narcissism. Had not Freud been harassed in this way on two fronts, might not he have felt able to maintain the distinction between ego instincts and libidinal ones, recognising merely that *part* of the ego's activity derives its energy from libidinal sources? It seems to have been left to Heinz Hartmann from 1937 onwards (Hartmann, 1939) to re-endow the ego with its own energies by establishing the concept of an autonomous ego with a conflict-free zone. Perhaps the refinement of Hartmann's formulations has tended to conceal the fact that his startlingly new ideas of 1937 were in a sense a return of what Freud had 'repressed'; and some of the resistance they have aroused perhaps needs to be understood in the light of this fact. If this is correct, then it may be important to get this unconsciously motivated resistance out of the way before we can criticise Hartmann's theory purely on its merits.

Just now, however, I wish to return to the development of Freud's last instinct theory and its crucial importance in relation to aggression. I have expressed the view that at the time it was germinating, between 1910 and 1914, Freud was under pressure from two sides. But we have his own statements to convince us that one of the weighty considerations for him was his conviction of an essential bipolarity in mental life (Freud, 1920, p. 53), a bipolarity which he felt sure must be reflected in the nature of instincts, so that these must belong to two great classes in mutual conflict and opposition. True, he justified this view clinically by stressing the universality of conflict in mental life; but it is difficult to avoid the conclusion that his conviction of essential bipolarity (which is not a necessary deduction from conflict) contains an important element of what Wisdom would, I think characterise as *Weltanschauung*, namely an implicit assumption which is not clinically testable. Indeed, this notion seems to be derived from conscious and unconscious human thinking and feeling, as revealed in myth and religion, and having nearly always an evaluative overtone – in such opposites, for example, as light and darkness, good and bad, God and Devil. But if we look at the first example it becomes evident that in this case the bipolarity is spurious (objectively, that is); for darkness is not really the polar opposite of light, but is simply the relative or absolute *absence* of light, in other words merely one end of a scale of lightness. This idea may be applicable in a number of other areas of apparent bipolarity.

Perhaps more important in determining Freud's conviction of in-stinctual bipolarity was the manifest existence of bipolarity in the sexual area – male versus female, active versus passive, etc. Indeed there is an unmistakable family resemblance between Freud's concept of an essential bisexuality of the individual (that is, a fusion of male and female, not merely of masculine and feminine) and his other great concept of the fusion of libido and aggression. If such bipolarity was for Freud a self-evident truth then, quite apart from the problems presented by Jung and Adler, it was essential to find an adequate instinctual counterweight and adversary to the libido. During the ten years from 1910 to 1920 aggression and finally the death instinct became more and more firmly consolidated in this role. Of course, even if my suggestion is correct that in reaching his conclusion Freud was strongly influenced by an untestable *Weltanschauung*, this would by no means prove that his conclusion was mistaken, though perhaps it should cause us to scrutinise it with more than average caution.

Clearly two independent hypotheses are contained in Freud's last instinct theory: first, that aggression is an instinct, equal and opposite to the sexual instinct; and second, that aggression originally takes the form of a self-directed death instinct derived ultimately, on the homeostatic principle, from the fact that living organisms developed out of inorganic matter. Most analysts, I believe, have long since accepted the first proposition, and possibly somewhat too uncritically if it is assumed that ultimately all mental activity expresses either Eros or Thanatos, and nearly always a fusion of both. But Hartmann has argued cogently for the existence of other forces in the mind, forces which would probably at one time have been described as ego instincts.

No doubt some of the difficulty arises from the instinct concept itself. However useful it may be to ethologists, perhaps it is beginning to be less so for analysts. Indeed when we try to apply Freud's (1915) views on instinct as developed in 'Instincts and their Vicissitudes' to the postulated aggressive instinct we get into trouble. For example, what 'somatic process' in which 'part or organ' is its source? The musculature was once suggested, but clearly that is merely the instrument, not the source.

Curiously enough, when we proceed to the second hypothesis, that of the death instinct, these difficulties diminish, provided we are prepared to follow Freud in assuming that all living matter is clamouring to lose its organic status and return to the inorganic. In that case, there *is* a somatic need for death and the source of the death instinct is indeed the entire body; it then becomes possible to imagine that this source should give rise to some kind of 'demand made upon the mind for work' (Freud, 1915). The piece of mental work might well include the effort to reconcile the demand for death coming from the soma with the conflicting demand, namely to avoid death until the appropriate moment; and this mental task might readily be combined with and achieved by externalisation of the aggression, as suggested by Freud. Perhaps another piece of the work that is demanded is concerned with the need to reconcile the demands of the death instinct with the libidinal ones. Thus, in what may seem a paradoxical way, the apparently so unbiological death instinct theory seems to be more easily reconciled with Freud's original, biologically oriented, libido theory than is the theory of primary aggressive instinct. It may well have become apparent to Freud that in this way he could retain his biological framework by altering biology through the introduction of a new principle, namely a death instinct pervading the whole biological universe. This grandiose concept is undoubtedly attractive in some ways, and we know that Freud found it increasingly so and increasingly convincing. But it seems doubtful whether Freud considered that the life and death instinct theory had any *direct* clinical application. He may well have thought it too remote from ordinary life to lend itself to interpretative use. Such use would surely run the risk of a kind of short-circuiting operation, glossing over so many intermediate stages and neglecting so much mental content that its therapeutic effect, if any, would probably be on a suggestive basis.

As we have noted, most analysts have compromised with the death instinct by accepting the theory of a primary instinct of aggression, but rejecting or at least ignoring the self-directed death instinct theory. But this was by no means true of Melanie Klein. Although it is doubtful if Freud appreciated this fact, she was in this matter more royalist than the king, in that she took the death instinct as a vitally important fact in the psychology of the individual, rather than seeing it as a cosmological concept. Not only did she follow Freud in conceiving of manifest aggression as a turning outwards of the immediately life-threatening death instinct; she also conceived of the infant as feeling persecuted in consequence of the internal threat, and then in turn persecuted from outside, following the externalisation of the death instinct. The use that she made in this connection of the adjectives 'good' and 'bad' is interesting; the 'bad' object, of course, is the one onto or into which the aggression has been projected. Seen from this point of view, the ultimate 'badness' is the death instinct which is an integral part of the infant himself – a sort of original sin. Of course, Klein was also perfectly well aware that the object experienced as good is the one that satisfies, and that the bad object is the frustrating one, which arouses an aggressive response, destructive fantasies, etc. But the explanatory use she makes of the death instinct theory inevitably gives the impression that ultimately it is this inherent 'bad' element in the infant that gives rise to trouble, rather than, for example, any failure in mothering. I think that for some analysts it is this acceptance of the death instinct and its clinical application as an explanatory concept which constitutes a very serious stumbling block, separating them from the Kleinian approach and making it difficult for them to profit from the very real and valuable contributions that have been made by many adherents of the Kleinian school. The fact that this aspect of Kleinian theory appears to be so literally derived from Freud's own post-1920 views makes the matter particularly confusing. This confusion, indeed, is my main justification for writing the present paper.

166

Jones (1957, p. 287) in his biography of Freud says that of fifty or so papers devoted to the topic of the death instinct, half of those published during the first decade after 1920 supported Freud's view, in the second decade only a third, and in the third decade none at all – thus implying that it is dying a natural death. I do not know how many analysts have written on the subject since 1950, nor in what sense. But what Jones failed to mention is that virtually every publication of Klein and her followers has contained an explicit or implicit endorsement of the death instinct theory; so that it is by no means dead.

Leaving aside the death instinct at this point, let us turn our attention to aggression; for even if we feel justified in discarding the former, we must still come to terms theoretically with the latter. No one will deny that the study of aggression is vastly important in any effort to understand the problems of human behaviour and feeling – so vitally important that it is essential to avoid fundamental mistakes if we can. To elevate aggression to the status of one of the two primary instincts or driving forces in organic life may not, however, be the best way to take account of this importance, particularly when this is combined with Freud's idea that aggression and destructiveness is primarily directed against the self (a view contrary, of course, to his earlier one). In a sense it is highly explanatory, but does it not explain too much and too facilely, like the hypothesis of God and Devil? Yet this explanation seems to have been adopted by Melanie Klein and her followers. On this basis certain things are held to be primary (envy is a good example) which seem anything but primary to those who do not start off with the premise of a primary self-directed death instinct.

The objection may be raised that up to this point my criticism has been essentially negative and unconstructive, and it may perhaps be thought that I am under an obligation to propose some kind of alternative theory. In the first place, however, this would be much too vast an undertaking for the present occasion; and secondly (a far more cogent point) I am in no way equipped for the task. Nevertheless one or two suggestions of a more constructive kind may be attempted here.

The growth of cells, their division, multiplication and differentiation, the limitation of the growth of organs, and the later further development of these organs and of their functions by maturational processes – all of this is evidently built into the constitution of the fertilised ovum from the start by mechanisms which are becoming increasingly understood by biochemists and others, and these developments are hardly instinctual in Freud's sense. A point we must consider in connection with Freud's concept of instinct is this: when does anything we can consider mental begin to come into the developmental sequence? When is there for the first time a mental apparatus upon which the soma can make demands for work?

Let us assume a primary undifferentiated state at birth, dominated by primary-process functioning. The neonate certainly has a number of automatic homeostatic mechanisms; and some of them, such as crying, are adapted to bring about homeostasis through the intermediary of another person. Thus, crying when certain kinds of homeostatic balance are upset (as in hunger) may reasonably be regarded as an instinctual pattern of behaviour in Freud's sense. When the homeostasis is not achieved the crying will be intensified and will take on what we tend to interpret as an angry or aggressive quality. In the Kleinian view or terminology, the object has turned from good to bad; and in death instinct theory, whether Kleinian or Freudian, the upset balance of homeostasis threatens survival, because of the danger of annihilation from the baby's own death instinct; the customary defence against threats from within is brought into operation by projecting the threat and feeling it as coming from an external persecutor (Klein's bad breast) in relation to which the barrier against stimuli can be put in action (Freud). But is this formulation in terms of death instinct really necessary?

Suppose we agree to assume that all instincts (*Triebe*) are essentially homeostatic. The newborn baby will then be instinctually concerned to keep himself in the same state as before birth – not, be it carefully noted, in the same state as before conception, when he was *not* inorganic but was *non-existent* as an entity (an entirely different thing). His instinctual concern, then, is to remain supplied with ample oxygen, with warmth, and with all the nutritive materials hitherto brought to him by the placental circulation.

Oxygen is taken care of more or less efficiently by the automatic homeostatic mechanism of breathing. But both warmth and nutrition have to be supplied by the mother, and if necessary she will be reminded of her duties by the baby's cries. The homeostatic character of instinct was implicit in Freud's (1915) original formulation that an instinct (*Trieb*) has a source, an aim, and an object. For clearly the source is an upset in the balance, a temporary failure of homeostasis; the aim is to redress the balance and achieve homeostasis, thereby substituting pleasure for unpleasure; and the object is that through which this aim may be achieved. From this point of view, unless we reject the above formulation of instinct, we must agree that all instincts are homeostatic. But should we necessarily accept Freud's formula as universal? It fits very well the paradigm hunger. But what of love? Or to put it more soberly, what of the sexual instinct? And what of aggression?

First, as regards the sexual impulse, I think that at the time of Freud's first formulations the source was guessed to be some sort of bodily tension, say in the seminal vesicles (but where, then, in the female?). Later, Freud considered chemical rather than physical sources and thus anticipated the discovery of sexual hormones. Nowadays the activity of hormones is certainly recognised as an important part of the mechanism, but not, I think, as the source of the impulse, in any simple sense. For example, Michael (1968) has shown that sexual activity in the *male* Rhesus monkey is dependent on the hormonal status of the *female* partner.

When we consider aggression the problem of a source becomes even more difficult. The discovery of 'centres' in the brain does not solve the problem, any more than we can implicate the musculature, for a centre is hardly a source, but rather a nodal point in the neural mechanism. And clearly if we cannot identify the source we are in no position to specify the aim in accordance with Freud's formula.

One way out is to change the focus, and this is what Freud did in 'Beyond the Pleasure Principle'. He changed his microscope for a telescope and contemplated the living universe rather than the human individual; he envisaged it as a vast contest between life instinct and death instinct, and he then applied these ideas to the human individual, whose inner conflict he saw in terms of such a struggle.

But if we cannot accept this way out of the difficulty, what then? The most obvious alternative (and the one favoured by Fenichel (1945, p. 59)) is the view that aggression is a *way* of doing things rather than an activity in its own right – war as a continuation of policy, to use a familiar analogy. The policy may be ultimately sexual in origin, or may be egoistic. If 'egoistic' and 'narcissistic' must be equated, then perhaps we may have to accept a unitary instinct theory. Even though this was, as Jones puts it, anathema to Freud, if his feeling was due to his *Weltanschauung* instead of being based on tested empirical data, then surely we are entitled to take a different attitude. Perhaps the death instinct theory might reasonably be left to rest in peace had it not come, in certain quarters, to be applied clinically and to be used in support of clinical theories. The other fact to note in this connection is that the majority of analysts seem to have compromised with the theory, accepting primary aggression as an instinct but rejecting the death instinct. Is it not possible that this compromise acceptance is due to our reluctance to say that in this area Freud departed from the line of development which he himself had so brilliantly initiated and carried through, and the line that most of us have tried to follow?

The theoretical and practical problems posed by aggression are indeed formidable; my purpose in this contribution has been to suggest that a simple declaration that we are dealing with a fundamental, irreducible element in the human constitution may be in the nature of a pseudo-solution.

Note

1 Invited contribution to the 27th International Psycho-Analytical Congress, Vienna, 1971.

13

Some regressive phenomena in old age[1]

The subject of our symposium is vast, for the concept of regression is a fundamental one. A simple way of looking at it is to regard regression as the antithesis of those processes of progression, growth, maturation and adaptation which are characteristic of individual development from the moment of conception up to maturity; it is movement in a backward direction instead of a forward one.

When deciding which aspect of regression I should choose for discussion in this symposium, I had to consider that I was sharing it with two acknowledged authorities on the subject, and that I should try to avoid covering the same ground. It seemed best to concentrate on some area which had attracted my own particular interest, and one that was unlikely to be touched on by the other contributors. Perhaps the very nature of our theme, regression, played a part in turning my thoughts back to work I did some thirty years ago, hitherto unpublished. Just now, I contrasted regression with the processes of progression that continue from conception to maturity. It was, in fact, when I wrote that phrase, and found I must write 'maturity' and not 'death' that it occurred to me that the study of regression in old age might be a suitable theme for this symposium.

At an early stage in my psychiatric and psychoanalytic career an appointment at Tooting Bec Hospital gave me the opportunity to carry out a study in a field at that time little cultivated, a field that has now acquired the name of geriatrics. During the three years I spent there something like a thousand patients were under my care at one time or another, and of these some 75 per cent were over 70 years of age. Psychiatric material of this kind is commonly regarded as uninteresting and unrewarding; but to anyone interested as I was in psychopathology, this proved to be far from true. I found that all that was necessary was to listen, for it was characteristic of many of these patients that they were very ready to talk freely about their pathological preoccupations; rich material was ready to hand.

Thirty years ago it was generally taken for granted that psychiatric illness manifesting itself for the first time in old age consisted essentially of senile or arteriosclerotic dementia, characterised mainly by intellectual deterioration. But although Tooting Bec Hospital was designed specifically for this type of patient, nevertheless, a considerable number of the patients were not in fact notably deteriorated in the intellectual sphere but had other psychiatric abnormalities; and these occurred also in a great many of the patients who did show signs of dementia. Examination of a representative sample of 207 male and 204 female patients whose illness began after the age of 60 showed that only about half were suffering from simple dementia, some 40 per cent were demented and in addition showed other marked psychiatric abnormalities, and 12 per cent appeared quite well preserved intellectually, but suffered from psychiatric disturbances of other kinds. In all, then, rather over 50 per cent had psychotic features other than dementia.

This unexpected finding led me to make a study of the psychotic manifestations of my elderly patients, and to attempt to discover if there were any features of these psychotic illnesses specially characteristic of old age, and if there were any typical psychopathological findings.

The commonest psychotic manifestations were found to be:

1 *Persecutory ideas in the widest sense.* They vary greatly in form and degree, and at the lower end of the scale of intensity they merge into normal grumbles about food, noise at night, or enforced captivity. Then there are ideas of having been kidnapped and plotted against by relatives who have stolen the patient's money. At the other end of the scale are the most intense and painful states of apprehension and terror, often of would-be murderers, who appear in the form of auditory and visual hallucinations and attack the patient by poisoning his food, blowing gases on his bed at night, or accusing him of having committed a crime, or of being diseased. Some patients make attacks on their supposed tormentors, who may be identified with the patient in the next bed or with the nurse. The commonest idea in the more fully developed cases is that the patient is going to be murdered. The patient himself often hears voices accusing him of having committed a murder, frequently of a child; or else he is accused of sexual immorality of all kinds and of being infected with venereal disease. There is nearly always an indignant denial of these charges.

2 *Depression of varying degree.* Very severe depression is rather uncommon, for the affect of the senile patient is typically labile. He is easily moved to tears when he thinks about himself and his unfortunate condition, particularly when the persecutory ideas just mentioned are prominent, and a moderate degree of dull depression is very common; but one has the impression that the patient is somewhat apathetic and does not feel very keenly the depression which he shows in his expression and his

tears. Apart from actual cases of paralysis agitans, which are not infrequent, and are often combined with depression, lesser degrees of the Parkinsonian facies are quite common among these depressed patients. Others appear more typically melancholic. Agitation and restlessness is very common and may reach an extreme degree, more particularly in patients who have also persecutory ideas. They feel they must get away, and are continually getting out of bed and wandering about in an aimless way.

3 *Hypochondriacal ideas and delusions.* These most frequently concern the bowels, and they are very common. Many otherwise sensible patients will tell one that their bowels have not moved for a week, when there is no foundation whatever for the statement. Less commonly there is a definite delusion that there is a blockage of the bowels, and that nothing can pass through. Other hypochondriacal ideas are fairly frequent, as that the whole body is rotten and stinking, or that the genitals are falling off, usually associated with the idea of venereal infection.

These three groups of symptoms are of course not mutually exclusive, but rather the reverse. The most typical picture consists of a combination of all three. It is particularly the combination of persecutory ideas with depression that seems to be most characteristic of the senile psychoses. The two mechanisms of melancholia and paranoia seem to be interwoven and to have modified each other. Thus, the patient is depressed and agitated, he believes something dreadful is going to happen to him, probably he is to be killed; but he denies that he has done anything to deserve this fate. As a rule he has no feeling of guilt or unworthiness, believes himself to be unjustly accused or attacked, and has a grievance against someone, from whom he desires to escape. On the whole, the mechanism of projection is more favoured, but there is all the time the tendency to introjection, depression, suicidal ideas and hypochondria. The projection seems to function as a defence against this. Other types of reaction are distinctly less common. A small group of patients shows elation, and quite a considerable number have ideas of grandeur, often of a grotesque nature.

In order to obtain a rough idea of the relative frequency of the commonest types of reaction, I made an analysis of the case papers of the psychotic patients in the group chosen for study (106 male and 111 female patients), with the following result:

	Depressed	Persecuted	Hypochondriacal
Males (%)	23	57	24
Females (%)	31	47	18

It will be seen that there is little difference between the male and female figures; there is probably more tendency to persecution in the males, and to depression in the females.

It will not be possible to quote extensive clinical material, but the following extracts from the notes of two typical patients will serve as illustration.

The first case is that of a very miserable, depressed and solitary old woman of 76, who is partially blind from bilateral cataracts. She was apparently well mentally until her admission two years earlier. The following is a typical example of her conversation.

They're not going to murder me, now then! (How did you think they would do it?) They are going to cut me up and burn me. They are going to take out my organs. I am not going to be murdered, to have my insides taken out. If I'm to be killed, why don't you take me down to the courtyard and shoot me and be done with it? No, they're not going to burn me either. They put things on my bed and burn it at night.

They say I'm mad. They're all down on me. The action has been stopped. If the bowels are stopped, what is the consequences? That's the cause of a good deal.

I didn't think I was coming to this end – to this sort of thing – to be murdered, and it's not a natural sleep, that's certain. My sleep isn't like it used to be. It is strange. They seem to say I talk and I do all sorts of things.

I had a touch of paralysis, and my mother died of paralysis. That's how I came into the infirmary over there. Bronchial is another thing I had. I got over that splendid – that was four years or more ago.

Why, this is terrible. All this steam and boiling water and freezing in the ward, taking my head out and my chest. They say I say all this. How could I get out of bed and talk like that? It's an absurd idea.

My face is not the same as it used to be – it don't feel the same. It's as if I was bilious. They're taking out wrappers – sheeting – out of the body – when you're born, I suppose. Stockinette, then. That is stockinette on my thumb, fine tiny spots, fine as fine can be.

They say I look like the Devil and all that sort of thing. It's dreadful. I don't want to be killed. Lusty, they call you. I'm as lusty as ever. I don't do that sort of thing.

This case is a good example of that mixed clinical picture which seems to be typical of senile psychoses. In the first place, there is a mixture of psychosis and dementia. The dementia is of a peculiar type, and one is tempted to call it pseudo-dementia. Thus, retention is very good for an address, but when it comes to repeating the gist of a story the patient fails completely. There is a strong tendency to refer the story to herself, and perhaps this explains the difference of reaction to the address on the one hand and to stories on the other. She also denies knowledge of the date, and of her age, though she has a good idea of how long she has been in hospital.

The psychosis itself is also mixed in type. Ideas of persecution and influence preponderate, yet the general impression the patient makes is that of melancholic depression. She is very unhappy, solitary, weeps a good deal, and has the melancholic facies. She believes something terrible will happen to her, that she will be murdered; indeed she believes that these things are already happening to her. Thus, we get many hypochondriacal delusions. The action of her bowels has been stopped. Her sleep is unnatural and is evidently equated with death. Her face feels different, she is being frozen, she is having things taken out of her body.

But instead of accepting all these things as the just punishment for some misdeed, she rebels violently and considers herself grossly abused and ill-treated. Everything is attributed to activities of vague persecutors. It is true, she is accused of misdeeds – hallucinatory voices accuse her of being 'lusty' and of doing 'all sorts of things' – but these accusations are indignantly denied. The bad people are all in the outer world. There is a suggestion of insight into her projective mechanism – 'They say I say all this. How could I get out of bed and talk like that – it's an absurd idea.'

Passing to the content of her delusions, it is to be noted that they are chiefly concerned with the idea of being murdered, this idea being elaborated in various ways. The elaborations are bizarre, and bear a very striking resemblance to well-known infantile phantasies. Thus, she believes she will be burned, cut up, have her internal organs torn out, have her bowels stopped up. These correspond very closely to some of the infantile anxieties that have been described by Melanie Klein as being the most terrifying, particularly for the female child; she considered them as representing the punishment for phantasied attacks on the mother's body. This patient says: 'If I'm going to be killed, why don't you take me down to the courtyard and shoot me?' Evidently 'shooting' (which we may take to represent symbolically the father's form of aggression) is preferable to the torture that the mother inflicts. The idea of things being taken out of the body is evidently connected with birth phantasies ('when you're born, I suppose'). The connection of birth phantasies with ideas of death can be found in a number of senile patients.

The second patient was a man of 82, who up till recently had appeared quite normal, being quiet, of temperate habits and very keen on his work as a tent-maker. He left work three or four years ago, and it was then that he started to break up and to become queer mentally. He had lost his wife thirty years earlier, but got over this and devoted himself to his two daughters.

For some years he had complained about trouble with his water. Later, he started threatening to do away with himself, and one morning he was found on the side of a canal, saying he was going to jump in. He said he was not fit to live, that he had some rotten disease. He was sent to a general hospital, where he became worse, saying that he was going to be cut up, and that they were going to stew him. Opposite his bed was a chimney from which steam issued all day, and he said they were getting up sufficient steam to cook him.

All his life he was extremely clean and would never sit down to table without washing his hands. He worried a lot about venereal disease, and had been thoroughly examined with negative results. He was not satisfied, and now still says he is infected, and that maggots crawl out of him and attack the other patients. He also talks about being the father of cats and dogs, and being responsible for their death.

On examination he is a morose, reticent, depressed and introverted little man, who likes to sit in a corner by himself, with face averted, picking the skin off his fingers and showing other signs of agitation. He is unwilling to converse and is retarded. He is very worried and apprehensive, evidently as a result of hearing hallucinatory voices, which make accusations and threaten him with various punishments, but chiefly with castration or blinding, which seem to be quite synonymous for him. The following is an example of the form taken by his delusions.

> They say they're going to give me a bath, and then I'll lose my eyesight. If they cut me, I will. I'm in proper danger here, I am. I wish I could get out of it. (What's the matter?) I've had a bad disease (he shows his genitals). It's here – kind of a pox or something like that it is. I got it sitting on a W.C. I think. It keeps on going, this complaint. I feel like little lumps down there, little spots. (What are you afraid of?) I don't want to lose my genitals. I don't want to lose my eyesight. (How will that happen?) They will take it off. I hope they don't do it tonight. I don't know why they want to take it off at all. It will be semi-blind, won't it? I don't want it. I shan't be able to see to do anything, shall I? They won't take my legs away, will they? They'll only take one thing away. I don't want them to take it off.

As in a large number of male senile patients, mental breakdown occurred only after he gave up his work on account of age. There are probably several reasons for this, as for example that general mental deterioration is the cause of retirement. Then again there is increased opportunity for introspection and speculation; but I would suggest that an important factor is the impression made on a man by his retirement that he is done, good for nothing any more, and that he might as well be dead.

The most prominent feature of this case is anxiety, and it takes the form of undisguised castration anxiety. This is typical of a large group of male patients, and next to worry about the bowel function it is the commonest way in which they express their anxiety. As in this case, it is usually combined with the idea of venereal infection, either accepted as a fact or projected in the form of hallucinatory accusations. Delusions and fears with regard to the genitals occur also among the female patients, but they are not nearly so common, or at least they are much less frequently expressed.

But other fears are also present in this case. There are more general ideas of being cut up, or stewed, there is the fear of the water in the bath, and there is the fear of losing his eyesight. At first one is perhaps inclined to regard this last merely as a symbolic expression of his castration anxiety. It seems possible, however, that the converse might equally well be true – that is, the castration anxiety might be really a more tolerable substitute for other more primitive fears. I am inclined to think that the castration anxiety of seniles is to be regarded as in part defensive, and that the underlying anxieties are more primitive ones – the fear, for example, of having the whole body destroyed, cut up, burnt or stewed. One might thus conceive of the phallus being offered up as a sacrifice in order to ensure the survival of the rest of the body. In this way, the typical anxieties of the female would be covered up and obscured in the male by castration anxiety.

Let us pass now to some psychopathological considerations.

Most observers agree that the first change noted in senescence is an intensification of already existing character traits; this is well illustrated in our second case, and implies a quantitative rather than a qualitative change. Such character traits are determined to an important extent by reaction formations, that is, by permanent alterations in ego structure designed to serve as defences against instinctual impulses which would be dangerous or useless to the ego. Hence, if we find an intensification of such defensive character traits, we may surmise that the anticipated danger against which these defences are directed is the danger that the unconscious phantasies may break through into consciousness, and that the instinctual impulses may attempt to find gratification in reality. In this first stage, then, the defensive forces are successful, and the result is merely an exaggeration of character peculiarities.

The next change to be noted in senile patients is their increasing lack of interest in external objects, whether persons or things. At the same time, their thoughts tend to centre more and more on themselves, and every-thing in connection with their own persons becomes invested with undue importance. In other words, libidinal interest regresses to a narcissistic level.

This increase of narcissism involves relative independence of the external world and facilitates a more or less complete withdrawal from reality. Thus the soil is prepared for psychosis formation. It becomes possible to neglect the reality principle and arrange things in accordance with the pleasure principle. Unpleasant facts can be denied, and the patient retires into the world of phantasy. The mechanism of repression is of prime importance here. Such denial of reality and repression is most obvious in the manic reactions, but it can be seen to operate also in the depressed and persecuted types; what they fear is not the real danger but a phantasy substitute.

Perhaps the most striking feature of the senile psychoses is the very clear way in which they show libidinal and ego regression. There is a great increase of interest in the excretory functions and in food, reflecting anal, urethral and oral regression. But it is in the phantasies and delusions of these patients that we get the clearest evidence of regression. It would thus appear that at this stage of the illness the exaggeration of character traits has failed as a means of defence, and the phantasies against which it was directed have broken through into consciousness.

Along with this libidinal regression we find a predominance of the mental mechanisms characteristic of the pregenital phases of development, notably the mechanisms of projection and introjection. Projection is used of course in accordance with the pleasure principle; thus, everything distasteful is projected. If a senile patient falls and hurts himself, the usual story is that someone hit him. But the most striking thing is that the idea of death is projected. Natural death comes from something inside, whether it be disease or 'death instinct'; but the typical senile psychotic patient is apparently oblivious of this real internal peril, and is convinced that he is going to be murdered by some outside agent.

Introjection is most obvious in the hypochondriacal cases. A very hypochondriacal patient told me that he had a little man inside his head who caused him a lot of trouble. It is not always easy to observe this mechanism in the depressed cases, possibly owing to the nature of the introjected object, which will be discussed presently. The characteristic mixed paranoid and depressive picture seems to be brought about by the combination of these two mechanisms.

There does not seem to be anything about the phantasies, fears and delusions themselves which can be regarded as specific for senile psychosis, unless it is that they are so largely concerned with ideas of death in one form or another. Very similar delusions and hallucinations were described by Bromberg and Schilder as characteristic of alcoholic hallucinosis.

We have now to consider why the abnormal mechanisms we have observed have been called into play. It has already been noted that the narcissistic regression natural to old age acts as a facilitating factor. Perhaps it may do more than this.

In general, regression tends to follow libidinal deprivation, that is, the loss of a loved object. In such a situation libidinal and aggressive tensions rise and produce anxiety. If the situation becomes intolerable for the ego, it takes refuge in the defence measures we have mentioned. One of these is regression, and the resulting clinical picture will depend upon the level to which the libido and ego have regressed.

But if, as in senile persons, the libido is largely narcissistic, it is clear that the object is the self. The deprivation or disappointment to be looked for in seniles would therefore be a narcissistic one; the lost object must be the self. A senile dement has ample cause for such disappointment with himself – he has only to observe his own physical and mental deterioration. Freud has left open the question whether pure ego damage can cause a melancholic depression. Hollós and Ferenczi made this hypothesis the basis of their theory of the psychic disorder of general paresis.

But what of the cases where there is no dementia and hence no ego deterioration? The traumatic agent here appears to be not so much actual deprivation as the threat of it. The threat is ultimately the threat of death, and the fear of death is the anxiety that has to be dealt with. The fear of death clearly requires further analysis, for in so far as death is equated with a state of peace and complete absence of tension it should be felt as desirable. But it is evident that death is liable to be envisaged in an entirely different way, namely as a withdrawal, not of all pain, but of all pleasure, as the state of complete deprivation to which Ernest Jones gave the name 'aphanisis'. Castration anxiety may be regarded as a special form of this fundamental dread, which is common to both sexes. The idea of complete annihilation is foreign to the human mind, at any rate to the unconscious mind, so that this dread is not modified by the reflection that in the case of his death the person will not be there to feel the deprivation.

This fear that everything worth having is to be taken away may be called forth in its maximal intensity by the idea of approaching death. It may be aroused by bodily illness, but also in a number of other ways, especially by circumstances which impress upon the patient the fact that his former capacities are leaving him. Thus, he finds himself unable to obtain employment owing to his age, his sight is failing, his potency impaired; in short, he sees himself approaching the stage of 'sans everything'.

Apart from general theoretical considerations, the clinical facts which led me to regard the fear of death as the most typical (I do not suggest universal) traumatic factor in the production of senile psychoses are two. First, the abundant evidence of repression of the idea of natural death in senile patients; and secondly, the 'return of the repressed' in the form of delusions of being killed.

I would also suggest that the traumatic, precipitating factor may be relatively more important in senile psychoses than in other types of psychosis. Heredity seems to play comparatively little part, and it seems improbable that a person with a strong predisposition to psychosis should reach the age of 60 without breakdown. The ordinary stresses and strains of life have not upset the equilibrium of these patients. It therefore seems reasonable to seek a precipitating cause in some more or less specific senile factor.

Acknowledgement

I am much indebted to the University of Edinburgh for permission to publish in this paper parts of a thesis accepted for the degree of MD in 1934.

Note

1 Read at Symposium on Regression, Annual Meeting of British Psychological Society, Bristol, 1962.

14

The end of life

The obvious meaning of my title, 'The End of Life', is that I am going to talk about getting old and dying; and this is true. However, the word 'end' has, of course, another important meaning apart from that of termination. Anyone who was exposed in youth to the Shorter Catechism will remember the question: 'What is the chief end of man?' Well, it is 'end of life' in that sense that I want to discuss, as well as old age and death. Something will be said about the end or aim of life in general, but more particularly about the end or aim of human life – which I suppose amounts to much the same as the question from the Shorter Catechism. And I want to try to bring these two subjects together and see if we can learn anything from such a confrontation. If I may choose a little poetry to illustrate and embellish my theme it is this from Robert Browning's 'Rabbi ben Ezra':

> Grow old along with me,
> The best is yet to be,
> The last of life for which the first was made.

Besides dealing with these two aspects of 'the end of life', my remarks will also fall into two parts in another way. One part will be theoretical, whereas the other part will consist of clinical material which I hope you will find relevant and illuminating in relation to the theoretical issues.

First, then, let us take a look at some psychoanalytical theories and speculations which might be thought to have a bearing on the subjects I want to discuss, especially theories about the instincts. Freud didn't in fact often use the word 'instinct' but rather spoke of '*Trieb*', a German word meaning approximately 'drive'. What he had in mind was something very different from much that biologists understand when they speak of 'instinct'; a typical example of biological instinct is the highly complex but largely unlearned nest-building activities of birds. Yet what Freud meant by '*Trieb*' has one important thing in common with animal instinct, namely its innate, unlearned quality. James Strachey decided to use the word 'instinct' in the Standard Edition of Freud's works and I will follow his example; but please remember not to think too much in terms of animal instinct.

To put it vulgarly, what Freud was concerned with in studying 'instincts' was to find out what makes people tick. He was convinced that they had, so to speak, an internal mainspring or mainsprings, rather than that they responded merely to external stimuli. From an early stage of his researches he tried to find a satisfactory way of classifying the instincts and he has told us how much he felt at a loss here, for he was looking for a very broad basis of clarification. As he says (in 'Civilization and its Discontents' (1930)):

> In what was at first my utter perplexity, I took as my starting point a saying of the poet-philosopher Schiller, that 'hunger and love are what moves the world'. Hunger could be taken to represent the instincts which aim at preserving the individual; while love strives after objects, and its chief function, favoured in every way by nature, is the preservation of the species. Thus, to begin with, ego–instincts and object-instincts confronted one another . . . Neurosis was regarded as the outcome of a struggle between the instinct of self-preservation and demands of the libido.

The fact that this idea of the essential dichotomy of instincts was suggested by a great poet did not, we may be sure, detract from its value in Freud's eyes, for he often paid tribute to the superior power of poets in such matters, scientists often plodding behind to demonstrate scientifically what has already been grasped intuitively by a creative genius. Even in 1930 Freud could still see merit in this way of looking at instincts, namely that hunger and love not merely move the world, but strive to move it in different directions. It was something different that made him abandon it, namely his discovery of the importance of narcissism. The phenomenon of self-love, and Freud's growing belief that this may be something earlier than love for things or people outside oneself, made it plausible to suppose that what he had been classifying as non-libidinal, non-object-related egoistic instincts were indeed libidinal and did really have an object (not just a subject), the object being the self or ego. Thus it looked as if all the instincts he had postulated might turn out to be libidinal; in that case psychic energy should be equated with libido, as Jung had been proposing for some time. Freud recoiled from this conclusion because of a deep-seated conviction that there is an essential duality or bipolarity in human life. Clinically, he felt this was shown by the universality of conflict of one kind or another, but fundamentally internal conflict in the individual himself. Conflict, however, can clearly come about in various ways and it is not always between just two opponents. It need not in principle be based

181

on a conflict between two opposing instinctual drives, though of course this is certainly an obvious way in which conflict *might* come about.

But Freud's certainty about bipolarity seems to have been something inherent in his way of seeing things. One area in which a dichotomy is obvious is the existence of two and only two sexes. It is a remarkable fact that another of Freud's deepest convictions was his belief in the universality of bisexuality, so that every man has something of the female in him, every woman something of the male. This is undoubtedly true, but Freud meant it in a curious, fundamental sense that many would not go along with, and I do not myself think that the very interesting recent advances in our understanding of sex differentiation during development will really be found to support the notion of universal bisexuality in the sense in which Freud meant it.

Professor J.O. Wisdom has propounded the view that every scientific theory contains at least two distinct parts. One part is based on the empirical data of the science, derived from observation or experiment, and this part is in principle capable of being put to the test and, if it is false, disproved. However, in Wisdom's view, there is always another part, even though the scientist himself may be unaware of it, because it is something he implicitly takes for granted. It is, as Wisdom puts it, part of his *Weltanschauung*, his general way of looking at things and apprehending them. Thus, before relativity, it was generally assumed that space had the qualities attributed to it by Newtonian physics. This part of any scientific theory may correspond to the truth or may not, but this cannot in principle be proved or disproved, as it is usually assumed can be done with a theory if it is truly scientific.

Now if this is true of scientific theory in general, it must be true of psychoanalytic theories, and I am suggesting that Freud's conviction, namely that there is an essential bipolarity in human beings, indeed in life generally, is a good example of the part played in any scientific theory by unprovable and irrefutable preconceptions. Of course such a theoretical bias may indeed correspond with the fact, but it lacks the compelling quality of the other element in scientific theory, that is, the parts that can, in principle, be refuted if false.

With this in mind, let us go on to consider the further development of Freud's instinct theory. The next step was his recognition of the enormous importance of aggression in its myriad forms, and his division of the instincts once again into two great classes – the sexual instincts in the widest sense, and the aggressive instincts, whose aim is to destroy. Now if we assume that just as narcissism or self-love comes before the love of external people and things, so also the destructive impulse is originally an internal affair, directed against the self, then we have gone a long way to explain the almost inexplicable phenomenon of masochism, which leads a person to court pain deliberately in order to experience sexual pleasure. And since self-directed aggression is clearly a biological danger to survival, it can readily be supposed that some means must be found by nature to circumvent this danger; such a device might well be the capacity to turn the aggression outwards and direct it against other people or things, instead of against the self.

Although there are advocates of other concepts of the nature of aggression, most psychoanalysts have accepted Freud's view that aggression is the counterpart and more or less equal opponent of libido in the realm of instincts. But the idea that aggression is originally an internal, self-directed affair goes much further than this, and leads on to Freud's next theoretical development, which he introduced as long ago as 1920. Oversimplifying it grossly, as I must do, I will say that Freud once again, in his characteristic manner, brought together and integrated a number of ideas. One was the theory of originally self-directed aggression. Second, the principle of homeostasis applied to instincts: that is to say that an instinct always subserves a fundamental tendency to return to a former state – a kind of psychic inertia or equilibrium. This has much in common with modern notions of cybernetics and feedback mechanisms. Freud also adduced in this connection what he called the compulsion to repeat past experiences, even though they may be painful ones. A shattering experience, for example, is often repeated over and over again in dreams. Next, there is the generally accepted assumption that all living matter or organic life arose at some very remote time from inorganic, lifeless material. Fourth, there is the fact that virtually all living creatures eventually die. And fifth, there is the second law of thermodynamics, which *seems* to suggest that everything is steadily running down – a kind of death of the universe.

Now fascinating as this line of thought may be, and despite its wonderful achievements in uniting so many different facts under one master concept, namely that of the death instinct or principle, nevertheless some of it is open to damaging criticism and has indeed been criticised vigorously ever since it was propounded. For example, the second law of thermodynamics applies only to closed systems, whereas living organisms are *necessarily* open systems; further, the repetition of a painful experience is not really analogous to the homeostatic principle because it is actually the reinstatement of the disturbed equilibrium, not of the original undisturbed one. The fact that living creatures eventually die may merely reflect how difficult it is to stay alive, what complicated processes it requires – just as one falls off a bicycle as soon as one ceases to make the complex adjustments needed to keep going.

Biologically, of course, death and reproduction are opposite sides of the same coin. If there were reproduction but no death, then death would need to be invented in order to make the world possible to live in – a problem with which we are becoming only too familiar. Perhaps what Freud identified as the death instinct or principle ought not to be viewed in this way as the opposite pole to the life instinct, but should be understood as its necessary complement, not its opponent. The two together constitute something fundamental to organic life, whose mechanism we now know depends on DNA; something which I suggest we might call the *replacement principle* – not fundamentally a death principle at all but one of revivification.

You may now be inclined to ask the question: 'Does all this really matter in practice, or is it all an academic exercise, without practical consequences?' The answer is that this depends on how you choose to take it. Most psychoanalysts have accepted the view that the role of aggression is overwhelmingly important in any attempt to understand human problems, and there is at least a case for giving it the status of a primary instinct on the same level as the libidinal drives. However, the actual death instinct theory is a different matter, and opinion here is very much divided. Most analysts have had reservations on theoretical grounds and have certainly not seriously attempted to use this part of the theory in their endeavours to work with and understand patients. But there is an outstanding and important exception, namely Melanie Klein and the influential group of analytic thinkers whose work is fundamentally based on hers. Mrs Klein did in fact take over Freud's view of a destructive urge directed originally against the individual's own life; one may relate this to the newly born infant's vulnerability and the fact that real efforts must be made if he is to be kept alive, efforts which are thought of as being directed against the strong urge inherent in the infant to die, to 'return to inorganic'. And from the psychological angle it seemed to Mrs Klein that this urge to die must be experienced by the infant as a terrifying threat, a threat that he soon begins to cope with by regarding it as a threat coming from outside – a persecutory attack rather than something inherent in his own constitution. This leads to the most far-reaching consequences in Kleinian theory.

At this point I cannot refrain from interrupting my own presentation in order to point out that the newly born child can very well be thought to have an urge to reinstate so far as possible his former condition, that is, his state whilst in the womb, and good mothering is essentially an effort to produce the nearest approximation to that condition by warmth, feeding, etc. And even if it is held that the infant wants to proceed further still, let us say to the state of affairs before he was conceived by the union of sperm cell and ovum, then I must point out that what he would in that case be striving for would be not an inorganic state of existence, but a state of total non-existence as an entity.

Now even if one is unwilling to entertain the notion of a newborn child whose urge to live is already in combat with a perhaps even stronger urge to die, one may nevertheless be ready to concede that an urge to die is not foreign to the human mind, and that it normally manifests itself in old age, though sometimes at a much earlier age, as shown by suicidal inclinations. As regards suicide, this is really a very complex problem and cannot be seriously discussed in this context – but I would say in passing that the conscious wish for death is generally a wish to escape pain of one sort or another and to this extent is a manifestation of the pleasure principle rather than of anything 'beyond' it. But the study of old people might be expected to throw some light on the question whether a death instinct exists. I leave theory at this point, and turn to an investigation of old people which I carried out many years ago.

At the end of 1931 I became an assistant medical officer at Tooting Bec Hospital, which at that time was unique in that it was the only mental hospital in England that was empowered to admit patients over 70 years of age without certification. It contained also a large number of chronically ill elderly patients who had been transferred from other mental hospitals. In all, 75 per cent of the patients were over 70 years of age. Finding myself, largely by chance, amongst this clinical material and having just come from Vienna where I had started training as a psychoanalyst, I naturally asked myself how patients like this might be approached with a view to understanding their psychopathology. Nothing could be easier in principle than the answer I found to this question – namely just to listen to the patients and record what they said, with a minimum of prompting or prodding on my part. In this way I readily uncovered marvellous material, which could be said to be 'untouched by hand', uncontaminated by analytic interpretation or intervention. I want now to quote some of this material, and I must limit it to three patients; but they are fairly representative ones.

1 Mrs Katherine S., aged 84.   Three years earlier she began to lose her sight from cataracts, but refused an operation because she was afraid she might die. When seen, she could only just perceive light with one eye. She continually felt persecuted in bizarre ways and was very suspicious, particularly at meal times, for she was convinced that there was a conspiracy to poison her and she protected her plate with her hands, lest anyone should put 'soil' on it or squirt 'petrol' on it. At night, she said, petrol is squirted on her bed by her nephew Dan. To prevent this she has a fire alarm under her bed. Sometimes there is a fire and one night she got out of bed and 'outed' it four times. She also has a brother called Dan who likewise persecuted her.

Asked her age, she gave it correctly, but added: 'I'm looking forward to live to be as old as my aunt, who was 202 when she died the other day. Laurie ripped her stomach up with a paper-knife. She was taken very bad through that, and she went into a trance. They thought she was dead but she wasn't dead at all.' She stated also that her father's sister is 104 years old. Her father's brother left £90 million and this should come to her.

The ideas of persecution in this case are combined with a distinctly elated type of reaction and with ideas of grandeur. Many of her statements can be regarded as extravagant fantasies that she enjoys playing with, but they greatly influence her behaviour. It seems likely that the development of her cataracts, with the idea of operation and the fear of death that this aroused, led directly to her mental illness. The fear of death has been dealt with so thoroughly by her defences that it appears no longer to exist: she is sure she will live to be 202, in spite of all the attacks and murderous attempts made upon her – attacks that can be readily understood as projection, that is, the result of attributing to outside forces what is really an internal threat, which could without much difficulty be seen as a manifestation of the self-directed death instinct of Freud.

2 Mrs Marion K., aged 74.   This patient was perfectly well mentally till five years before I saw her and she lived with my informant, a married daughter. At that time, when 69, she had an attack of shingles which terrified her; she thought she would die and that perhaps she had cancer. Following this she began to have attacks of depression and would often say that she wanted to die but couldn't. She became self-centred and showed a certain lack of good judgement, but her memory was unimpaired. Soon after this she attempted to gas herself and after recovering from this she became much worse, agitated and restless, expressing ideas of being burnt and of constipation and often saying that the Devil was after her.

When first seen she appeared to me depressed in a dull, apathetic way. However, her condition varied and she was sometimes profoundly depressed with delusions of a melancholic and hypochondriacal type. Her ideas were nearly all connected with death, the main theme being that her mother was a cruel and wicked woman and on this account had abnormal children. Twin sisters, she said, were born before the patient and died because they had no back passage (this may be true, for all I know). She believes, however, that she is the same, or at least that there is some impediment so that she is unable to pass anything; she is different from everyone else and has always wanted to die. She ought to have died years ago, but she can't. She has had pneumonia and diphtheria twice and didn't die, and she is a curse to everyone because she lives. Death will never come to her unless she is destroyed, preferably by fire. She wants to go home and kill herself, otherwise she might suffer a worse death. She ought not to have had any children, for the same destiny awaits them. When her son was killed in the war she believes he didn't die – they must have buried him alive. The shock of being in battle must have made him go unconscious

186

and they must have buried him alive (here you will remember about Mrs S.'s aunt, who didn't die, just went into a trance).

Among much else, Mrs K. said:

I want to die but I can't. I think I ought to have died years ago. If I had known what I know now I'd have committed suicide. I am perfectly sane. I have senses enough to hear what they say, and I know that *they* died – they die properly [referring to other patients]. I don't think I shall ever do that – I'll have to be killed. I'll be burnt. I'm sure I'll never die a natural death – positive.

Another time:

I wish I could understand life. (What about it?) The end of life – death. Death will never come to me unless I am destroyed. The harm done through my birth – I don't think I was ever meant to live . . . I was to be like my two sisters. Ever since I remember I have had great difficulty in evacuating anything – sometimes I would take 8 pills a day. I never had a child delivered naturally – the last one I was nearly a whole month.

And again:

My sisters said our mother is so damned wicked, they didn't wonder she had children like that. My mother said I'd have to be burnt alive because I'd never be at rest. You couldn't drown yourself because you wouldn't sink in water. The rescuers might get drowned and you might be saved. Albert, my son, came home to me that night he was killed.

In the case of Mrs K., the preoccupation with ideas related to death is overwhelming. Again we have denial of her own possible death, but a very paradoxical denial. She is convinced that she can never die a natural death, that disease cannot kill her, because, as she once said, she has not enough vitality. Therefore she must die a violent death and she oscillates between the idea of drowning herself and of being burnt alive. However, if she tried to drown she would float, and this seems to mean that she is a witch, so that burning is the appropriate death. The close psychological connection between fantasies about death and those about birth is clear in this case. Like her sisters who died, she was born imperfect in her anus and should also die. She showed too that she had the fantasy of birth through the anus. She blames her mother's cruelty and aggression but does not answer it in kind. Her own aggression is clearly turned against herself – she ought to have died years ago, she and her children ought to be burned alive for she is handing on her abnormal destiny to them. The identification with a bad mother leads to her depression.

3 Thomas T., aged 69.   In earlier life his only known peculiarity was abnormal jealousy about his considerably younger wife. When about 50 he had an accident at work in which his eyes were burnt and after this his sight gradually deteriorated, so that he had to take a job in charge of a public lavatory, where further damage was done to his eyes when some sailors set upon him; this led to prolonged litigation with his employers, who finally decided in his favour. When 65 he began to show signs of mental illness; he became suspicious and developed the belief that he was being per-secuted – that a man living opposite flashed a light into his room; also that an older man had an intrigue with his wife, and would come out at 2 a.m., clap, and say 'Come out, Pearl, I'm waiting for you.' Later he became afraid that he was going to be murdered and put down the sewer. He also believed people were accusing him of having venereal disease. In hospital, he heard voices on the telephone saying he is rotten and poxed, and he believed his wife and children were being told this. He would spend hours shouting out of the window at these persecutors. Also when I spoke to him he would shout and gesticulate violently all the time, beating his own body or pulling at his genitals to demonstrate their soundness. The following are extracts from his talk:

> I'm tired of life – I wish they would put me out of it. A man has brought a crime against me of dirty filthy habits – they turn round and say I'm stinking and rotten and that I've got the bad disorder here. I want you to put the tube up the front of me – you can do what you like, you can kill me if you like. Put me to sleep and don't let me wake no more, and cut me open and see if I've got any bad disease. My downfall is here where the food-bag goes – my liver's gone to blazes, that's what causes me to smell. And I shall never be no good till they cut it out of me. If you're going to murder me as they said – put his eyes out, cut his head off, cut off his arms and legs, cut him in two – if they're going to murder me, murder me in a proper manner. They say I done something to a dog – to a cat. Now if you can prove I've got a dog under my heart or a cat in my stomach you can murder me at once.

His genitals bulk very large in the picture – he is continually talking about being poxed, showing them to the examiner, and offering them, in what seems a passive homosexual way, for his 'satisfaction'. But it seems even more probable in Mr T.'s case that these genital fears and reassurances are merely a facade. He reassures himself by proclaiming the integrity of his externals, his penis and skin generally, against the deeper fears, of being rotten inside 'where the food-bag goes'. There is something rotten and stinking inside him (his liver) and he will never be any good until it is cut out. Often he denies that there is anything bad about himself and attributes the badness instead to his persecutors. Running through it all, in one form or another, is the fear of being murdered.

Indeed, to sum up the common characteristics of these three and many other cases, we may say that ideas of death and murder are very common in them all, and that these ideas show themselves mainly in two forms – a denial of natural death, and fear of murder. They also show a great wealth of regressive infantile fantasy in a remarkably clear and undisguised form. It is as if some lid had been taken off and we are given a clear view of what in younger and healthier people is so carefully buried and concealed, not only from the world but from the person's own awareness.

After this excursion into the clinical field, let me return to the problems I discussed earlier – problems of life and death and theories of instinct, and in particular Freud's theory of the death instinct. I want you to consider these matters now not simply theoretically, but in the light of my investigation of the old patients at Tooting Bec Hospital. Whatever view one may take of the clinical facts, no one can fail to notice that these mentally disturbed old people are preoccupied with the subject of death to a quite remarkable degree. Why were my patients so vulnerable in this area – why did they need to deny the facts and defend themselves against them with such vigour?

Let us look again at the view of life and death which Freud proposed for our consideration in 'Beyond the Pleasure Principle'. At one point he says:

It is possible to specify this final goal of all organic striving. . . . It must be an *old* state of things, an initial state from which the living entity has at one time or other departed and to which it is striving to return by the circuitous paths along which its development leads. . . . Then we shall be compelled to say that the 'aim of all life is death' and, looking backwards, that 'inanimate things existed before living ones'.

And a few sentences later:

These circuitous paths to death, faithfully kept to by the conservative instincts, would thus present us today with the picture of the phenomena of life. If we firmly maintain the exclusively conservative nature of instincts, we cannot arrive at any other notions as to the origin and aim of life.

Incidentally, Schopenhauer, seventy years earlier, had said that death is the true result and to that extent the purpose of life.

So what of the self-preservative instincts? Freud now saw them as merely assuring that the organism shall follow its *own* path to death, avoiding any possible ways of returning to inorganic existence other than those which are immanent in the organism itself. Thus far, then, Freud seems to be saying quite clearly that the end, that is, the aim, of life is death, and that our vigorous efforts at self-preservation, however instinctually powerful they may be, are directed merely to dying in the orthodox way through old age.

However, the argument so far has ignored the sexual instincts and the phenomena of reproduction, which of course do lead to a kind of potential immortality; so that here we find the direct antagonist of the death instinct which is called for if the principle of bipolarity is to be upheld. As soon as Freud brings the sexual instinct into the discussion and reminds us of the facts of self-love or narcissism and the bearing of this on self-preservation, he finds himself forced to revise his first suggestion that self-preservation is a manifestation of the death instinct – instead, he now declares that the self-preservative instincts are essentially libidinal.

Freud's own view as to what is the end of life now emerges as an ambiguous one. Is it death? Or is it reproductive immortality? Or is it, as I should like to suggest, a combination of both, united in what I have christened the 'principle of replacement'?

Other writings and references

PART THREE

Other writings and references

Full chronological list of writings, published and unpublished, by William H. Gillespie

1929 **Essay:** 'The Symptoms and Sequelae of Encephalitis Lethargica with their Appropriate Treatment'. Essay awarded Prize by British Medical Association for competition by final-year medical students in all Scottish medical schools, 1928–29. Unpublished.

1933 **Abstract:** 'Federn, P. Das Ichgefühl im Traume'. *International Journal of Psycho-Analysis* 14:507.

1934 **Thesis:** 'A Clinical and Psychopathological Study of Senile Psychoses'. Thesis accepted for degree of MD, University of Edinburgh. Unpublished.

1935 **Abstract:** 'Pfister, O. Neutestamentliche Seelsorge und Psycho-analytische Therapie'. *International Journal of Psycho-Analysis* 16:361.

1935 **Abstract:** 'Deutsch, H. Don Quijote und Donquijotismus'. *International Journal of Psycho-Analysis* 16:375.

1936 **Abstract:** 'Erickson, M. A Study of an Experimental Neurosis Hypnotically Induced in a Case of Ejaculatio Praecox'. *International Journal of Psycho-Analysis* 17:365.

1936 **Abstract:** 'Schilder, P. Psychopathologie der Zeit'. *International Journal of Psycho-Analysis* 17:515.

1937 **Book review:** 'Gardiner, D.E.M., The Children's Play Centre'. *International Journal of Psycho-Analysis* 18:486.

1938 **Abstract:** 'Kubie, L. Modifications in a Schizophrenic Reaction with Psychoanalytic Treatment'. *International Journal of Psycho-Analysis* 19:348.

1939 **Abstract:** 'Tidd, C. A Note on the Treatment of Schizophrenia'. *International Journal of Psycho-Analysis* 20:188.

1940 **Book review:** 'Goldstein, K., The Organism'. *International Journal of Psycho-Analysis* 21:369–70.

1940 **Paper:** 'A Contribution to the Study of Fetishism'. *International Journal of Psycho-Analysis* 21:401–15.

1940 **Abstract:** 'Menninger, K. The Psychological Factor in Disease'. *International Journal of Psycho-Analysis* 21:87.

1940 **Abstract:** 'Eisner, E. Phantasy in Mal-adjusted Children as Observed in Three Classes at the Southard School'. *International Journal of Psycho-Analysis* 21:93.

1940 **Abstract:** 'Brown, J. Reactions of Patients in a Frustrating Situation'. *International Journal of Psycho-Analysis* 21:222.

1940 **Abstract:** 'Menninger, K. Emotional Factors in Hypertension'. *International Journal of Psycho-Analysis* 21:342.

1940 **Abstract:** 'Crank, H. The Use of Psychoanalytic Principles in Out-patient Psychotherapy'. *International Journal of Psycho-Analysis* 21:349.

1941 **Paper:** 'Discussion on Psychiatric Aspects of Effort Syndrome'. *Proceedings of the Royal Society of Medicine*: 34:537–8.

1941 **Book review:** 'Rippon, P. and Fletcher, P., Reassurance and Relaxation'. *International Journal of Psycho-Analysis* 22:88.

1941 **Book review:** 'Brain, R., Diseases of the Nervous System'. *International Journal of Psycho-Analysis* 22:88–9.

1942 **Book review:** 'The Inter-relationship of Mind and Body. (Vol. XIX of the Proceedings of the Association for Research in Nervous and Mental Diseases. London: Baillière Tindall)'. *International Journal of Psycho-Analysis* 23:45–6.

1942 **Book review:** 'Berg, C., War in the Mind'. *International Journal of Psycho-Analysis* 23:182.

1943 **Book review:** 'Maslow, A. and Mittelmann, B., Principles of Abnormal Psychology'. *International Journal of Psycho-Analysis* 24:79.

1943 **Book review:** 'Allen, C., The Sexual Perversions and Abnormalities'. *International Journal of Psycho-Analysis* 24:79.

1943 **Book review:** 'Pavlov, I., Conditioned Reflexes and Psychiatry'. *International Journal of Psycho-Analysis* 24:80.

1944 **Paper:** 'A Paranoid Reaction Associated with Oculogyric Crises and Parkinsonism'. *Journal of Mental Science* 90:582–7.

1944 **Paper:** 'The Psychoneuroses'. *Journal of Mental Science* 90:287–306.

1945 **Book review:** 'Masserman, J., Behaviour and Neurosis'. *International Journal of Psycho-Analysis* 26:81.

1945 **Book review:** 'Sargant, W. and Slater, E., Introduction to Physical Methods of Treatment in Psychiatry'. *International Journal of Psycho-Analysis* 26:82.

1945 **Book review:** 'Horsley, J., Narco-analysis'. *International Journal of Psycho-Analysis* 26:83.

1945 **Book review:** 'Strachey, A., A New German–English Psycho-analytical Vocabulary'. *International Journal of Psycho-Analysis* 26:83.

1945 **Book review:** 'Berg, C., War in the Mind'. *International Journal of Psycho-Analysis* 26:83 (2nd edition – see 1942).

1948 **Book review:** 'Hall, M., Psychiatric Examination of the School Child'. *International Journal of Psycho-Analysis* 29:137.

1951 **Chapter:** 'Le Dévelopment Affectif et ses Troubles'. Chapter 5:39–43 in *Psychiatrie Social de l'Enfant. Le Centre International de l'Enfance.* Travaux et Documents II. Paris.

1952 **Paper:** 'Notes on the Analysis of Sexual Perversions'. *International Journal of Psycho-Analysis* 33:397–402.

1952 **Book review:** 'Bowlby, J., Maternal Care and Mental Health'. *International Journal of Psycho-Analysis* 33:73.

1953 **Chapter:** 'Extrasensory Elements in Dream Interpretation'. Chapter 29:373–83 in *Psychoanalysis and the Occult*, Devereux (ed.), International University Press, New York.

1954 **Book review:** 'Ehrenwald, J., New Dimensions of Deep Analysis'. *International Journal of Psycho-Analysis* 35:365.

1954 **Book review:** 'Boss, M., Sinn und Gehalt der Sexuellen Perversionen'. *International Journal of Psycho-Analysis* 35:368.

1956 **Paper:** 'The General Theory of Sexual Perversion'. *International Journal of Psycho-Analysis* 37:396–403.

1956 **Chapter:** 'The Structure and Aetiology of Sexual Perversion'. Chapter 1:28–42, in *Perversions: Psychodynamics in Therapy*, Lorand and Balint (eds), Random House, New York.

1956 **Paper:** 'Experiences Suggestive of Paranormal Cognition in the Psychoanalytic Situation'. In *Extrasensory Perception 204–214*, Wolstenholme and Millar (eds), London: J. & A. Churchill.

1957 **Book review:** 'Tanner, J. and Inhelder, B. (eds), Discussions on Child Development (World Health Organisation), Vols 1 and 2'. *International Journal of Psycho-Analysis* 38:365–6.

1958 **Paper:** 'Neurotic Ego Distortion'. *International Journal of Psycho-Analysis* 39:258–9.

1958 **Paper:** 'Sleep Disorders in the Child and in the Adult'. *The Medical Press* 240:699–702.

1958 **Obituary:** 'Ernest Jones'. *International Journal of Psycho-Analysis* 39:304–5.

1959 **Book review:** 'Tanner, J. and Inhelder, B. (eds), Discussions on Child Development, Vol. 3'. *International Journal of Psycho-Analysis* 40:352–3.

1960 **Paper:** 'A Psychoanalytic Comment on Mental Health'. *British Journal of Medical Psychology* 33:255–7.

1960 **Presidential address:** '21st Psychoanalytic Congress, Copenhagen'. *International Journal of Psycho-Analysis* 41:169–72.

1963 **Paper:** 'Some Regressive Phenomena in Old Age'. *British Journal of Medical Psychology* 36:203–9.

1963 **Book review:** 'Wangh, Martin *et al.*, Fruition of an Idea'. *International Journal of Psycho-Analysis* 44:118.

1964 **Paper:** 'Contribution to Symposium on Homosexuality'. *International Journal of Psycho-Analysis* 45:203–9.

1964 **Chapter:** 'Psychoanalytic Theory of Sexual Deviation with Special Reference to Fetishism'. Chapter 5:123–45 in *The Pathology and Treatment of Sexual Deviation*, Rosen (ed.), Oxford University Press, London.

1964 **Talk:** 'Retrospect and Prospect. Jubilee Oration to Commemorate Foundation of British Psychoanalytical Society in 1913'. Uunpublished.

1965 **Obituary:** 'Max Gitelson'. *International Journal of Psycho-Analysis* 46:244.

1966 **Paper:** 'Dreams, Psychopathology and Mental Apparatus'. Proceedings of IVth World Congress of Psychiatry, Madrid. Excerpta Medica International Congress Series No. 150:162–7.

1968 **Chapter:** 'The Psychoanalytical Theory of Child Development'. Chapter 5:51–69 *Foundations of Child Psychiatry*, Miller (ed.), Pergamon Press, London.

1969 **Paper:** 'Concepts of Vaginal Orgasm'. *International Journal of Psycho-Analysis* 50:495–7.

1969 **Book review:** 'Hartmann, E., The Biology of Dreaming'. *International Journal of Psycho-Analysis* 50:413–14.

1969 **Book review:** 'Stoller, R., Sex and Gender'. *International Journal of Psycho-Analysis* 50:251–4.

1969 **Obituary:** 'Willi Hoffer'. *International Journal of Psycho-Analysis* 50:263–4.

1970 **Speech** at unveiling of Freud Statue in Swiss Cottage. Unpublished.

1970 **Essay:** 'Discussion of "The Psychopathology of the Psychoses: A Proposed Revision" by Arlow and Brenner'. *International Journal of Psycho-Analysis* 51:160–2.

1970 **Book review:** 'Freud, A., Indications for Child Analysis and Other Papers'. *British Journal of Psychiatry* 116:228.

1971 **Paper:** 'Aggression and Instinct Theory'. *International Journal of Psycho-Analysis* 52:155–60.

1971 **Lecture:** 'The End of Life'. Public lecture given under auspices of the Institute of Psychoanalysis, London. Unpublished.

1971 **Obituary:** 'Donald Winnicott'. *International Journal of Psycho-Analysis* 52:227–8.

1972 **Obituary:** 'Lothair Rubinstein'. *International Journal of Psycho-Analysis* 53:329–30.

1973 **Paper:** 'The End of Life'. *Bulletin of the British Psycho-Analytical Society* 70:1–12.

1975 **Paper:** 'Woman and her Discontents: A Reassessment of Freud's Views on Female Sexuality'. *International Review of Psycho-Analysis* 2:1–9.

1975 **Book review:** 'Schur, M., Freud: Living and Dying'. *International Journal of Psycho-Analysis* 56:118.

1975 **Obituary:** 'Walter Joffe'. *International Journal of Psycho-Analysis* 56:477–9.

1976 **Lecture:** 'The Legacy of Sigmund Freud'. Inaugural lecture as Freud Memorial Professor of Psychoanalysis at University College, London. London: H.K. Lewis.

1976 **Public lectures** at University College London as Freud Memorial Professor of Psychoanlysis. Unpublished:
Freud and Science.
Freud and Culture.
Symbolism and Language.
Freud and Sexuality.
Structure and Structuralism.
Controversial Issues.

1978 **Talk:** 'The Relations between Psychoanalysis and Hypnosis'. Address to British Society of Medical and Dental Hypnosis. Unpublished.

1979 **Book review:** 'Holbrook, David, Gustav Mahler and the Courage to Be'. *International Journal of Psycho-Analysis* 60:540–2.

1979 **Talk:** 'Freud and Culture'. Address to Goethe Institute. London.

1979 **Essay:** 'Jones, Ernest: The Bonny Fighter'. *International Journal of Psycho-Analysis* 60:273.

1980 **Book review:** 'Segal, Hannah, Klein'. *International Journal of Psycho-Analysis* 61:85–8.

1982 **Obituary:** 'John Klauber'. *International Journal of Psycho-Analysis* 63:83–5.

1983 **Paper:** 'Fifty Years with Freud'. Memorial address on Freud's birthday anniversary at Hampstead Clinic. *Bulletin of the Hampstead Clinic* 6:233.

1987 **Book review:** 'Grosskurth, Phyllis, Melanie Klein: Her World and Her Work'. *International Journal of Psycho-Analysis* 68:138–42.

1989 **Book review:** 'Elizabeth B. Spillius (ed.), Melanie Klein Today. Developments in Theory and Practice'. *International Journal of Psycho-Analysis* 70:740–5.

References

Abraham, K. (1910). 'Remarks on the Psychoanalysis of a Case of Foot and Corset Fetishism'. In *Selected Papers*. London: Hogarth Press, pp. 125–36.

Arlow, J. (1954). 'Perversion: Theoretical and Therapeutic Aspects' (Panel Report). *Journal of the American Psychoanalytic Association* 2:336–45.

Bak, R. (1953). 'Fetishism'. *Journal of the American Psychoanalytic Association* 1: 285–98.

——(1956).'Aggression and Perversion'. In *Perversions: Psychodynamics in Therapy*, Balint and Lorand (eds). New York: Random House, pp. 231–40.

Beach, F.A. (1949). 'A Cross-species Survey of Mammalian Sexual Behaviour'. In *Psychosexual Development in Health and Disease*, Hoch and Zubin (eds). New York: Grune & Stratton.

Bergler, E. (1951). *Neurotic Counterfeit Sex*. New York: Grune & Stratton.

—— (1954). *Kinsey's Myth of Female Sexuality*. New York: Grune & Stratton.

Bergler, E. and Eidelberg, L. (1933). 'Der Mammakomplex des Mannes'. *Internationale Zeitschrift für Psychoanalyse* 19.

Binet, A. (1887). 'Le Fétichisme dans l'amour'. *Revue Philosophique* 24:143.

Boss, M. (1947). *Meaning and Content of the Sexual Perversions (Sinn und Gehalt der Sexuellen Perversionen)*. (1947, 2nd edition 1953; English translation 1949.) Zurich.

Burlingham, D. (1935). 'Child Analysis and the Mother'. *Psychoanalytic Quarterly* 5:69–92.

Carington, W. (1946). *Telepathy*. London: Methuen.

Chasseuguet-Smirgel, J. (ed.) (1964). *Female Sexuality: New Psychoanalytic Views*. Paris: Payot. English translation. Ann Arbor: Michigan University Press, 1970.

Decter, M. (1973). *The New Chastity*. London: Wildwood House.

Deutsch, H. (1933). 'Homosexuality in Women'. *International Journal of Psycho-Analysis* 14:34–56.

Ehrenwald, J. (1948). *Telepathy and Medical Psychology*. New York: Norton.

Eisenbud, J. (1946). 'Telepathy and Problems of Psychoanalysis'. *Psychoanalytic Quarterly* 15:32–87.

—— (1947). 'The Dreams of Two Patients in Analysis Interpreted as a Telepathic Rêve à Deux'. *Psychoanalytic Quarterly* 16:39–60.

Ellis, H. (1905). *Studies in the Psychology of Sex*, Vol. 2. Philadelphia. Reprinted New York: Random House, 1940.

Fenichel, O. (1930). 'The Psychology of Transvestitism'. *International Journal of Psycho-Analysis* 11:221–7.

—— (1931). *Perversionen, Psychosen, Charaktersörungen*. Vienna: Internationale Psycho-analytische Verlag.

—— (1934). 'Defence Against Anxiety, Particularly by Libidinization'. *Collected Papers, I*. New York: W.W. Norton, 1953.

—— (1945). *The Psychoanalytic Theory of Neurosis*. London: Routledge and Kegan Paul.

Ferenczi, S. (1914). 'On the Nosology of Male Homosexuality'. In *First Contributions to Psychoanalysis*. London: Hogarth Press, 1952.

—— (1926). 'The Problem of the Acceptance of Unpleasant Ideas'. In *Further Contributions to Psychoanalysis*. London: Hogarth Press, pp. 366–70.

Freud, A. (1951). 'Homosexuality'. *Bulletin of the American Psychoanalytic Association*, 7:117–18.

—— (1954). 'Problems of Technique of Adult Analysis'. In *The Contributions of Anna Freud*, Vol. 4. New York: International Universities Press, pp. 377–401, 1968.

Freud, S. (1893). 'Charcot' SE 3.

—— (1894). 'The Neuro-Psychoses of Defence'. SE 3.

—— (1895). 'On the Grounds for Detaching a Particular Syndrome from Neurasthenia under the Description "anxiety neurosis" '. SE 3.

—— (1901). 'The Psychopathology of Everyday Life'. SE 6.

—— (1905). 'Three Essays on the Theory of Sexuality'. SE 7.

—— (1908). 'On the Sexual Theories of Children'. SE 9.

—— (1909). 'Analysis of a Phobia in a Five-year-old Boy'. SE 10.

—— (1910). 'Leonardo da Vinci and a Memory of his Childhood'. SE 11.

—— (1914). 'On Narcissism: An Introduction'. SE 14.

—— (1915). 'Instincts and their Vicissitudes'. SE 14.

—— (1919). 'A Child is Being Beaten. A Contribution to the Study of the Origin of Sexual Perversions'. SE 17.

—— (1920). 'Beyond the Pleasure Principle'. SE 18.

—— (1922). 'Some Neurotic Mechanisms in Jealousy, Paranoia and Homosexuality'. SE 18.

—— (1923a). 'The Ego and the Id'. SE 19.

—— (1923b). 'The Infantile Genital Organization of the Libido'. SE 19.

—— (1924). 'The Economic Problem in Masochism'. SE 19.

—— (1925a). 'Some Notes on Dream Interpretation as a Whole'. SE 19.

—— (1925b). 'Negation'. SE 19.

—— (1925c). 'Some Psychical Consequences of the Anatomical Distinction Between the Sexes'. SE 19.

—— (1927). 'Fetishism'. SE 21.

—— (1930). 'Civilization and its Discontents'. SE 21.

—— (1931). 'Female Sexuality'. SE 21.

—— (1933). 'New Introductory Lectures on Psycho-Analysis. Femininity'. SE 22.

—— (1940a). 'An Outline of Psycho-Analysis'. SE 23.

—— (1940b). 'Splitting of the Ego in the Process of Defence'. SE 23.

—— (1950a). 'Extracts from the Fliess Papers'. Draft G. 'Melancholia'. SE 1.

—— (1950b). 'Extracts from the Fliess Papers'. Letter 75. SE 1.

Gillespie, W.H. (1940). 'A Contribution to the Study of Fetishism'. *International Journal of Psycho-Analysis* 21:401–15.

—— (1952). 'Notes on the Analysis of Sexual Perversions'. *International Journal of Psycho-Analysis* 33:397–402.

—— (1956a). 'The General Theory of Sexual Perversion'. *International Journal of Psycho-Analysis* 37:396–403.

—— (1956b). 'The Structure and Aetiology of Sexual Perversion'. In *Perversions: Psychodynamics in Therapy*, Lorand and Balint (eds). New York: Random House, pp. 28–42.

—— (1963). 'Some Regressive Phenomena in Old Age'. *British Journal of Medical Psychology* 36:203–9. (Symposium with Anna Freud and D.W. Winnicott at Medical Section Meeting.)

—— (1964a). 'Contribution to Symposium on Homosexuality'. *International Journal of Psycho-Analysis* 45:203–9.

—— (1964b). 'The Psychoanalytic Theory of Sexual Deviation with Special Reference to Fetishism'. In *The Pathology and Treatment of Sexual Deviation*, Rosen (ed.). London: Oxford University Press, pp. 123–45.

—— (1969). 'Concepts of Vaginal Orgasm'. *International Journal of Psycho-Analysis* 50:495–7.

—— (1971). 'Aggression and Instinct Theory'. *International Journal of Psycho-Analysis* 52:155–60.

—— (1975). 'Woman and her Discontents: A Reassessment of Freud's Views on Female Sexuality'. *International Review of Psychoanalysis* 2:1–9.

Glenn, J. and Kaplan, E.H. (1968). 'Types of Orgasm in Women: A Critical Review and Redefinition'. *Journal of the American Psychoanalytic Association* 16:549–64.

Glover, E. (1932). 'On the Aetiology of Drug Addiction'. *International Journal of Psycho-Analysis* 13:298–328.

—— (1933). 'The Relation of Perversion Formation to the Development of the Reality Sense'. *International Journal of Psycho-Analysis* 14:486–504.

Greenacre, P. (1953). 'Certain Relationships between Fetishism and Faulty Development of the Body Image'. *Psychoanalytic Study of the Child* 8:79–98.

—— (1955). 'Further Considerations Regarding Fetishism'. *Psychoanalytic Study of the Child* 10:187–94.

—— (1960). 'Further Notes on Fetishism'. *Psychoanalytic Study of the Child* 15:191–207.

—— (1968). 'Perversions: General Considerations Regarding their Genetic and Dynamic Background'. In *Emotional Growth: Psychoanalytic Studies of the Gifted and a Great Variety of Other Individuals, Vol. 1*. New York: International Universities Press, pp. 300–14, 1971.

Hartmann, H. (1939). *Ego Psychology and the Problem of Adaptation*. New York: International Universities Press, 1958.

Horney, K. (1926). 'The Flight from Womanhood'. *International Journal of Psycho-Analysis* 7:324–39.

—— (1932). 'The Dread of Woman'. *International Journal of Psycho-Analysis* 13:348–60.

—— (1933). 'The Denial of the Vagina'. *International Journal of Psycho-Analysis* 14:57–70.

Johnson, A. and Szurek, S. (1952). 'The Genesis of Antisocial Acting Out in Children and Adults'. *Psychoanalytic Quarterly* 21:323–35.

Jones, E. (1927). 'The Early Development of Female Sexuality'. *International Journal of Psycho-Analysis* 8:459–72.

—— (1933). 'The Phallic Phase'. *International Journal of Psycho-Analysis* 14:1–33.

—— (1953). *Sigmund Freud. Life and Work, Vol. 1*. London: Hogarth Press.

—— (1957). *Sigmund Freud. Life and Work, Vol. 3*. London: Hogarth Press.

Kallman, F. (1952a). 'Twin Sibships and the Study of Male Homosexuality'. *American Journal of Human Genetics* 4.

—— (1952b). 'Comparative Twin Studies of Genetic Aspects of Male Homosexuality'. *Journal of Nervous and Mental Diseases* 115:283–98.

Kemper, W.W. (1965). 'Neue Beiträge aus der Phylogenese zur Bio-Psychologie der Frau'. *Zeitschrift für Psychosomatische Medizin* 11:77–82.

Kinsey, A.C., Pomeroy, W.B. and Martin, C.E. (1948). *Sexual Behaviour in the Human Male*. Philadelphia and London: W.B. Saunders.

Kinsey, A.C., Pomeroy, W.B., Martin, C.E. and Gebhard, P.H. (1953). *Sexual Behaviour in the Human Female*. Philadelphia and London: W.B. Saunders.

Klein, M. (1932). *The Psycho-analysis of Children*. New York: Norton.

—— (1946). 'Notes on some Schizoid Mechanisms'. *International Journal of Psycho-Analysis* 27:99–110.

Kolb, L. and Johnson, A. (1955). 'Etiology and Therapy of Overt Homosexuality'. *Psychoanalytic Quarterly* 24:506–15.

Krafft-Ebing, R.V. (1893). *Psychopathia Sexualis*. Stuttgart.

Kronengold, E. and Sterba, R. (1936). 'Two Cases of Fetishism'. *Psychoanalytic Quarterly* 5:63–70.

Lang, T. (1940). 'Studies on the Genetic Determination of Homosexuality'. *Journal of Nervous and Mental Diseases* 92.

Mahler, M.S. (1965). 'On the Significance of the Normal Separation–Individuation Phase: With Reference to Research in Symbiotic Child Psychosis'. In *Drives, Affects, and Behavior, Vol. 2*, Schur (ed.). New York: International Universities Press, pp. 161–9.

—— (1967). 'On Human Symbiosis and the Vicissitudes of Individuation'. *Journal of the American Psychoanalytic Association* 15:740–64.

—— (1968). *On Human Symbiosis and the Vicissitudes of Individuation, Vol. 1*. New York: International Universities Press.

Mahler, M.S., Pine, F. and Bergman, A. (1975). *The Psychological Birth of the Human Infant*. New York: Basic Books.

Masters, W.H. and Johnson, V.E. (1966). *Human Sexual Response*. Boston, MA: Little, Brown.

Michael, R.P. (1968). 'Gonadal Hormones and the Control of Primate Behaviour'. In *Endocrinology and Human Behaviour*, Michael (ed.). London: Oxford University Press.

Nacht, S. (1938). 'Le Masochisme'. *Revue Française de Psychanalyse* 10:172–291.

Nacht, S., Diatkine, R. and Favreau, J. (1956). 'The Ego in Perverse Relationships'. *International Journal of Psycho-Analysis* 37:404–13.

Nunberg, H. (1938). 'Homosexuality, Magic and Aggression'. *International Journal of Psycho-Analysis* 19:1–16.

Payne, Sylvia (1939). 'Some Observations on the Ego Development of the Fetishist'. *International Journal of Psychoanalysis* 20:161–70.

Rado, S. (1940). 'A Critical Examination of the Concept of Bisexuality'. *Psychosomatic Medicine* 2.

—— (1956). 'An Adaptational View of Sexual Behavior'. In *The Psychoanalysis of Behavior: The Collected Papers of Sandor Rado*. New York: Grune & Stratton, pp. 186–213.

Rosenfeld, H. (1949). 'Remarks on the Relation of Male Homosexuality to Paranoia, Paranoid Anxiety and Narcissism'. *International Journal of Psycho-Analysis* 30:36–47.

Sachs, H. (1923). 'Zur Genese der Perversionen'. *Internationale Zeitschrift zür Psychoanalyse*, 9:172–82. 'On the Genesis of Perversions'. English trans. (Hella Freud Bernays, 1964) in C. Socarides, *Homosexuality*. New York: Jason Aronson, pp. 531–46, 1978. English version also in the New York Psychoanalytic Institute Library, New York City.

Sadger, J. (1921). *Die Lehre von den Geschlechtsverirrungen (Psychopathia Sexualis) auf psychoanalytischer Grundlage*. Leipzig and Vienna: Internationale Psychoanalytische Vereinigung.

Sandler, J. (1960). 'On the Concept of the Superego'. In *The Psychoanalytic Study of the Child*. New York: International Universities Press, 15:128–62.

Sherfey, M.J. (1966). 'The Evolution and Nature of Female Sexuality in Relation to Psychoanalytic Theory'. *Journal of the American Psychoanalytic Association* 14:28–128.

Slater, E. (1962). 'Birth Order and Maternal Age of Homosexuals'. *The Lancet* 13 January.

Socarides, C. (1960). 'The Development of a Fetishistic Perversion: The Contribution of Pre-oedipal Phase Conflict'. *Journal of the American Psychoanalytic Association* 8:281–311.

—— (1962). 'Theoretical and Clinical Aspects of Overt Female Homosexuality'. *Journal of the American Psychoanalytic Association* 10: 579–92.

—— (1968). *The Overt Homosexual*. New York: Grune and Stratton; republished New York: Jason Aronson, 1974.

—— (1978). *Homosexuality*. New York: Jason Aronson.

—— (1979).'A Unitary Theory of Sexual Perversions'. In *On Sexuality: Psychoanalytic Observations*, Karasu and Socarides (eds). New York: International

Universities Press, pp. 161–80. Also in *The Preoedipal Origin and Psychoanalytic Therapy of Sexual Perversions*. New York: International Universities Press, 1988.

—— (1988). *The Pre-Oedipal Origin and Psychoanalytic Therapy of Sexual Perversions*. New York: International Universities Press.

—— (1990). 'The Homosexualities: A Psychoanalytic Classification'. In *The Homosexualities: Reality, Fantasy and the Arts*, Socarides and Volkan (eds). Madison, CT: International Universities Press, pp. 9–47.

Sperling. O. (1956). 'Psychodynamics of Group Perversions'. *Psychoanalytic Quarterly* 25:56–65.

Stoller, R. (1969). *Sex and Gender*. New York: Science House.

Thorner, H. (1949). 'Notes on a Case of Male Homosexuality'. *International Journal of Psycho-Analysis* 30:31–5.

Weissman, P. (1962). 'Structural Considerations in Overt Male Bisexuality'. *International Journal of Psycho-Analysis* 43:159–68.

Winnicott, D.W. (1953). 'Transitional Objects and Transitional Phenomena'. *International Journal of Psycho-Analysis* 34:89–97.

Wisdom, J.O. (1969). 'Scientific Theory: Empirical Content, Ontology, and *Weltanschauung*'. In Proceedings of the 14th International Congress of Philosophy. Vienna: Herder.

Name index

Abraham, Karl 96
Arlow, J. 39, 99
Astor, David: endowed new chair of
    Psychoanalysis 33
Attenborough, David: T.V. programme
    on courtship 144

Bak, Robert 40, 44, 45, 46, 47, 87, 89,
    91, 116
Beach, F. A. 121
Bernays, Hella Freud 41
Bergler, E. 126, 127
Binet, A. 113
Bleuler, Eugen: lecture 17
Bonaparte, Princess Marie 29
Boss, Dr Medard 81
Bowlby, John 23, 26
Browning, Robert 180
Burlingham, Dorothy: on supernatural 160
Bychowski, Gustav 40

Carington, W.: on telepathy 160
Chamberlain, Neville 21, 23
Chasseguet-Smirgel, J. 144
Churchill, Winston 3

Decter, M. 145
Deutsch, H. 126, 141
Devereux, George: *Psychoanalysis and the
    Occult* 28

Eder, Dr 59, 61
Edward VIII, King 14
Eisenbud, Jule: on extrasensory
    communication 158, 159
Elizabeth II, Queen 29

Ellis, H. 102

Federn, Paul 15
Fenichel, Otto 40, 87, 97, 115, 169
Ferenczi, S. 90, 97, 120
Fliess, Wilhelm 124, 131, 135
Freud, Anna 29, 32, 43, 130; close
    collaboration in the IPA 27; invitation
    to William Gillespie 33
Freud, Sigmund: anatomical distinction
    140; on bisexuality 120; castration
    threat 87, 115; 'Child Beaten' 82, 83,
    94, 95, 97, 106; civilisation 163, 181;
    correspondence with Fliess 135, 136;
    on female sexuality 130, 131, 142,
    143; fetishism 84, 89, 97, 114; instincts
    165, 168, 181, 182; on jealousy 96; on
    Leonardo 94, 106; mental bipolarity
    164; narcissism 163; negation 89, 97;
    negative of perversion 81, 94, 106;
    'Phallic Phase' 97; pleasure principle
    162, 163, 183; sexual theories of
    children 140; splitting of consciousness
    98; splitting of the ego 79, 90, 98, 110;
    on telepathy 157; 'Three Essays' 81,
    82, 93, 94, 102, 106, 108, 117 120,
    121, 131, 137, 139

Gillespie, Sadie (Sadie Mervis) 33;
    marriage to William Gillespie 31;
    training analyst 3
Gitelson, Maxwell 29
Glover, Edward 40, 49, 69, 83, 88, 97, 110;
    on drug addiction 95; interviewed by
    17; opposition to Klein 22; on reality
    sense 96; wrong diagnosis by 19

205

Subject index

Preliminary Note: *bis*, *ter*, *quater* after a page reference number denotes that the item is separately mentioned two, three or four times on the same page; *passim* denotes that the references are scattered through the pages indicated; n after a page reference denotes the item being in a note at the end of a chapter; William Gillespie's name is abbreviated to WG throughout.

9 780415 128056

Lightning Source UK Ltd.
Milton Keynes UK
UKHW02f1955201217
314841UK00011B/717/P